SHY BUT NOT RETIRING

Shy But Not Retiring

The Memoirs of
The Right Reverend Eric Waldram Kemp

edited and prepared for publication
by Jeremy Matthew Haselock

continuum
LONDON • NEW YORK

Continuum UK
The Tower Building, 11 York Road, London SE1 7NX

Continuum US
80 Maiden Lane, Suite 704, New York, NY 10038

www.continuumbooks.com

First published 2006

British Library Cataloguing-in-Publication Data
A catalogue record for this book is available from the British Library.

ISBN 0–8264–8073–X

Typeset by YHT Ltd, London
Printed and bound by Antony Rowe Ltd, Chippenham, Wilts

Contents

Foreword

On various occasions since 1990 I have been urged to write my memoirs and so in 1995 I began. I was initially much helped by my two secretaries, Jo Parkinson and Ros Manketelow, and I am grateful to them for all they did. After retirement I was able to give rather more time to the project and completed a text which to those to whom I showed it seemed worthy of publication. Bishop Geoffrey Rowell, one of those who kindly read the first draft, felt at times I had been too discreet, so suggested I ask one of my former chaplains, Canon Jeremy Haselock, the Vice-Dean of Norwich Cathedral, to work on it with me. The following pages are the product of that collaboration and I am very grateful to Jeremy for the enormous amount of time that he has given to it which has greatly improved the book.

I dedicate the finished work to my wife and children who have enabled me to keep reasonably sane during the last fifty years. I hope they will not be disturbed by anything I have written about them, nor I hope will anyone else.

EWK December 2005

1

A Lincolnshire 'Yellow-Belly'

I was born at 3.30pm on Tuesday, 27 April 1915, the only child of Tom and Florence Kemp. Like most babies of that time, I was delivered in my parents' bedroom at home. For my mother and father, home was Grove House in Waltham, a village five miles to the south-west of Grimsby, in Lincolnshire. I am, therefore, by birth a Lincolnshire 'yellow belly' and a native of what Henry VIII called one of 'the most brute and beastly counties of the realm'. To have been called that by such a monster must be regarded as an accolade of which to be proud and, indeed, I am. So far as I know there is only one other person born in the village to have become an episcopal yellow belly, namely John of Waltham in the fourteenth century. He was a distinguished civil servant – Master of the Rolls, Keeper of the Privy Purse, Lord High Treasurer of England – and Bishop of Salisbury from 1388 to 1395. By order of his master, Richard II, he was buried in Edward the Confessor's chapel at Westminster Abbey, the only person not of royal blood buried there. There is a small brass, dated 1400, in All Saints, the parish church of Waltham, commemorating his father and mother. There is a larger brass there, dated 1420, of a Joanna Waltham, with her unmarried son and daughter, who I suppose was his niece. The family tomb or vault was in the north aisle.

In those days, Waltham was a small village. Its most significant nearby landmark was a magnificent working windmill built in 1880 by John Saunderson, the famous millwright from Louth. It served the surrounding farms as a wind-powered flour mill until 1962. In the mid-1970s it was bought by the local district council and thoroughly restored. It is still producing flour today, not as a commercial enterprise but as a major tourist attraction for the area.

Significantly for my parents, there was a tea garden with a tennis club near the centre of Waltham and it was there my father's family met my mother and her father and one or two of her cousins who came to play tennis. A village romance must have ensued for Tom Kemp and

Florence Waldram were soon engaged and they married in All Saints at 8.30am on 25 April 1914.

Grove House, into which my parents moved, was my mother's family home, and lay at the southern end of Waltham. It stood in the middle of a considerable area of ground with a garden to the west and south, in the yard behind it stood the coach house, wash house, stables and coalhouse, and behind that was a hard tennis court. Behind the tennis court was a broad ditch called the Beck, which ran through the village and close to the tannery. (The only really serious illness I had as a child was caused by falling into the Beck and swallowing some of the water.) Between the tennis court and the back of the coach house a wooden garage was built when the family acquired a car – a Ford Standard – in the early 1920s.

I grew up, therefore, in an environment characterized by plenty of space. My earliest memory concerns the garden at Grove House: of being given a toy anti-aircraft gun and taken out on the lawn to shoot at Zeppelins. I think I was three years old at the time so it must have been 1918. There were air-raids on the east coast as well as bombardment from the sea and so in the village we began to hear much about the war.

In my very earliest years the house was lit by 'Aladdin' oil lamps but gas was soon installed and by the 1930s we had progressed to electric lighting. Water came from a pump in the backyard which was employed every morning to lift water up to a tank in the attic. There was also a well in the cellar which in wet weather was apt to flood. We lived mainly in a large sitting room on the south side of the house and rarely used the formal drawing room which was just beyond it but, when I was about five, I re-arranged the furniture in this room to resemble the layout of the parish church, with pews, lectern and pulpit and pretended to conduct Matins. We used the front door, entered from the garden on the west side, just as rarely. Normally, we came into the house from the back yard, up some steps and through a door which opened directly into the large kitchen. The house had one bathroom at the top of the stairs. The stair hall was dominated by a large reproduction of Turner's *Fighting Temeraire* being tugged on her last voyage to be broken up. The sitting room had a large sideboard, the upper part of which was a big mirror. (This piece of furniture went with me from house to house through my life until we moved to the Deanery at Worcester where it proved to be too big for any of the rooms and was consigned to the cellar. While we were there some changes to the plumbing entailed the installation of a water pipe across the cellar steps. When we moved out to go to Chichester we discovered the new pipe had made it impossible to get the sideboard out. For all I know it is still in the Deanery cellar at Worcester.)

As was the custom of the time, my parents employed a small staff to help with running the house and grounds. We had a gardener called Gutteridge, of whom I was very fond, but the household depended much on a maid called Louie Hutton who came to us at the age of sixteen having, as they then put it, 'misbehaved herself'. She was with us for several years and looked after me in my early childhood. In later years after she had left us to get married, I used to go and visit her whenever I was in the neighbourhood. She was succeeded as maid by her younger sister, Edna, who similarly stayed with us until she was married. Throughout my childhood, my family also included a dog. The first was an Alsatian, but I have no clear recollection of it as it was run over when I was quite small. The second was a mongrel called Vic whom I adored. It was with us for many years until its death.

The house was bought by my maternal grandfather, Walter Waldram. He was an estate agent with a house and office in Grimsby. His wife died in 1896 when my mother was twelve years old and she was, in effect, her father's mainstay since, though in Grimsby he had a housekeeper, Miss Ethel Hall, one of 12 children distantly related to us. My mother always remembered my grandmother on her deathbed murmuring the hymn 'Peace, Perfect Peace' again and again. The Waldram family came to Grimsby from Leicester some time in the second half of the nineteenth century and my great grandfather, Job Waldram, was Chief Constable. I never knew him, but I gathered that he was a fine, handsome man, intelligent and well read, who lost a leg while trying to stop a riot at Grimsby docks. He was also a prominent Freemason. We had a half-length oil painting of him in full regalia as Provincial Grand Sword Bearer, which I think is in the possession of the Grimsby Police. I still have the handsomely bound, complete works of Dickens which belonged to him. He was also a devotee of John Ruskin, the influential art critic, architectural theorist and social reformer. This enthusiasm he passed on to my mother, who left me several of Ruskin's works.

Walter Waldram was also a Freemason but never seemed to me to take it terribly seriously other than socially. He would go regularly to Masonic dinners in Grimsby and tell us about the after-dinner entertainment, which was usually provided by some moderately well-known comic. I remember him speaking particularly of Stainless Stephen, who became famous for his original comic method of speaking punctuation – an idea later adopted and refined by Victor Borge. At his funeral, I recall, several Masons appeared, sang a hymn and threw things into the grave. There was never any suggestion that I should become a Mason and I have not done so. I remember many years later, when I was a curate in Southampton, being consulted by a young man, an articled clerk in a firm of solicitors, who told me that he was being pressed by the partners to become a Freemason on the grounds that it would be a great advantage to him in his career. Masons I have met in recent years tell me that the application of such pressure to join is contrary to their rules.

The mainstay of my grandfather's business was as agent for Hewitt's brewery, managing the portfolio of house property they owned in Grimsby. On Mondays my mother drove round collecting rents on my grandfather's behalf and on Tuesdays my father did the same. As a small boy, I often went with them. I do not remember any evidence of serious poverty and, on the whole, relations between tenants and rent collectors were good. Indeed, I remember only one untoward incident when a woman, who came to the office to pay her rent, stole my mother's handbag. Over the years my grandfather and my parents had invested in property, so there were rents of their own to be collected. In addition to the rent collecting, my grandfather also acted for the Inland Revenue and for the Grimsby Corporation. I remember going round with one or other of my parents to nail up notices relating to income tax matters on church notice boards.

Grandfather Waldram was a dominating figure in my early life; indeed, until his death in 1942. Grove House, in which we lived, was very much his house. He came home every Wednesday and stayed one night. He returned to Waltham on Saturday to stay until Monday. He had to be fetched from Grimsby and there was a great row if we were ever late. While he was at home everything revolved round him and most of our holidays involved him. He was a big man with a violent temper, generous by nature but rather given to drink. Relations with him placed a great strain on my mother's life. I think that it was as a result of his reliance on her that my mother had a nervous breakdown in 1925, shortly after I had gone away to school.

To recover and convalesce, my mother was advised to go to Harrogate to see Dr Kathleen Rutherford. This first visit lasted for some weeks and she stayed in a boarding house kept by a Mrs Stothart in the King's Road. We joined her after a short while and, as my mother's consultations with Dr Rutherford continued for some years, I began a long acquaintance with Harrogate and developed a lasting fondness for the place. For a short time I saw Dr Rutherford myself, and found her very helpful in dealing with my shyness. After we ceased to stay at the boarding house, we frequented the Spa Hotel. The general standards maintained at the Spa Hotel were excellent, but I am sure an influence on my developing personality was the fuss my grandfather made about the food. This was a constant source of anxiety and embarrassment to me and may have had something to do with my dislike of publicity and reluctance to speak unnecessarily in public.

At that time the Hastings Orchestra, conducted by Basil Cameron, played in Harrogate for part of the year and we went often to their concerts. On Thursday nights was the Symphony Concert and it was there that I first became acquainted with the great pieces of classical music. It was long before I heard them elsewhere. Basil Cameron went on to conduct first the San Francisco and then the Seattle Symphony Orchestras.

Lincolnshire is a very large county and the north-eastern corner around Grimsby did not have a great deal of contact either with the south round Boston, or the south-west round Grantham. From Grimsby there was a railway line going south past the east-coast towns of Mablethorpe, Skegness and Boston, joining the mainline from Edinburgh to London at Peterborough. This was closed as part of Dr Richard Beeching's drastic master plan for the railway network in the early 1960s. There was also a line going west to Sheffield and I remember the announcements made over the station loudspeakers when the train was due to arrive: Retford, Sheffield and Manchester. This, after I went to Oxford, was one of my main lines of communication as I could get a train from Oxford to Sheffield and change there for Grimsby and home.

In my early years we did not go very far away from the north-east of Lincolnshire, other than the occasional holidays across the Humber to Bridlington and south to Mablethorpe. Another of my earliest memories is while on holiday at Bridlington of being turned out of a cinema for crying. I must have been getting on for nine or ten before I went to

Lincoln and I remember being impressed by the cathedral and being taken on a pilgrimage by my mother to the grave of Bishop Edward King. Later, when we acquired the car, we had the greater adventure from time to time of driving down to London. When we reached the outskirts of London, my father would always arranged for us to be met by a representative of the Automobile Association (AA) who drove us in our own car into the centre where we were to stay, usually, I think, at the Regent Palace Hotel. At the end of our holiday the AA driver then collected us and returned us to the point we had met him, where my father took the wheel again.

The Waldram family had long been connected with St James' church, the parish church of Grimsby. The curate in 1915 was the Reverend Fred Burgess, subsequently Vicar of Brigg. It was he who baptized me and although I had no contact with him in my early childhood, he was to enter my life very influentially when I was at school. My mother used to speak of an incumbent called Mr Bullock who attracted large congregations, including at special services for men only. I think this Mr Bullock must have prepared my mother for confirmation, but the great thing in her life was that she had been confirmed by Bishop Edward King. When we went to Lincoln Cathedral, she would always say that the statue of Bishop King in the south-west transept was exactly as she remembered him at her confirmation.

King became Bishop of Lincoln in 1884, having been the first Principal of Cuddesdon Theological College and then Regius Professor of Moral Theology and Canon of Christ Church at Oxford. At the University his personality attracted many undergraduates to the services he held in an outhouse in his garden on Friday nights. In Lincolnshire, his personal holiness and his pastoral care for his people were remembered long after his death in 1910. William Wright, the squire of Wold Newton with whom I became very friendly as a boy, told me that he was never flustered or impatient about anything. If a train was late, he would sit happily with a book, waiting patiently for it to arrive. On one occasion, when King was visiting a village in his diocese, the vicar complained to him about the lack of piety among his parishioners: 'There is a boy whom you confirmed when you were last here whom I questioned about the preparation he had made for his Easter Communion. All he said was, "I've cleaned me boots and put them under me bed."' To which the bishop replied, 'Don't you think that the angels would delight to see them there?' He had an instinctive understanding of the outlook of ordinary farming people. A Methodist, who had once been to one of King's ordination services in Lincoln Cathedral, was asked whether he was not put off by the bishop's cope and mitre. He replied, 'No, I only saw the holiness of the man.' The then Bishop of London, AF Winnington-Ingram, returning from King's funeral, said, 'We have buried our saint.' Many years later, I was told by a Lincolnshire country parish priest of a man he visited who never went out and never spoke to anyone. They had sat in silence for some time and then the man looked up and asked, 'King still at Lincoln?' It was 40 years after King's death. William Wright, whose recollections of Bishop King helped form my opinion of him, became a great friend and I used to visit him to talk about historical subjects. He had been at Oxford, at St John's, with Canon SL Ollard, the distinguished church historian, with whom he had visited many of the great French cathedrals. Wright was a considerable historian in his own right. We would talk about local history, about John and Joanna Waltham buried in the parish church, and the Waltham family connections in the fourteenth century. He possessed an Anglo-Catholic outlook and must have helped shape my own views. He told me he looked forward to the day when Lincoln Cathedral would use Eucharistic vestments and had bought some chasubles to give to the Cathedral when that happened.

My grandfather's brother, George Waldram, also an estate agent, was churchwarden of St James'. He had two children, Horace and Kythé, who made an innovation in the family by both going to Cambridge which, I think, inspired my mother with a determination that I, too, should go to university. Two sisters completed the older generation of the Waldram family. One went on to marry a sergeant in the Grimsby Police, and they had a daughter who later became the village schoolmistress at Fimber on the Yorkshire Wolds. The other also married and had a daughter, Alice, who married a Jack Baumber, a clerk in the head office of Hewitt's brewery. Their son, Ralph, was closest to me of our generation.

So much for my mother's family, the Waldrams. My father's family, the Kemps, were recorded as living at Waltham at the beginning of the nineteenth century. How long they were there before that I do not know. The head of the family worked, for two or three generations, as the village butcher. My Kemp grandfather, John Kemp, had sold the business and moved to a large house at the top of the High Street by the time I was born. The family also owned a small farm, the village tannery and an interest in the village brickyard. The elder son, William, known as Will, lived next to the tanyard, which he managed with my father and the husband of their elder sister, Leonard Lowis. One of my boyhood recollections is of going with my father by horse and cart to Grimsby on Fridays to collect a load of sheepskins for the tanyard. I can still recall the smell as I lay on top of the pile on the way back to Waltham.

My father had another sister, Annie, who married and moved three miles away to Scarthoe, so we saw very little of her. I was particularly fond of Will's wife, my Auntie Rose. The lives of Will and Rose Kemp were later touched by tragedy as their daughter, my cousin Vera, married unhappily and eventually committed suicide by hanging herself at the tanyard. Their son, Michael, far more happily, moved to Sussex with his family and once I moved there with my family, we were able to meet conveniently from time to time. To complete the picture, I had another cousin, Rex, the son of the Lowises. He worked for some years in Sierra Leone then came back to England and settled in Lincolnshire, where I saw him fairly often until his death.

As a young man, my father left home and went to work as a journalist in Farnham, Surrey, where he found lodgings with a Mr and Mrs Speake. Speake was secretary to the Bishop of Winchester, Randall Davidson, who at that time lived in Farnham Castle, the official residence of the Bishops of Winchester. When Bishop Frank Woods moved the episcopal residence to Winchester in the 1920s, Speake must have moved with him as he remained the bishop's secretary until the time of Cyril Garbett in the 1930s. He was living in retirement at St Cross Hospital when I was ordained at Winchester in 1939.

My father was born in 1885 and can only have been in his teens when he went to Farnham, as he remembered going from there to London for Queen Victoria's funeral. How long he stayed in Farnham I do not know, but I suspect that it was no longer than a few years. He was certainly back home at Waltham by 1912, probably earlier.

My father received no formal education other than that of the village school but he read widely. This must have included Bergson, Quiller Couch, Swift, Gibbon, Buckle, Bagehot and Henry James as I still have some of these books from his library in my possession. Father had an older friend in the village, a Mr Watkinson, with whom he used to spend a good deal of time and by whom, I suspect, he was encouraged in his reading. He told me that Mr Watkinson was a friend of the churchwarden of Cleethorpes, Mr Ernest de Lacey Read, who instigated the prosecution of Bishop King for allegedly performing illegal ritual acts when celebrating the Holy Communion. The Cleethorpes wardens had earlier made a formal complaint to the bishop concerning certain changes in ritual introduced by their new rector. According to my father, Mr Watkinson claimed to have suggested to Mr de Lacey Read that he should take the matter further in view of his dissatisfaction with the lenient action of his diocesan in vetoing the prosecution of the incumbent.

Our Christmas celebrations followed a regular pattern. Walter Waldram came to us for the whole holiday period. An elderly lady – the caretaker of the Masonic Hall in Grimsby – came to lunch, and in the afternoon we were joined by my mother's Pearson cousins, their husbands and children. These were cousin Alice, cousin Annie, who was married to Sidney Telling, a butcher in Rotherham, and unmarried cousin Doris, who lived with the Tellings and who, with Annie, ran a dress shop in Rotherham.

Boxing Day was a reverse of Christmas Day and we all gathered at Jack Baumber's house at Fairfield, half way between Waltham and Grimsby. We were joined by Jack's two elderly sisters, ladies who were rather Puritan in outlook and put a damper on things if Christmas fell on a Sunday. Some members of the family were rather strictly Sabbatarian. I remember that for some years I was not allowed to ride a bicycle on Sundays and there was also talk of an elderly member of the family who would stay up until midnight on Sundays so she could begin the week's washing at the first hour of Monday. The procedure on Christmas Day and Boxing Day was the same in both houses. Desultory family conversation was followed by high tea, after which there was more talk, various members of the company sang or performed their party pieces, some played whist, and at about nine o'clock, after some more refreshment, the visiting parties returned home. Cousin Ralph and I found it all very dreary and did not look forward to Christmas. The life and soul of the party tended to be my uncle, Sydney Telling. He was the only one of the men who served in the war and was full of stories which Ralph found more exciting than I did. He was also a great singer, though I only remember one of his songs, 'The Little Tin Soldier'. For me, these Christmas occasions filled with war reminiscences were the beginning of a great hatred of war and a lack of enthusiasm for the glamour some people see in it.

In the 1920s, the Waltham Christmas party was joined by my grandfather's brother, George Waldram and his wife Kate, their lively daughter Kythé, their married son, Horace and his wife Marjorie, and their two sons, George and John. These boys were younger than Ralph and I and we never felt much in common with them at that stage. Horace was a master at Brentwood School, a public school, whereas by that time Ralph and I had gone, as boarders, to Brigg Grammar School. Kythé was much involved with a local repertory company and when she learnt of my developing interest in Gilbert and Sullivan, one year she made for me a *Mikado* costume.

My father was not called up to fight in the Great War, as he had lost the top of one of his fingers in a farming accident, so my earliest years had the benefit of home life with both parents. They were concerned about my education and keen that I should have what they had not. My mother was undoubtedly prompted by the fact that her cousins, Horace and Kythé, had both been to Cambridge. I was, therefore, not sent to the village school my father and three of my cousins attended, instead myself and cousin Ralph were sent, in 1920, to Levalley School in the Abbey Road in Grimsby. This was a private school, owned and run by a Mr and Mrs Bryan. Wilfrid Bryan was a frail, lame man, crippled I believe in the war. The school was dominated by his wife, a massive cheerful lady. We had lunch at the school and one of the few things that I remember about it is that Mrs Bryan always drank something called Big Tree Burgundy. The label on the bottle showed a large tree split at the bottom with a car driving through it.

During the school holidays, Grimsby was almost as much the centre of my life as Waltham because on Mondays I would go there to collect rent with my mother and sometimes again on a Tuesday with my father. On Wednesdays we would go to fetch my grandfather and on Thursdays take him back again. On Fridays I would go with my father to fetch the sheepskins for the tanyard and on Saturdays back again to fetch my grandfather. It was during these trips to Grimsby I came to know well my grandfather's housekeeper, Miss Ethel Hall, who, with her sister Jessie, lived in the back part of his house at 113 Victoria Street. My grandfather occupied the two front downstairs rooms, one as the clerk's office and the other as his office and living room. There was a front staircase which led up to his bedroom and bathroom. The rest of the house was occupied by the Halls.

Ethel and Jessie were two of twelve children – the others lived in different parts of Grimsby. It was through them that I came to know Mr and Mrs Drakes of Manor Farm, Tealby, where I spent many happy childhood holidays. Will Drakes had married a second time, a wife younger than himself. By his first wife he had a son, Reg, who farmed elsewhere in Tealby. Each summer, for several years, I spent some weeks at Manor Farm, and sometimes part of the Christmas and Easter holidays also.

I grew up very much a part of the North Lincolnshire farming community, becoming familiar with the milking and the separating machine in the dairy, the annual bull show, horse racing at Market Rasen, ferreting and other such rural pursuits. A particular friend was the cowman, Mr Dale, and I spent hours with him in the crewyard. I was most attached to Mr Drakes, who treated me as a grandson. After he died I felt unhappy at the farm and only stayed there once more. Manor Farm introduced me to two special Lincolnshire features. The farm house stood on the edge of the Wolds and from the front windows one looked straight across to Lincoln Cathedral, fifteen miles away. It was a few years later that I actually went to Lincoln but the sight of that glorious building standing on its hill made an impression which is renewed every time I go to Lincoln. Below the farm, nearer the village, was Bayons Manor, a romantic early nineteenth-century construction in the style of a moated baronial castle. It was built by one of the Tennyson family and during my years at Tealby was occupied by the Tennyson d'Eyncourts. I remember that Mrs Tennyson d'Eyncourt was always complaining about the Manor Farm bulls being in the fields between the farm and Bayons Manor. That was my introduction to Tennyson, of whose poetry I have since become very fond. I was gratified many years later to be invited to deliver one in the series of annual Tennyson discourses at Bag Enderby. Bayons Manor has now been pulled down.

Another memory of those early years of school holidays is of being taken to the theatre for the first time, on my seventh birthday, to see *Iolanthe*, performed by the D'Oyly Carte second touring company, with Frank Steward as the Lord Chancellor. From that afternoon I have been a Gilbert and Sullivan fan. A year later the company came to Grimsby again and we went to see *The Mikado*, and the arrival of the

Lord High Executioner, with his great sword, quite frightened me. It did not, however, put me off the opera. In fact, I made a model theatre in a hut which served the tennis court at the back of our house, and I used to give Gilbert and Sullivan performances accompanied by gramophone records. When I was 13 I joined the Gilbert and Sullivan Society, of which I am still a member. We discovered that the Spilsby Amateur Operatic Society did a Gilbert and Sullivan opera each year and it was there that I saw *Patience* and *Ruddigore* which have remained two of my favourites. Sometime in the early 1930s, my mother, grandfather and I went on holiday to Bournemouth and I was delighted to discover the first D'Oyly Carte Opera Company performing there for two or three weeks, almost the whole of the time we were there. I was able to see some of the famous period stalwarts of the Company, particularly Sir Henry Lytton, Bertha Lewis and Darrel Fancourt. The visit to *Iolanthe* had another lasting result as it started for me a life-long interest in the law, and for many years thereafter my ambition was to become Lord Chancellor.

After I turned eight, I became aware that my parents were talking about a change of school. While I had been going to Levalley School in Grimsby with my cousin Ralph, they were keen that I should have the opportunity of greater educational advantages. From what my mother subsequently told me, they considered Sedbergh, but it was too expensive. They then explored Giggleswick and Worksop but my father discovered that they were of Anglo-Catholic foundation and so rejected them firmly. It is rather ironic that, as Bishop of Chichester, I was Visitor of the whole Woodard Foundation to which those two schools belong. Finally, my parents settled on Brigg Grammar School, reasonably local but with a small boarding house, and I started there in the summer term of 1924, having just turned 9.

The reaction in the village was not entirely favourable. The rector remonstrated with my mother because the headmaster of Brigg Grammar was a Methodist minister, but she was able to reassure him that the housemaster of the boarding house where I was to stay was a staunch Anglican. In fact, the headmaster, HE Bryant, was no longer functioning as a minister and certainly made no attempt to influence the boys in a nonconformist direction. The housemaster of School House, the boarding house, was HA Shute. A staunch Anglican he may have been, but he was also a stern disciplinarian, who once caned me, I remember, for some misdemeanour.

The School was founded in 1669 by a local squire, Sir John Nelthorpe of Scawby, the first Nelthorpe Baronet. He had been born in Brigg, trained as a lawyer but turned soldier in the Civil War. He never married so decided to make his permanent memorial a school in Brigg where boys were to be 'taught the Lattin, Greeke and Hebrew languadges, to write alsoe, and Arethmaticke'. Provided they were drawn from an area defined in his will boys were to 'have their learning gratis'; those from other localities had to pay. In his will, Sir John left land in various parts of the county to provide an income for the school, as well as a capital sum to fund the provision of buildings. The school was proud of its history and a member of the Nelthorpe family was chairman of the governors during the time that I was at school and for a number of years afterwards. When I joined, there were about 250 boys, 25 of whom were also boarders, the rest were day boys. In 1976, I believe, the school amalgamated with nearby Brigg Girls' High School and the resulting comprehensive is now known as The Sir John Nelthorpe School. I was pleased to be invited to speak at the last Speech Day before the school went comprehensive and I enjoyed the occasion thoroughly.

The core of the school was its original building, a large hall erected in 1680 by William Catlyn, a master builder from Hull. It is, I think, now the school library. There were some adjacent classrooms and running north from the west end was a one-storied block which housed the physics and chemistry laboratories. During my time at the school, a two-storied block was built parallel to it at the east end. East of the main building was the boarding house and beyond that the playing field. When I started there was also a tin hut which housed the two lowest classes, who were presided over by a Miss Couldrey, the only woman on the staff. In the boarding house there was a large common room called the Day Room and a dining room, together with a room for the two assistant housemasters. Mr Shute's wife presided over the domestic side of things and, along with their two children, the family had their meals with us. It was regarded as an insult to Mrs Shute if we did not eat all the food provided. On the first and second floors were the dormitories and the matron's room. (My first love affair was an attachment to the matron, a young nurse from Weston-super-Mare.) As one got older and moved from the first to the second floor dormitory, one had to go through an initiation process which consisted of swinging across the room on the two iron bars which supported the roof.

Mr Shute was the dominating figure of my early years and, being the master of the boarding house, we saw more of him than of the rest of the staff. He was also the chemistry master. In those days there was much learning by heart. I have never forgotten the jingle:

Little Willy's dead and gone,
His face we see no more,
For what he thought was H_2O
Was H_2SO_4.

A broom handle was kept in the chemistry laboratory; one end of it would be put on a boy's nose, a question asked, and the handle pressed until it was answered correctly. That was rather typical of the standard of teaching in my early days, though things were changing rapidly. The Physics master was called Thumwood, and he went to live in Vienna after he retired but returned to England and settled in Chichester in a hotel following a heart attack. To occupy himself he learned to read sixteenth- and seventeenth-century handwriting and went every day to the Record Office to transcribe documents. I was delighted to find him there when I became Bishop and saw a good deal of him until he went to live with his sister.

One of the best teachers was the mathematics master, AE Knight, called, for some obscure reason, Bumper. AJ Gregory, known as Prague, taught French rather ineffectively until the subject was taken over by a newcomer by the name of Morris. In my last two years, Prague also taught me German. William Lamb, who was at the School from 1919 to 1937, taught me Latin, again rather ineffectively, until a younger man replaced him teaching the senior forms. Lamb had been an undergraduate at Worcester College, Oxford, and claimed to have occupied the rooms in which Amy Robsart's body had been laid before her funeral in St Mary's, the University Church. She was the wife of Robert Dudley, afterwards Earl of Leicester, a favourite of Queen Elizabeth I. On 8 September 1560, Amy was found dead at the foot of a staircase of Cumnor Place near Abingdon. The circumstances were suspicious and Dudley was widely rumoured to have been responsible for her death. William Lamb would have us boys believe that on the anniversary of her death all the bedclothes were suddenly whipped off him in the middle of the night without any sign of anyone else being there. Why Amy Robsart's ghost should have done this piece of mischief was not explained but the *frisson* of the story was much enjoyed.

Mr Bryant retired in 1927 and was succeeded as headmaster by JT Daughton, a lively little man who had poor sight and for some therapeutic reason wore blue-tinted glasses. His wife was as large as he was small and together they rather reminded one of Ko-Ko and Katisha in the second act of *The Mikado*. When Mr Shute, the housemaster, left to be headmaster of Sleaford Grammar School, the Daughtons moved into School House and the headmaster became the boarding master also.

In 1930, towards the end of the summer holidays, I was taken ill. Appendicitis was diagnosed, and I went into a nursing home in Grimsby for an operation. I had experienced surgery before. When I was about ten years old, the village doctor decided that I should have my tonsils and adenoids removed. This operation he performed at my home, on the dining room table, which was taken upstairs to one of the bedrooms for better light. I do not think this surgery was entirely successful as I have suffered occasional soreness on one side of my throat ever since, but the removal of my appendix seems to have been accomplished without problem. I recovered rapidly from the operation. By that time, I had discovered Wagner and I was given the vocal score of *Die Walküre*, which occupied my attention while I was bedridden. It was, however, some years before I was able to go and experience Wagner on stage for the first time, travelling to Golders Green to see Florence Austral and Walter Widdop in *Tristan* under Thomas Beecham. Musically it was very fine, I remember, but, as both the soloists were rather large, the tragic climax at the end when Isolde dies on top of Tristan was rather a ludicrous spectacle.

Surgery and convalescence delayed my return to school at the beginning of the new term and when I got back I found there had been a number of staff changes. The new senior history master, Mr Henthorn, became a considerable influence on my life, and until his death was someone with whom I met regularly on the council of the Lincoln Record Society. There were new French and Latin teachers, the latter known as 'Tiger' Richards, and a new Physics master. There seemed to be a general change in the tone of teaching and it became much more professional. However, I still think I have suffered all my life due to the very inadequate teaching of English Literature and Scripture. The master in charge of both subjects was a former congregationalist minister. His teaching method consisted principally of making us read texts for which he provided next to no literary or historical explanation. It may have been because of his lack of inspirational teaching that I have very little memory of what I read in those years. Certainly at an early stage I read *Alice in Wonderland* and later Dumas – *Twenty Years After* and *The Three Musketeers*. At some stage I made the acquaintance of John Buchan, some of whose books, especially those featuring that most unlikely of heroes, Dickson McCunn, have remained regular reading. Classics such as Jane Austen did not feature until I was at Oxford but I encountered Shakespeare at school and I appeared as Shylock in the trial scene from *The Merchant of Venice* at my last Speech Day.

At quite an early age I learned to read music and play the piano. At Brigg we had a music teacher called Rowbottom who had rather old-fashioned methods. I sat on a tall piano stool with my hands high above the keyboard. I remember he was very proud of his gramophone and had four loudspeakers, one in each corner of the room. When I later went for piano lessons with the organist of St James', Grimsby, Stanley Robson, he had me sit on an ordinary-level piano stool with my hands in a different position from that to which I had grown accustomed. I made no real progress with him and rather lost interest for a time until I went to a piano recital which so inspired me that I resumed playing, practising three hours a day and learning some Chopin. When I went back to Mr Robson he said, 'I never thought I would ever hear you play like that.'

My two-and-a-half years in the sixth form at Brigg were the most interesting of my school life, largely because of the changes in the staff and the improvement in the style of teaching that took place. I also engaged with the life of the school in other ways when, in due course, I became Senior Prefect and Head Boy. I remember with particular appreciation the work of Mr Henthorn, the history master. For the Higher Certificate examination I studied eighteenth and nineteenth century English history, together with European history of the same period. During that time I also completed my first piece of serious writing as an entry for a school prize – an essay on the events leading up to the Great Reform Bill of 1832. I won the prize. I had, however, been studying the same period for some years before and I got rather tired of it, so when I had taken the Higher Certificate and it was suggested that I should stay on at school for another year before going up to Oxford, I decided to widen my historical interests. I started to study the history of the Reformation and was advised to take, at least, the history section of the Higher Certificate again in the hope of getting a distinction. I still have in my possession the English translation of Ranke's *History of the Reformation in Germany*, which I read carefully and which did a great deal to fill me with an intense dislike of the Reformation. However, I was not destined to complete that course. I had been studying the syllabus that I would have to cover for the Pass Moderations examination at Oxford and decided to take three languages, including German, which would excuse me from half the set books. It seemed important, therefore, that my German should be considerably improved beyond what I had so far learned at school and it was arranged that I should go to Germany for the period from May to August of 1933.

I had only been out of England once before when in 1927 my father took me for a week's holiday to Paris. I remember that we went by ferry from Newhaven to Dieppe and then by train, but I cannot recall where we stayed. That visit was enhanced by my having recently seen a film version of Dumas' *Twenty Years After* and having read *The Three Musketeers*. I saw the characters and setting of those two books everywhere, and I experienced Paris through the eyes of Dumas. In France we visited Fontainebleau and Versailles, and saw a performance of *Around the World in Eighty Days* at Le Chatelet. It was a most exciting and enjoyable week. I returned to France with a school friend, Peter Campbell, in 1936 but apart from that brief visit I was not to go to Paris again until 1948.

As an impressionable young man, just out of school, not widely travelled and from a rural part of England, I came to Germany at a time of particular interest as well as growing concern. It was at a crucial stage in the development and rise to power of the Nazi movement. Adolf Hitler had become Reichskanzler in January, shortly before I arrived, and the first developments of his policy were taking place together with some indications of what was to follow. I, however, knew little about Germany before this visit other than that Hanover, my destination, was the state from whence came George I and the Hanoverian dynasty on the throne of Great Britain. I must have been aware through the newspapers of Hitler and the rise of the Nazi movement but my thoughts about going to the country were not affected as they might have been later on. In 1933, to all outward appearances, things were relatively quiet politically and my thoughts were dominated by the prospect of visiting an opera house and seeing a performance of Wagner.

A former Brigg pupil by the name of Lovelock had a year or two before gone to live with a family in Hanover called Hartmann, and arrangements were made that I should go to stay with the same family. My father travelled with me and we crossed from Hull to Bremen on a cargo boat and then went from there to Hanover by train. We were received by the family with which I was to stay and my father returned to England. I lived with the Hartmanns at No 14 Rumannstrasse until the end of August but during part of July and August we went to Osterode in the Harz Mountains to stay with Frau Hartmann's mother. The family in which I found myself consisted of the father and mother, and a ten- or eleven-year-old boy called Axel. The household also included two other lodgers, a young man of about my age, possibly a little older, who belonged to the Prussian *Junker* class which was absorbed into one of the Nazi organizations while I was there; and a young female student who was a militant Nazi. The family as a whole were strong supporters of the regime. Carl Hartmann was a school-master, a teacher of German Literature who had edited one of Schiller's plays. He had been a member of the Sturm Abteilung, the Brown Shirts, since 1929 and as I listened to the talk about Germany in the 1920s, the inflation and the other sufferings resulting from the Treaty of Versailles, I began to understand how the Nazi movement came to be seen by many as a great hope of recovery and renewal. There seemed, at that stage, to be a continuance of democracy with Hindenburg as President and the Reichstag. Young Axel Hartmann already belonged to the Hitler Jugend and could not believe that I was not familiar with the *Horst Wessel Lied* (*Die Fahne Hoch*), by now the official anthem of the Nazi party. I had been studying German for only a short time at school and had no great acquaintance with the literature but I knew about Goethe and Faust and had read Heine's *Die Harzreise*. I had not been long in Germany before I learned from the wife of the British Vice-Consul that Heine was a Jew and not to be regarded as a com-mendable German author. My ignorance of German culture was paralleled by a lack of knowledge of England among those with whom I came in contact. I remember being asked whether there were any distinguished English composers and, having recently sung in *Messiah*, I rather unthinkingly mentioned Handel. The immediate reply came back – but he was German! When I mentioned Edward Elgar and Arthur Sullivan, they had not been heard of.

Through a number of small incidents in the relatively sheltered life I shared with this typical German family, I could not help becoming gradually more aware of the growing influence of the Nazi movement. On one occasion, when I was out for a walk in the country with Carl Hartmann, we passed through a village and he said that this had once been a great centre of communism. I asked where they were now and he just smiled and we went on. On another occasion, when we were staying in the Harz Mountains, I went from Osterode for a whole day's walk and when I was well out in the country a young German student caught up with me and we got to conversing. When he discovered that I was English and could be trusted, he let himself go and told me about the sufferings and problems the Nazis were causing him and his fellow left-wing students. I gained an impression of the developing situation in other ways also. For a time I taught English to a lawyer who was, to a certain extent, sympathetic to the Nazis but not altogether happy with the developments that were taking place. He was nevertheless quite clear that it would be extremely frustrating and even dangerous for his career to make any public opposition. I, myself, had German lessons from the wife of the British Vice-Consul. He was English but his wife was German. It was interesting that all they felt they could talk about was the way in which Hitler had made the trains run on time and had cleaned up the literature on the station book stalls. On Sundays I went to the nearest Roman Catholic church and had one or two conversations with the priest there. He clearly knew nothing about the Church of England and was not particularly interested in learning more, but he was obviously very careful about what he said to a foreigner concerning the political state of things in Germany, and no members of the congregation ever tried to speak to me. On the last Sunday I was in Hanover, I think it must have been the last Sunday in August 1933, there was a great festival of German schools in the Hindenburg stadium to which the Hartmanns took me. The climax of the afternoon was when the children formed an outline map of Germany in the centre of the Stadium and outside the frontiers were groups representing Sudetenland, Danzig and the parts of Poland to which the Germans laid claim, and the Saar. To great applause and shouting, the frontiers were pushed out and all those outlying parts brought in. This left an impression that I have never forgotten as it clearly showed what the up-and-coming regime intended to happen. I have often wondered whether the British Vice-Consul reported that sort of thing to the Foreign Office, and, if he did, whether they took any notice. It so clearly indicated what the official policy was and it also showed what was being done in the education and formation of children's minds. I am sure that similar things must have happened elsewhere in Germany and that these contributed to the support of Nazi policy, and in subsequent years, eventually to the war.

When eventually I returned home, I felt glad to be back in England. My one real happiness in Hanover had been in going to the opera house, where I saw my first performances of *Die Meistersinger, Der Fliegender Hollander* and also *Teifland* by d'Albert, which I have only seen once since. The Wagner I saw made me realise how much a German performance added to the presentation. I must also have practised the piano quite hard while there, still enthused by my newly acquired skill, as I remember that someone asked Frau Hartmann whether I played the piano, to which she replied, 'Uberhaupt übungen' (mostly exercises). I had no further contact with the Hartmann family or they with me. Looking back over my stay with them, there are a number of inconsequential things I recollect that were rather typical of the atmosphere in that particular home. One is that the cheese was kept securely sealed in a kind of glass cake dish and they were insistent that the lid be replaced immediately after one had served oneself because of the smell of the cheese. Another was their insistence that you must not drink cold water after eating fruit as it was a very dangerous thing to do. They seemed always to be going on about it and I believe it was a general German superstition at that time. Fifty years later, my wife and I went for a holiday in Germany. We visited Osterode and the Harz mountains and then went on to Hanover. I was able to find Rumann-strasse, but half of it had been destroyed by bombing and numbers 1 to 14 had disappeared. What became of the Hartmann family, I do not know.

2

The Church of my Youth

My father's family were Primitive Methodists. Methodism was very strong in Lincolnshire, perhaps unsurprisingly given the Wesleys' family background at Epworth in the north west of the county. There were two Methodist chapels in the village. The grander and larger was the Wesleyan, attended by those of the upper-middle class who were not Church of England. The smaller was the Primitive Methodist chapel attended by the farm labourers and shopkeepers, such as my father's family. It was said, rather sneeringly, that Primitive Methodists always had a tea party to celebrate Good Friday. Many years later, when I was involved in the Anglican–Methodist Conversations, it was difficult not to call to mind the Waltham situation.

I do not remember my father having anything to do with religion. When it became known to him that I felt I had a vocation to be ordained, he is said to have remarked to my mother that he could not understand how anyone could think himself called to convert other people. Towards the end of her life, my mother told me my father was considering being confirmed but nothing came of it. It was the Church of England to which my mother belonged, and it was the Church of England that influenced my upbringing. On Sundays my mother and I, and sometimes my grandfather, went to Matins at Waltham parish church, where the rector was a retired headmaster, William Horn. When I went to school in Brigg, I found that the boarders were marched to the parish church there, dressed in Eton suits. The Vicar of Brigg was, by then, the same Fred Burgess who christened me at St James's, Grimsby. On the first Sunday of the month at St John the Evangelist, Brigg, the service was a sung Eucharist rather than Matins, and I found this much more interesting. For me, something seemed to be happening in the service rather than just the recitation of a lot of words. This impression may have been strengthened by the fact that at Matins the lessons were usually read by a local bank manager who seemed to have studied the mode of delivery of Sir Henry Irving, who was still regarded as a model. Indeed, I can remember as a small boy trying to imitate him myself.

When I was about thirteen I strained my heart cross-country running and for a time I became a weekly boarder. As a result, I was prepared for confirmation by the Rector of Waltham when I came home at the weekends. Mr Horn had been headmaster of Alford Grammar School, and was High Church in principle, though he felt himself too old, he said to me once, to make changes to the services. He assured me that he would have liked to have introduced a sung Eucharist and that there were some very fine settings by Mozart. Looking back, I cannot see Waltham parish church choir singing Mozart masses. When a Sung Eucharist was finally brought in by his successor, the music was by Caleb Simper, whom Ralph Vaughan Williams once coupled with John Henry Maunder remarking, 'Composers with ridiculous names: their names are about the one thing these composers couldn't help; other aspects of their activities are less innocent.' Simper's tuneful, Victorian melodies would have fallen sweetly on the ears of the congregation at Waltham. To help with my preparation for confirmation, Mr Horn gave me a moderate Catholic interpretation of the Book of Common Prayer and a helpful little devotional guide by Vernon Staley called *The Christian Way*. I was confirmed at Brigg parish church by the Bishop of Lincoln, Dr William Shuckburgh Swayne. I can remember little of the ceremony, only that as we were sitting beside the pulpit I could see and note with approval that the bishop wore an alb and girdle. When he resumed his cope after the sermon the morse fell and clattered to the ground.

When I returned to school after recovering from my operation for appendicitis, I found that the new history master, Mr Henthorn, had completely revised and updated the teaching of history, based on university methods. We wrote essays which were discussed in class. At some stage that year we studied the history of the Oxford Movement and its huge influence on the self-understanding of the Church of England. Following on from the confirmation preparation I had been given by Mr Horn, this opened my eyes to a bigger view of the Church of England than I had had hitherto. I came to see the Church of my baptism as part of the Western Catholic Church and accepted the teaching of John Keble, John Henry Newman and Edward Bouverie Pusey, the leaders of the Oxford Movement, as the true teaching of the Church of England. Some might, perhaps, regard this as a 'conversion' moment in my life. Certainly as a result, I formed the conviction that I ought to make my confession so I sought out the Vicar of Brigg, the same Fred Burgess who baptized me. After he heard my confession and gave me some advice, he set me a penance. I do not recall what it was I had to say or do, but I do remember him saying that the penance was one frequently set by Father Bell Cox for his penitents. Cox was one of the pioneer Anglo-Catholic incumbents in Liverpool, where he was persecuted for his teaching and practice.

At about that time a new incumbent was appointed to St Andrew's, Grimsby, a parish church beside the old market in the centre of the poorer part of the town and near the docks. Father Tom Warrilow was a devoted priest who rapidly transformed the worship of St Andrew's into that of a typical Anglo-Catholic church of the time. This attracted much publicity locally and nationally, and the son of the founder of the Protestant Truth Society, John A Kensit, came to hold meetings of protest in the market place. Kensit was a noted campaigner against ritualism in the Church of England and a populist agitator. At one of these gatherings Father Warrilow managed to get on the platform wearing his cassock and biretta and address the crowd. My Waldram relations at St James's were rather shocked by this and I remember there being talk about it at our Christmas gatherings. I had not come into contact with such popular opposition to ritual developments in the Church of England before, though I must have known of the much earlier prosecution of Bishop King through my father's stories of his friend Mr Watkinson. I first became aware of the activities of the Kensitites through listening to the Christmas broadcasts from St Hilary in Cornwall, and hearing of what Father Bernard Walke had suffered there in August 1932. I had read of the lawsuit brought against him by one of his parishioners, a Miss King, in collusion with the Protestant Truth Society and how they had succeeded in damaging the Church by the violent removal of altars and statues. A national newspaper described the scene on 10 August:

> The beautiful reredos at the back of the Altar, designed by Ernest Procter, ARA, was destroyed and the canopy torn down. Two tabernacles were removed, the Venetian bracket supporting the image of St Joseph was dug out of the wall and the images of St Anne and Our Lady removed. The fifteenth-century font was smashed and the plinth at the foot of the memorial to Canon Rogers, a former Vicar of Penzance, was broken.

How could one not be moved by reading of such a scene? Many years later, I visited St Hilary, now restored, and I read Father Walke's moving autobiography, *Twenty Years at St Hilary*.

I was able to attend St Andrew's, Grimsby, when I was at home, usually on a Sunday evening when Father Warrilow would preach powerfully for forty minutes. I introduced myself, went to see him, and we had several conversations. I discovered he used to go out visiting at 2pm every weekday and thereby visited every house in the parish. He told me that on one such visit a woman had said to him, 'I don't go to church because I never go out of the house for anything.' He replied, 'You will go out one day, feet first.' Eventually he left Grimsby and went to Frome. St Andrew's was never the same again.

The other church in Grimsby which developed along similar Anglo-Catholic lines was in the more fashionable southern part of the town, St Augustine's. It developed its tradition under a Father Bloomer and his curate, Father Richardson. Richardson had been trained at Nashdom Abbey, the Anglican Benedictine community in Berkshire, where a retired priest used to train those young men who, for various reasons, did not want to go to one of the ordinary theological colleges. Some years later, after I had been ordained and was at Pusey House, I looked after the parish while Father Bloomer was away. Amongst other things, I took the wedding of a parishioner who was marrying an American airman stationed at one of the airfields which abounded in Lincolnshire. I was fascinated by the amount of documentation produced, including a paper informing the girl of what she would and would not become entitled to by marrying an American airman. I remember it ended by insisting that she would not become entitled to free dental treatment!

Mr Horn died shortly after I was confirmed, and he was succeeded as Rector of Waltham by the Reverend GF Holme, who I had heard preach at Brigg on one occasion as he was the father of the school doctor. He was well over seventy when he was appointed but he was a man of great energy and determination who built churches and other parochial buildings wherever he went. He came to us after 30 years in Penshaw in the Durham diocese, where he had made the acquaintance of AEJ Rawlinson, subsequently Bishop of Derby, whose theology he admired. Holme's wife told me they had wanted for some time to move to Lincolnshire to be nearer to their son. When Holme saw that Waltham was vacant and discovered it was a Crown living, he immediately took a train to London, went to Downing Street and asked to be appointed. He was.

Having arrived at Waltham, Mr Holme found that there had been a great housing development in the parish, around the railway station, two miles from the main village. Mr Horn bought a plot of land with a view to eventually providing a new church and social centre. The new rector decided to work on this immediately. He made several thousand concrete blocks in the rectory garden, had them carried down to the new site and there, with the help of various roped-in tramps, he dug the foundations and built the walls of a church hall. He employed professional craftsmen and builders to put in the windows and build the roof. After I went to Oxford, I was able to help him during the vacations. I encouraged his desire to start a Sung Eucharist in the parish church, and bought two sets of vestments, which he was delighted to have. He wanted to wear them when the bishop dedicated the new hall so people could see that the bishop approved. I could tell from the structure and content of Mr Holme's sermons that he had been a fine preacher, but by the time he came to us the gospel message had rather deteriorated.

I have one more memory which rather illustrates the character of the rural church in Lincolnshire at the time. The parish church had a verger called Thornton who liked to be referred to as the sexton. One Sunday, when I was doing a good deal to help in the church, Mr Holme was rather late in coming from the rectory. Thornton and I were standing at the church door and he turned to me and said, 'If t'oad chap don't come, if you do th'up stuff I'll do down stuff.' By this he meant that if the rector did not appear I was to preach and he would read the prayers. It was common in the village at the time for the sexton to make most of the responses and I heard of one where when the lady of the manor was being churched after childbirth and the vicar said, 'O Lord, save this woman thy servant', the sexton replied, 'Who putteth Her Ladyship's trust in Thee.'

3

Oxford, 1933 to 1939

My mother's two Waldram cousins, Horace and Kythé, had both gone to Cambridge and she was determined that I, too, should attend university. Brigg Grammar School at that period in its history had little knowledge of universities, but the second headmaster during my time there, Mr Daughton, had been to Oxford. I was put in for scholarships at all three groups of colleges, unsuccessfully I fear, but I was offered a place at Exeter. At that stage it was still my firm intention to be a lawyer and become Lord Chancellor, but Cheshire, who was the law tutor at Exeter, advised his pupils to read another subject first. I was accepted to read History.

Not being offered a scholarship or exhibition by any college was a slight setback but I successfully sat an examination in Lincoln to win a Lindsey County senior scholarship. This was for the considerable sum of £100 per annum, which substantially helped my parents with the cost of university education. I sat for the examination along with Margaret Burgess, eldest daughter of the then Vicar of Brigg, who also won a scholarship and went to St Hugh's. She subsequently married Canon Herbert Waddams, the Archbishop of Canterbury's secretary for foreign relations and, later, a residentiary canon of Canterbury Cathedral.

As well as winning the scholarship, the other thing of great importance to happen at that time in Lincoln was that on one morning I went to Holy Communion in the Cathedral and, for reasons which I still do not understand, I knew quite clearly when I came out that I must be ordained. That, however, made no immediate alteration to my plans and I went up to Oxford for the Michaelmas term of 1933 to read history.

Before going up I found no shortage of encouraging advice from those at home. When he was at Oxford, Mr Daughton had been at St Catherine's, which during his time was a non-collegiate institution, so his perspective was more of the university as a whole than any specific college. I remember him sharing his enthusiasm about Sunday evenings and how after dinner, one should go to the sermon at the University Church and then to the Balliol Concert. These evening sermons had been started by FR Barry, Vicar of St Mary's, and were usually preached by a distinguished visitor.

The Rector of Waltham had a rather different picture of Oxford. He had been an undergraduate at Queen's in the 1880s and was full of stories about correct social behaviour, of waiting to be called on by second- and third-year men before he called on any of them. He told of how some seniors had collected the visiting cards of several second- and third-year men and left them in the rooms of some unfortunate freshman who then returned the calls, committing a social gaffe by doing so. Knowing where my mind was tending, he recalled that in his day men who hoped to be ordained were required to attend the divinity lectures and told me of one in which the lecturer had paused for a moment and, in the silence, a voice at the back of the room was heard to say, 'What's trumps?' He urged me to get in touch with Pusey House, which must have been founded in his time at Queen's. Mr Daughton, however, warned me against committing myself to any religious institutions, mentioning specifically Pusey House. So, it was with these two very different pictures and pieces of advice that a very shy and rather nervous youth of eighteen arrived at Exeter College in Oxford one Thursday in October 1933.

I found my rooms in College and was informed that dinner was at seven in the hall and that after dinner the sub-rector would speak to all the freshmen. At Exeter, I soon discovered, the sub-rector is what in some other colleges is called the dean, the disciplinary officer. There was some considerable time before dinner so after unpacking, I went out for walk into the Broad. At the Martyrs' Memorial, in the spirit of exploration, I turned into St Giles and to my surprise, soon found myself passing the very Pusey House about which I had received such contradictory advice. There was a notice on the door and I stopped to read it. While I was doing so, the door opened and a priest in a cassock emerged, on his way to post a letter. He stopped and asked who I was and to what College I belonged and rapidly ascertained that I was a practising Anglican. Without further ado, he then suggested that I should come back on Sunday and sing in the choir. This priest was Freddy Hood, the approach was typical of him and he was the first person to make me feel really welcome in Oxford.

Going back to college we had dinner and after dinner were addressed by the sub-rector, JPVD Balsdon, generally known in college as Dacre. He had been a scholar at Exeter in the early 1920s having come from Exeter School. After a brief period as a schoolmaster and then a tutor at Keble College, he had come back to Exeter as a fellow and saw himself as the epitome of the true spirit of the college and the representative of its authentic traditions. He had a loud and somewhat artificial manner of speech which was very off-putting to ordinary, shy people like myself. He remained sub-rector until Greig Barr became a fellow in 1946. Over the years, colleges have often depended on such bachelor fellows who live in college, become senior in its community, and represent the history and traditions of their particular institution. They were greatly respected and obvious candidates for headships when vacancies occurred.

The senior tutor at Exeter was EA Barber, a Latin scholar, and together, he and Dacre left one in no doubt that classical Mods and Greats were superior to all other subjects. He was regarded as the greatest scholarly authority on the Latin writer Propertius, a contemporary of Ovid and one of the greatest elegiac poets of the first century BC. Nevill Coghill, later best known for his lively modern English version of Chaucer's *Canterbury Tales*, once told me that in common room one evening after dinner, he had asked Barber's opinion of the literary merits of a recent English translation of Propertius and had received the reply, 'I have never concerned myself with the gush aspect of the subject.' This more or less prevented any further conversation between the two of them. Barber was my moral tutor. He was essentially a kind man who did his best to get to know the undergraduates in his care and entertain them. Somewhat to his colleagues' surprise, he had married a Swiss-French woman, whose English was never perfect, but she was a very friendly and amusing person. Barber was a typical classical scholar, demanding acute attention to detail not just in his subject but in all aspects of life. For example, when he later became Rector, there was an occasion when Greig Barr, the then sub-rector, had to go to tell him that one of the undergraduates had been arrested the previous evening, having been found in a ladies lavatory, dressed in women's clothes. Greig waited anxiously for the rector's reaction. When it came, it was: 'In which public convenience did this occur?' – the one detail that had been omitted from the account. I recall another vignette. At a meeting of the chapel committee, Nevill Coghill proposed that the undergraduate choirmen should wear cassocks at chapel services as well as surplices as the boy choristers did already. When Barber seemed reluctant to agree to this, Coghill asked him, 'Are your objections aesthetic or theological?' The reply was, 'Theological on the whole,' which so perplexed the rest of us that the subject was dropped. Many years later, after Barber retired, he and his wife lived near us in North Oxford. My wife and I saw them frequently and I did my best to minister to him in his last years but I could never discern what his religious beliefs really were.

The college was founded by Walter de Stapledon, Bishop of Exeter, in 1314 and had a number of scholarships and exhibitions for boys from schools in a restricted area – the original diocese of Exeter, namely the counties of Devon and Cornwall. This area was enlarged in the 1920s to include Somerset and Dorset. The then Rector, Farnell, had said somewhat inaccurately, 'We shall then be coterminous with the ancient kingdom of Wessex.' The Rector when I went up was RR Marrett, whose autobiography, A Jerseyman at Oxford, indicates his Channel Island origins. He was a classicist, originally, but had turned to the study of anthropology. He was a pioneer in the development of this subject at Oxford and the 'father' of the pre-animistic theory of the origin of religion. The 'mana theory' associated with his name has become an established feature of the religious studies vocabulary. He was a big, bluff man whose manner of speech often left one in doubt about the seriousness of what he was saying, as one story which circulated about him illustrates. According to the story he was said to have written a book on anthropology for the Home University Library, which was then published at a shilling a volume, and someone had pointed out mistakes in it, to which Marrett is said to have replied, 'You can't expect the truth for a shilling.'

After I had taken my degree, CT Atkinson, my tutor, invited me to dinner at high table on a Sunday evening. Marrett's portrait had recently been painted and was hanging over the fireplace on the north side of the hall. There was some discussion about it amongst the fellows around me and at the end of dinner Atkinson said, 'Let us go and look at it.' We stood in front of the picture and Atkinson remarked, 'The face in that picture is the face of a man at a loss for a word. Have you ever known the Rector at a loss for a word?' We then joined the others in the Old Bursary for dessert and I was seated next to the great man himself, who said to me magisterially, 'I have written a number of books and the critics have been kind enough to say that I have a fine style. I have maintained that in all forms of primitive religion there is an influence which I have called "mana". When this staircase was being rebuilt last year they found inscribed on one of the oldest beams the letters "Mana"!' Whether this was significant, coincidental or serendipitous was never revealed.

As I was to read history, I had first to take Pass Moderations. I had earlier discovered that if I did three languages I would be exempt from half the set books in each. Fresh from my four months in Germany, I did German, French and Latin and, with fewer set books to read, took the examination after one term instead of the usual two. This enabled me to start the history course in my second term. Modern History at that time consisted of what was called 'continuous English history to 1914'; a selected period of European history; constitutional history with set texts; political thought, examining Aristotle, Hobbes and Rousseau; and a special subject. Having been studying the eighteenth and nineteenth centuries for the last five years at school, I rather reacted against that period and therefore when I was offered a choice I selected the medieval constitutional period with Stubbs' *Charters* as my set text, European history from 918 to 1273, and St Augustine as my special subject.

My first tutor for the course on continuous English history and indeed my supervisor for the whole three years, was CT Atkinson, a remarkable man who had been elected a Fellow of Exeter in 1898. He was a military historian who had written various regimental histories but also a history of Germany in the eighteenth century. He delighted to remind us that a reviewer of his book on Germany had said that at the end it was 'like having gone through a charnel house'. With his pupils Atkinson always referred to the book as 'the charnel house'. As a tutor he was not particularly inspiring but he was very disciplined. No essay was allowed to be more than five pages long and he would insist it covered what he called 'the main points'. His teaching started with the Norman Conquest, on the grounds that English history before that was too difficult for a beginner, and he stopped at 1840 because, he assured us, there was no real history after that. He and a don at Lincoln College, called Carlyle, were, I believe, the last two tutors in Oxford to teach the whole of English history themselves, though whether Carlyle started at the beginning and went right up to 1914 (which at that time was the finishing date) I do not know.

Atkinson was one of the few remaining dons who would not lecture to women. He used to refer to the admission of women to degrees as 'when the University was polluted in 1920'. He would not attend any occasion in an academic gown if women were to be there in gowns. I remember when his former pupil Tom Parker was giving the Bampton Lectures, which are delivered as University sermons, knowing there would be women attending in gowns, Atkinson asked me if there was anywhere in the University Church where one could go without a gown as he felt he ought to attend at least one of Tom's sermons. This prejudice did not prevent him from examining women candidates and he delighted to tell how, on one such occasion, a niece and her mother had been staying with him and had asked to attend the *viva voce* examinations, which of course were public. At lunch he asked them what they thought of the morning and his niece had said, 'O Mother, aren't women stupid!' In spite of all this, he was not a misogynist as some thought. He had been happily married until his wife died in 1933. He objected only to academic women, as one soon discovered when one learnt it was unwise to refer to or quote any woman historian in any essay. He lectured only on a limited number of subjects of which the Peninsular War was one and after his retirement, when he was no longer officially obliged to obey University regulations, the lecture list used to read 'Mr Atkinson – The Peninsular War (for men only)'. He had a dog called Pincher, a very fierce Sealyham, and I was warned by the porter quite early on that if there was no reply when I knocked on the door to his rooms I should on no account enter lest Atkinson had been called away and left Pincher behind to attack all who went in. A story circulated that on one occasion when he had a class in his room he was called away and when he came back it was to find the class sitting on the table and Pincher going round and round it barking at them. If it was raining when he came down to college he brought a towel with him, and the first few minutes of any lecture or tutorial were spent drying Pincher. When dining in hall, he used to put some of the meat into an envelope to take home for the dog.

Atkinson was basically a very kind man and liked by his students. I remember his closeness to his younger brother, Leonard, who was employed in the Public Record Office and came to Oxford for most weekends when they used to dine together in the hall on the Sunday night. In later years, after I had become a Fellow myself, my wife and I used to invite Atkinson to lunch or tea and I visited him frequently at his house in Chadlington Road. It was a great blow to him when his brother

Leonard died. Atkinson had always said that he did not want any memorial service for himself but when eventually he died, the College insisted on holding his funeral in the chapel and I took the service.

Having worked through Atkinson's series of essays on English History and arriving at the nineteenth century, I moved on to European history from 918 to 1273. For this period I was sent to a young Research Fellow who had just arrived at Exeter, having spent most of the previous year in Paris at the Ecole Nationale des Chartes under Ferdinand Lot, and also spent a short time at Munich. This young scholar was Richard Southern, who received a First in History at Balliol, under VH Galbraith, and had then been elected a Junior Research Fellow at Exeter. Being taught by him was like moving into a new world. I have never known anyone like him for being capable of bringing something new and illuminating to any subject of conversation. I remember well the first two weeks of work with him. Atkinson had suggested that in preparation I might get a copy of Tout's *Empire and the Papacy*. I arrived with it but it was pushed aside and for my first assignment I was given a reading list almost entirely in French. On this list was Fournier and Le Bras, *Histoire des Collections Canoniques en Occident*, my first introduction to canon law. I was fascinated by it and my close involvement with the study and development of canon law dates from that time. Here was something which coincided with my vision since the age of seven of becoming a lawyer and eventually Lord Chancellor. Some time later, as I became more deeply immersed in the study of canon law, I came to know Gabriel Le Bras himself. As for the rest of my time with Southern, well, the reading list for the second essay was almost entirely in German and so we went on. Tout's book was never mentioned.

After two terms on the foreign period we moved on to the course on constitutional history to 1307 with Stubbs' *Select Charters* as the set book. I did not think that Dick Southern was very much interested in this field but I did enjoy the lectures on it by JG Edwards. These were the few lectures I remember clearly, though I must have gone to others as I still have notes on lectures by Ogg at Oriel, Wickham Legg at New College and Armstrong and Markham at Hertford, but there was no great encouragement to go to lectures, rather one read and wrote. For Political Science we were taken by the college Philosophy Tutor, WC Kneale, who was a very engaging and interesting person, and I thoroughly enjoyed working with him.

At the end of the course was the special subject, for which I had chosen St Augustine. For this Atkinson sent me to TM Parker, who had just arrived as a Librarian at Pusey House. Tom had been a pupil of Atkinson's at Exeter and had got a First before going on to read Theology. Studying St Augustine for my special subject paper started an interest which led to my writing an article called 'The Augustinian Tradition in the Religious Life' which was my first publication, being accepted by *The Church Quarterly Review*. At the time, I thought that I might have a vocation to the religious life and dreamed of founding an Anglican Dominican Order, but I was wisely told that I should first of all become a member of one of the existing orders. I eventually took the History School in 1936 and later that summer went on to St Stephen's House.

Perhaps because of my early decision to train for ordination, perhaps because of Freddy Hood's initial welcome, perhaps because of my own shyness, Pusey House rather than Exeter College was the centre of my undergraduate life and I made a number of friends there. One of the first was from Jesus across the road, Sidney John, who subsequently added the name Bernard by which he preferred to be called. We saw a good deal of one another and I went to stay with him at his home in Newport, South Wales. Another was Geoffrey Hunt of Wadham with whom I was to later have dealings when he joined the Oxford University Press. A third was Ronald Barrass, also of Wadham. I remember the three of them particularly because we were all involved in a project which took us down to Tredegar in Monmouthshire during several vacations. The inspiration for these visits was a priest, Father Kent White, curate at St George's, Tredegar. During my first year he came to Pusey House to talk about an unemployment centre he was opening in the disused offices of a former colliery. He appealed to us and to the Oxford University Church Union for help. A good many of us responded, organized ourselves and raised money to support the centre. I took on the role of treasurer and those of us who could, volunteered to spend at least part of our vacations helping there.

We discovered an appalling situation in South Wales in 1934. The unemployment rate was very high and the living conditions were pretty awful. I remember visiting some houses built into the mountain side and finding there was water flowing down the back wall. There was terrible poverty; children wearing shoes with great holes in them and whole families sleeping together in one room. Altogether, the conditions were such as I have never seen before or since. As far as we could tell, the government was doing very little to help or even show concern at that time, a factor which prompted many of us to become supporters of the Labour Party. In Kent White's centre, a certain amount of daytime shelter and a hot midday meal was provided for the unemployed. Father White encouraged some of us to become god-parents to children he was preparing for confirmation, and I acquired two goddaughters in this way, with whom, I regret to say, I have completely lost touch. I remember very clearly the confirmation which was taken by the Right Reverend Gilbert Cunningham Joyce, Bishop of Monmouth, an impressive-looking, tall, bearded man. His two addresses on wisdom and holy fear were hardly inspiring for miners' children.

Among other friends acquired through Pusey House were three New College men of different years, Donald Mackinnon, James Stewart and Cheslyn Jones. The oldest of this trio was Donald Mackinnon, of whom I first became conscious at the service of Devotions to the Blessed Sacrament, which was held late on Saturday evenings. What first struck me was his powerful voice but I could not help noticing that he would rarely sing through the whole of any hymn. He would sometimes start in the middle of a verse and sometimes stop before the end of the hymn and the sudden starting or stopping of this loud voice was very disturbing to the rest of the congregation. It must certainly have put off Freddy Hood who accompanied the hymns on the harmonium. This was very typical of Donald's many eccentricities. He would sharpen his pencils with a knife and if he happened to be sitting behind you in the lecture theatre while doing this, it could be quite alarming when his knife missed the back of one's neck by inches. Donald's particular philosophical position was not very evident in his relations with his friends. What was obvious to us, and to others at the time, were his politics and his pacifism. During the Spanish Civil War in the mid-1930s, he seemed to roam the streets, buying every issue of the evening paper as it came out, so great was his concern for the Spanish gov-ernment and his hostility to Franco. During the war he became an air raid warden and when I returned to Oxford, I found him sleeping in the Upper Library at Pusey House every night and reading a selection of the more abstruse books. His hostility to the war was obvious and took particular shape in an active hostility to Bishop Kirk, who had spoken of the rightness of the British government's attitude. He was also hostile to the Bishop of Dorchester, Gerald Allen, who was known as 'Puffles'. It was said that once, when they were together at some meeting, seated at a long table, it was noticed that Donald had disappeared from view and a few minutes later Puffles gave a yelp of pain and clutched his leg. Donald had crawled under the table and bitten him on the shin. He became a tutor at Keble, then a Fellow of Balliol before leaving Oxford for Cambridge, where he was Norris Hulse Professor of Divinity from 1960 to 1978. There are many other anecdotes about his eccentricities and, as with many such people, one can never be sure how many of them are genuine and how many stories are carried over from predecessors. With some justice, the Cambridge Divinity Faculty claims him as perhaps the greatest British philosophical theologian of the twentieth century. His thought and teaching were highly influential on a large number of the current generation of academic theologians, not least the present Archbishop of Canterbury, Dr Rowan Williams.

James Stewart was a friend more of my age who eventually began preparation for ordination at St Stephen's House at the same time as me. He had read Greats and, as many classicists did at the time, he had then read Theology for one year. After ordination, James went to India and joined the Cambridge Brotherhood in Delhi. I remember spending a short holiday with him in Brighton where, among the Anglo-Catholic delights of the churches there, he introduced me to St Wilfrid's. This parish was flourishing at that time under the leadership of Father Wilfrid Westall, who subsequently became Bishop of Crediton in Devon. Many years later, when I was Bishop of Chichester, I had to take the decision to close St Wilfrid's church and I recall that Bishop Westall came and preached at the last service held there. With Cheslyn Jones, of whom I shall have more to say later, we were all three associated with a number of others in a kind of guild of Christian social concern under the guidance of Father Harold Ellis CR.

Another great friend at the time was John Sutters, from St John's, with whom I remained in touch until he died in 2003. I think it was through him that I became involved in some social work organized by Sister Mary Ruth of St Thomas' Convent. This was a gathering of tramps and other unemployed men in Oxford which met at the Convent on Sunday afternoons for tea, chat and a short act of worship. A few undergraduates were involved and under the supervision of John Brewis, vice-principal of St Edmund Hall, we had to take the service and give an address on a text provided by him. Imagine my horror when the first time I led the worship the text given to me was 'Marvel not if the world hate you'.

Oxford undergraduate religion at that time was very much divided into a number of distinctive parties and traditions. It was in Oxford that I came into contact with evangelical Anglicanism for the first time, in those days centred at St Aldate's and at the less well-known St Ebbe's. Both then, and in later years as a college chaplain, I encountered it as a very divisive expression of religion. In my experience, it drew people away from the Church in which they had been brought up, as well as their college chapel, and its enthusiasts refused to co-operate with any other religious group or participate in a university mission. There was also the Student Christian Movement (SCM) which had some very fine people associated with it at the time but which had been a greater force in the earlier part of the century. In the view of my friends, the SCM tended to be rather wishy-washy. The High Church group, which was quite large, was divided into those who went to Pusey House, those who went to St Barnabas, those who went to the Cowley Fathers and a handful who went to other parish churches. Within this High Church alliance there was one main division, the effects of which are still, to a certain extent, with us now. Rather like the dispute between the Big-endians and the Small-endians in Swift's *Gulliver's Travels* over which end of a boiled egg to approach first, much heat but very little light was generated. This division of opinion concerned the liturgy of the Church of England. On one side were those who described themselves as followers of the English Use. They favoured the celebration of the English Liturgy according to the pattern laid down by Percy Dearmer, most popularly in *The Parson's Handbook* but also with more academic rigour in the publications of the Alcuin Club. The liturgical habits of this group were characterized by the other party as 'British Museum Religion' because they favoured the style of liturgical furnishing and vesture which had prevailed in the first years of the reign of Edward VI. Gothic vestments, so-called English altars, and the 'Use of Sarum', were sure signs of this tendency. On the other side were those who followed the Western Rite and ceremonial – in other words, the contemporary liturgical usages of the Church of Rome, but a little adapted to suit the ethos of the Church of England. Here there was further division between those who adapted the Prayer Book rite to fit the Roman pattern, and the more hard-line

Romanizers who basically used the Roman missal either in translation or in the original Latin. This group argued that taste in liturgical furnishings and vestments should be exactly that of the contemporary Roman Catholic Church, as if the Reformation had never happened and fashions had evolved in England in exactly the way they had on the Continent. Their position found its literary expression in the publications of the Society of Ss Peter and Paul. While today sartorial distinctions within the Catholic Movement in the Church of England are less polarized than they were then, there is still a division between those who are loyal to the liturgical formularies of their Church and those who use the Roman Missal in public worship and the Breviary for their Office. My own outlook was undoubtedly shaped by Freddy Hood and later confirmed by Arthur Couratin. It was definitely anti-papalist and liturgically focused on the Interim Rite – a permitted variant of the Holy Communion service in the 1662 *Book of Common Prayer*. I was content with this until the various official revisions of the Anglican liturgy began to appear.

There were other fascinating divisions which showed themselves in various societies, such as the Reunion Society and the Nicene Club, which were addressed from time to time by various senior people. One such was Dr CB Moss who lived in retirement just outside Oxford and who was the epitome of very traditional High Church Anglicanism. In contrast to him there was Dr Scott, the Rector of Oddington, who was very much of a papalist. I remember an occasion when Dr Moss had delivered a paper on something to do with the papacy, and in the discussion afterwards Dr Scott said, 'Twenty years ago I wrote a book in which I established conclusively that the Fathers of the first four centuries recognized papal authority. Nobody has answered it.' There was a pause and it seemed as if nothing more was to be said and then Dr Moss lumbered to his feet and said, 'I have read Dr Scott's book and I think that the reason why nobody has answered it is that no-one takes it seriously!' There were, however, more serious occasions than that to participate in and there were great preachers to be heard, particularly at the late Sunday evening service in the University Church. Two of the Canon Professors of Christ Church, Dr NP Williams and Dr KE Kirk, always attracted a good audience. Among speakers from outside the university. I particularly remember hearing Michael Bolton Furse, Bishop of St Albans, who at that time was prominent in defence of the orthodox doctrine of marriage and divorce. Archbishop William

Temple conducted a mission in the University during my under-graduate days but I cannot remember that it made any impression on me. I do, however, recall his speaking at a meeting in the Union one afternoon. Among the many questions put to him, he was asked if he believed in the existence of the devil. He replied, 'I do, and what convinces me is the fact that every missionary I have ever met who has worked in India or Africa has spoken of the sense of being opposed by forces of evil which were more than just evil men.'

In my first term I joined the Oxford University Church Union (OUCU) which had been founded in the 1880s by Cosmo Gordon Lang, then Vicar of the University Church. It had declined in the period immediately before the First World War, but after the war was revived by Dr JW Wand, Dean of Oriel, who left Oxford in 1934 to be Archbishop of Brisbane. Robert Mortimer, then a clerical student at Christ Church and later a distinguished Bishop of Exeter, was senior secretary and every Friday evening conducted a service of preparation for Holy Communion in the University Church. I was quite soon elected a member of the committee and that marked the beginning of a long connection with the OUCU. Canon Kenneth Kirk followed Dr Wand as President and the Principal of St Edmund Hall, AB Emden, was asked to be chairman of the committee, though my recollection is that Kirk presided over many of the meetings. We had to be careful to distinguish the OUCU from the Church Union founded in 1933 by the amalgamation of the English Church Union and the Anglo-Catholic Congress, a union promoted by Lord Halifax. I do not remember ever seeing that legendary figure, but I sang in the requiem that was held in Pusey House Chapel when he died a little later, and I recall the election of his son Lord Irwin as Chancellor of the University.

The Roman Catholics were definitely a visible presence in the University but, on the whole, they seemed to keep themselves much to themselves. I think I arrived during the last stages of Ronald Knox's chaplaincy. As an Anglican priest he had been chaplain of Trinity, the predecessor as such of Kenneth Kirk, and an associate of such leading Anglo-Catholics as Maurice Child, Sam Gurney and NP Williams. He had collaborated with them in the establishment of the Society of Ss Peter and Paul and wrote some of their earliest tracts. These were designed to be successors to the *Tracts for the Times* of the founding fathers of the Oxford Movement but were much more acerbic in their attitude to the occupants of the episcopal bench of the time. They called themselves 'Publishers to the Church of England' and named some of the products they marketed with conscious irony – 'Lambeth Frankincense', for example, and the 'Latimer and Ridley Pricket Stand'. Knox's conversion to Roman Catholicism in 1918 was a real blow to the Catholic Movement in the Church of England, as well as a great sadness to his father, a prominent Evangelical bishop. He wrote an account of his conversion in a book which he called *A Spiritual Aeneid*. Some reviewer commented that he had not, like Aeneas, carried his father on his back with him. He was one of four brothers, one other of whom Wilfred Knox became similarly prominent in the Catholic Movement. He went to Cambridge to join Alec Vidler and others in what came to be called the Liberal Catholic Group and helped to found a community of celibate priests called the Oratory of the Good Shepherd. Freddy Hood and others in Oxford had little time for this group and the community never attracted me. Ronald developed a talent for writing detective fiction and in the 1920s became nationally prominent through a spoof broadcast about a fictional general strike. He was later appointed Roman Catholic chaplain in Oxford and established the chaplaincy at the Old Palace in St Aldate's. I remember seeing him in the streets from time to time – a rather sad figure – but I had no occasion to meet him. The one Roman Catholic institution which did impress me was the Dominican house, Blackfriars, next to Pusey House, and I went to Compline there quite often. I also went to some lectures on canon law by Father Ambrose Farrell OP, whom I came to know quite well.

The other powerful religious influence in the University at that time was the OICCU, the Oxford Inter-Collegiate Christian Union. This was the Oxford branch of the Intervarsity Federation, a non-denominational evangelical body which was very strict in its rules and rigid in its non-cooperation with any other religious societies. When, as happened every three or four years, there was a University mission organized by the college chaplains in association with the SCM and the OUCU, the OICCU refused to take any part and chose to run its own mission, either at the same time or during the following year.

I have already recounted how Freddy Hood picked me up and recruited me into Pusey House choir on my first day in Oxford. From that moment on, the House became a central part of my life, certainly more so than Exeter. The Principal at that time was Dr Darwell Stone, a distinguished patristic scholar and editor of the *Lexicon of Patristic*

Greek. He had been Principal since 1909 and for most of that time, the House had remained a rather quiet institution not greatly known. He did not have much to do with undergraduates but it would be a mistake to assume he knew nothing about them. Freddy told me of one occasion when he had consulted Darwell about someone who had become involved with a young woman of doubtful reputation. Darwell asked her name and when Freddy replied he thought she was called Cowley Kate, Darwell commented, 'That name is not unknown to me!' Darwell wore a cassock always except during his holiday month and when going to London for Convocation. There was a story that some of the Pusey House lodgers had speculated about whether he slept in it and one young man had got up early and gone into the bathroom to find Darwell sitting in the bath, his long beard in a sponge bag with the strings around his ears. He usually spent his holiday month in North Africa and an undergraduate once asked him whether it was true that he had been seen sitting in a Moroccan café drinking wine and smoking a green cigar. The answer came, 'I don't think it was green.'

I made my first confession in Oxford to Darwell, as, I discovered later, had Robert Mortimer, but after that Freddy Hood became my confessor and remained so until I was ordained. I felt it a great privilege when in my second term, I was asked to serve Dr Stone's Mass which he offered every morning at 7.15. He had no book on the altar save the *Book of Common Prayer*, occasionally supplemented by the *Oxford Diocesan Service Book* but he recited the Roman Canon silently, from memory, on either side of the Prayer of Consecration.

The clerical staff of Pusey House were all known as librarians, the foundation being principally concerned with the care of Dr Pusey's library. Shortly after the House was founded, the librarians as a body were commissioned by the Bishop of Oxford to treat as parishioners any undergraduates who found their way there and chose to worship in the chapel. A sermon of Liddon's, preached in aid of the initial foundation, makes it clear that there was a fear around that the colleges of the University might not long remain religious foundations with chaplains. Pusey House was conscious to provision to cope with that change should it occur by the establishment of alternative pastoral care.

Darwell Stone had brought Freddy to Pusey House in 1922 from St Stephen's House where he had been Vice-Principal. Very quickly, Freddy persuaded Darwell to make some changes which he believed would open the House further to general members of the University.

Before Freddy arrived, the normal approach to the chapel was through the door in Pusey Street. Freddy had the door on St Giles unlocked and notices attached to it and on the wall beside. This notice was what had attracted my attention on my first day in Oxford. I do not know whether Freddy was responsible for bringing Leslie Cross to Darwell's notice, but the appointment of Leslie led to a marked development in the use of the library. In particular, he made one of the two downstairs rooms into a philosophy library, thereby attracting others besides theologians. I must add that later on, when I was in charge of the Library and dealt with the problem of missing books, we seemed to lose far more from the ethics section in that room than from any other.

Darwell retired in 1934 and Freddy became Principal. Humphrey Beevor, a protégé of Freddy's who had been appointed a librarian the previous year, devoted himself to the pastoral care of those who used the House and attended its chapel, leaving the library in the care of Leslie Cross. Freddy took charge of the general policy of the House and planned its preachers, as well as speakers at the weekday evening meetings he started. I heard him say many times that he believed that Pusey House should stand for the traditional Catholic faith presented with an understanding of critical theology and modern thought. He was always willing to invite preachers and speakers with whom he did not always agree. Dean Inge was a fairly regular preacher on Sundays, as was one of his successors at St Paul's, Walter Mathews. Among other speakers I particularly remember, there was Charles Williams, with his strong cockney accent, who talked about the main themes of some of his books. *The Descent of the Dove* I found especially memorable, and I recall being influenced by his theology of coinherence.

Quite early on in my time at Oxford I asked Freddy if I could have instruction in the Catholic religion to enlarge and clarify the knowledge I already had. I went to him once a week for a number of months and also to the 'Quiet Afternoons' and his locally conducted retreats. I learned much from him about prayer and the spiritual life, as well as about Christian doctrine. Early on, again, I asked Leslie Cross to recommend something I should read about the philosophy of religion as I felt very ignorant about it. He suggested a book by AE Taylor which I read and enjoyed but later, as Oxford was dominated by Logical Positivism, I came to feel that philosophy had little to contribute to the understanding and practice of the Christian religion. It seemed to be just the theories of individuals who frequently contradict one another. Something similar might be said about a great deal of modern theological writing. I gradually came to the conclusion that history is the most important discipline and that lessons from the past have so much to teach us in the present and as we look to the future.

Freddy Hood had been an undergraduate at University College where he had been taught theology by NP Williams, at that time Chaplain of Exeter, and who had inculcated into him a very strict intellectual approach. This formation led him to be clear and precise in his arrangement of material and a stickler for accuracy. From his example, I learned a great deal in these respects. It was through him that I later came into direct contact with the Williams family. When NP Williams died in 1943, he left instructions that his body be laid overnight in Christ Church and that Vespers of the Dead be sung. As this service was unfamiliar to Thomas Armstrong, he asked my help and this led eventually to my being asked to become an honorary chaplain to the cathedral.

Freddy had a marvellous capacity for picking up people as he had picked up me, and he must have acquired a great many friends this way. Many of us were invited to stay with him during the vacations in a house he had at Porthcawl in South Wales. It was near enough to where his mother, Mrs Clay, lived and we often used to be taken over to see her; a very fine, amusing, old lady. On the way to Porthcawl we would often stop at Gloucester to visit Philip Usher, who was chaplain to Arthur Cayley Headlam, the Bishop. Freddy had engaged in a public conflict with Headlam about the Church of South India and when on one occasion Headlam heard that Freddy had been to see Philip and had not called on him, he said, 'Not sulking is he?' At Porthcawl, Freddy was much involved with the work of his friends, the rector and his curate, and so we saw something of the life of a South Wales seaside parish. The times at Porthcawl were great fun. In the evenings Freddy would play the piano – I remember his versions of the more ebullient Stanford settings of the *Te Deum*. He also used to read amusing authors to us and it was through him that I came to know *The Autobiography of Augustus Carp*, which remains a great source of pleasure and amusement to me. In this context of friendship as well as spiritual direction, it was to Freddy that I confided my first thoughts concerning ordination. It was he who suggested that after finishing History at Exeter I should go to St Stephen's House and read for the Theology School while preparing for ordination. That was sound advice and so it was eventually arranged.

Freddy had been closely associated with CAH Green, the first Bishop of Monmouth. Green wrote what became the standard history of the disestablishment and constitution of the Church in Wales. He became its second Archbishop and was translated from Monmouth to Bangor. At Monmouth he was followed briefly by GC Joyce and then by AE Monahan, brother of the WB Monahan who wrote two books on St Thomas Aquinas, and whose daughter I later came to know at Worcester. Bishop Monahan made me one of his examining chaplains after I returned to Pusey House in 1941. Freddy already was one and in that capacity had done much for the diocese of Monmouth. When Monahan died, his successor, AE Morris, simply did not reappoint us and there was no word of thanks for all that Freddy had done.

Freddy was also a member of the governing body of the Church in Wales and, as such, was sure that had the Crown appointments system operated in Wales, rather than an elective system, he was very likely to have become a bishop. He knew all the Welsh bishops well and they were all among the regular preachers at Pusey House. Freddy was a good preacher himself and, at times, very Welsh in his manner of delivery. He would frequently ask rhetorical questions in a sermon and told me that he had once been interrupted when he had said, 'If we ask for the prayers of our mother on earth, should we not ask for the prayers of our Lord's Mother in heaven?' and a man at the back of the church had answered loudly, 'No.'

Pusey House's great period was under the principalship of Freddy Hood. He was not without private means and quietly supported the work of the House from his own income. How much became only too apparent after he moved. When Freddy decided to retire from Pusey House, he went to live in a house in London. At this time, the Archbishop of Canterbury asked him to provide pastoral care for priests who had misbehaved in some way and had been placed under discipline. Freddy developed a new ministry in this way, which involved finding secular employment for such priests and keeping in close touch with them until such time as he was able to assure the Archbishop that they could be restored to ministry. This important work continued when he became, first, priest-in-charge of St Mary Aldermary in the City, and then a Residentiary Canon of St Paul's. He also continued to exercise a valued and more general ministry in London and with the wide circle of those who sought his counsel. After his final retirement, the ministry to those under discipline was continued by Kent White and then by Michael Dean.

I, like many others, owe Freddy a great deal in ways I cannot fully express. He gave me all that I needed when I was young and searching after truth, a mode of being and the right mental furniture for life. There is an incident I heard about illustrates Freddy's outlook. At some point in the late 1920s EW Barnes, the Bishop of Birmingham, notorious for his scientific rationalism with regard to the faith and his persecution of Anglo-Catholics in his diocese, was announced to be coming to speak in Oxford. When Freddy heard that some members of the Pusey House congregation were proposing to go and interrupt the proceedings, he persuaded them that it would be much better to spend the time in chapel praying. He never seemed to change and it is a pleasure to record that in 1974, on his way down to Chichester for my enthronement, he again picked up a young person, this time in the train. It was my eldest daughter. I took his funeral at St Mary Aldermary on 26 January 1975, and celebrated the requiem. He was buried in South Wales near his mother.

During my last few years at school I had taken music lessons, initially piano and, a little later, organ and composition, from Stanley Robson, the organist and choirmaster of St James's in Grimsby. He had studied at the Royal College of Music during the time when Sir Hugh Allen was Principal. At the time I was studying, Allen was Professor at Oxford and a Fellow of New College. When I was preparing to go up, Stanley Robson wrote to introduce me to Sir Hugh. When I arrived in Oxford, I received a note asking me to call on him on the following Friday evening. Naturally, I went to see him, but with some apprehension as I had heard stories of his stern way with choral societies. He received me very kindly and after a few minutes' conversation said that I ought to join the Bach Choir and should go to a voice trial next day. This was held in the vestry at New College and seemed to me very formal but I do remember that Sir Hugh, who listened to our voices, played bits of the Mendelssohn Wedding March in between the various candidates' trials. To my surprise, I passed the test easily and was singing second bass in the Oxford Bach Choir on the following Monday evening. Thus began a most enjoyable connection which, except for the short period that I was in Southampton as a curate, lasted until I left Oxford in 1969. It was my good fortune that when I joined the choir it was starting to rehearse the Bach B minor Mass in preparation for a concert the following year and I cannot think of any work that provides a finer introduction to choral singing. Sir Hugh himself came and gave us a lecture on it, and I still have some notes. He had just ceased to be the regular conductor of the choir but came occasionally to take a rehearsal and in 1935 he conducted us in the Brahms Requiem at a memorial concert for King George V. I think we learned that work in just five weeks. The regular conductor was Thomas Armstrong, who had just arrived in Oxford as organist and choirmaster of Christ Church. Tom was a most interesting person and his talks on the works we were doing, and other things, taking up part of every rehearsal, were always instructive and amusing. I learned a great deal about music from those rehearsals. He was not regarded as the best of conductors but I can still recall a later performance of the B-minor Mass conducted by him, in which the Sanctus was a wonderful spiritual experience. Membership of the Oxford Bach Choir is something that I shall always treasure.

I have no recollection of attending the theatre in Oxford during my undergraduate days but I must have gone to the New Theatre, and I certainly made a regular annual visit to see the D'Oyly Carte Opera Company with Henry Lytton and some of my other favourite singers. I better recall the plays held in college gardens, particularly those directed by Nevill Coghill. I remember vividly his production of *The Tempest* staged on the edge of the lake in Worcester garden. Caliban appeared as if from out of the lake and, at the end, Prospero and the others sailed away over the lake with Ariel running as if across the water to bid them farewell.

I enjoyed my undergraduate years but, I have to say, my nervousness and shyness prevented me from taking much part in the life of the college. I do not think that I ever went once into the Junior Common Room. I did, however, go regularly to chapel out of a sense of duty, but I had no real liking for the chaplain, HP Kingdon, who had been appointed when still in deacon's orders in 1933. For that first year, before Kingdon was ordained priest, the Reverend VJK Brook, Censor of St Catherine's, came to celebrate on Sundays. Kingdon's obituarist in the *Daily Telegraph* of 24 June 1989 takes the view that he had 'a remarkable capacity for creating misunderstanding and often left a trail of havoc behind him'. This goes some way to explaining why he was not particularly popular as chaplain. He was an expert in the liberal theology of the Tübingen school but he lectured in language so obscure that few of his students felt up to the task of understanding him. I eventually succeeded him as chaplain in 1946, when the college devised an acceptable way of removing him from office by presenting him to the living of Great Somerford in Wiltshire, where, alas, he proved to be no more popular. But all this lay some time in the future. In 1937, I followed the advice of Freddy and for the next stage in my life moved to St Stephen's House.

In those days, theological colleges had four terms a year so after I had finished the History school, taking an upper second, I enjoyed a short holiday before starting the long vacation term at St Stephen's House. This was the last term with Dr Mitchell as Principal and I am glad to have had the opportunity to know him. He was a shy but kind man and a distinguished scholar, particularly in the field of liturgy. He gave a devotional address in chapel every Friday evening. The House was then in North Oxford, in Norham Gardens, and the chapel was next to the University Department of Education. Evening meetings held in the department would often interrupt our devotions with applause, sometimes tiresomely, but occasionally appropriately, as on one instance I recall, when Dr Mitchell was urging us not to postpone carrying out good intentions.

Arthur Couratin had joined the staff as chaplain in the Trinity term to succeed Dr Mitchell as Principal. He had been a student at St Stephen's House under Mitchell in the 1920s and recently Vicar of St Stephen's, Lewisham. He remained as Principal until he was appointed a Residentiary Canon of Durham in 1960. That meant that he trained priests in his distinctive manner for over 25 years. In his disciplined life and clarity of thought, Arthur was typical of many Anglo-Catholic priests of the time, but he was not a papalist and was more liberal in his theology than many of his contemporaries, having been taught Greats at Corpus by the philosopher Schiller, whom he greatly admired. After the death of their parents, his sister Marian came to keep house for him and the rest of the house. She eventually moved to Durham with him.

The day at St Stephen's House started with silent meditation in chapel, followed by Mass. After breakfast the morning was given to work, and the lesser silence was observed from 9.30am to 12.30pm. After lunch we were free until tea and then there was work again and lesser silence until Evensong at 6.30pm. After dinner we were free until 8.30pm, at which time we said Matins of the following day. The greater silence was then observed until Mass the next morning. Wednesday evenings were free and we were allowed to go to the cinema or the theatre. This was a very disciplined life but we prided ourselves on being less formal than Cuddesdon and, unlike the students there, we did not wear cassocks and surplices until we had been ordained.

After that Long Vacation term, during which I got to know the routines of the House and those who were joining it with me that year, I embarked on work for the Theology School. The first question to be faced was who was to teach me. Due to what I had heard from others at Exeter, I was quite clear that I did not want to have Paul Kingdon as my tutor. I would have liked to have had Harry Carpenter, then chaplain of Keble and one day to be Bishop of Oxford, but he felt it would be embarrassing to take on a pupil from another college which had a theology tutor in post. In the end, Tom Parker was asked to be my tutor and he agreed. He had himself taken the Theology School under NP Williams, so I received the benefit of his views and scholarship at second hand, as it were. I think, however, that it was Tom himself who was exceedingly critical of many of the contemporary commentators on the gospels. He pointed out, with some reason, that here were four very small books and that unless new material could be produced from outside, gospel criticism was entirely the opinions and guesses of individual teachers.

Tom was a great character. I first met him when Atkinson sent me to him to be tutored in St Augustine for my special subject. Later, he and I were to be colleagues on the staff of Pusey House. He was very strict and disciplined in his life and beliefs. I never saw him in anything but clerical dress and he recited the Roman Breviary daily. He was a member of the Society of the Holy Cross (SSC) in the days when many of its members took vows of celibacy. Over the next two years, Tom and I became great friends. We went together on a holiday to Ireland in 1938, sailing from Fishguard to Cork, where we were met by an acquaintance of Tom's called O'Nolan. Tom had met him during his curacy in Somers Town under Father Sir Percy Maryon Wilson, Bart. O'Nolan met us when we arrived, early on Sunday morning, having crossed by night, and before allowing us to go to the hotel where he had booked rooms for us, he insisted on taking us from church to church in Cork, 'to see the religion of the people'. On the Monday morning we hired a car and drove up to Limerick, calling at Killarney on the way, but we avoided kissing the Blarney Stone. We were late in stopping for a meal and it was after 2pm when we found somewhere to order lunch. 'Too late for lunch,' we were told, 'but you can have tea if you wish.' As this prospect seemed better than nothing, we accepted, and were served a hot three-course meal – with tea! The next morning at breakfast we were asked whether we would prefer tea or coffee, and having ordered coffee were then served with tea. Coffee seemed non-existent during that trip. My abiding recollection of Ireland in September 1938 is of being unable to get any meal without tea. As things were building up on the international scene with the Munich Crisis, Tom felt his parents would be getting anxious, so from Limerick we went back to Cork and then home, a brief visit of just two days. I was not to return to Ireland until the late 1960s.

Tom Parker's parents, who kept a grocer's shop in Stratford-upon-Avon and lived at nearby Bidford, were in some ways as remarkable as Tom himself. They were very kind and hospitable and had me to stay for three weeks' recuperation after I joined Pusey House in 1941 and suffered an illness which the doctor said was simply exhaustion. Tom himself had strings of stories to tell. One knew that by prompting him to recount one of them, he could be relied on to follow it with several others, loosely connected. I always think of him when I say or hear the *Te Deum*, for one of his stories was of a priest who had been asked to baptize the twins Cherubim and Seraphim on the grounds that 'they continually did cry'. The sermon at his memorial service in the University Church was preached by Richard Southern, who began, 'It is not easy to speak of one who for the last fifteen years was my confessor', which must have startled some of the hearers.

While at the House I did go to occasional lectures, including *pastoralia* from the Principal, and when we had occasional visitors. I remember we had a guest from Canada who told us about a *pastoralia* lecturer there whose subject was, 'How to hold our elder girls'! The person I remember best of visiting lecturers was Father Cyril Tomkinson, who had just resigned as parish priest of St Bartholomew's, Brighton, and who lived with us for a term before going to Little St Mary's, Cambridge. He told fascinating stories about St Bartholomew's – how on Easter Day it was packed and there would be ladies sitting in the pulpit looking as if they were in a box at the opera; of the silver altar in one of the side chapels, which is still there, and which Cyril called 'Gladys Cooper's dressing table'.

As my first degree was in History, I was permitted to take the

Theology School in two years. The course I followed began with Biblical studies, first the Old Testament, followed by the New Testament in Greek. I did no Hebrew but had to learn New Testament Greek for the second part of the course. Greek is not a language I have ever liked, feeling it contrasts adversely with Latin. A language which changes words at the beginning as well as the end is tiresome. After the Bible, one went on to study early Christian doctrine to AD 461 and Church history for the same period. I cannot remember much else save that after I had taken schools, in which I got a good second, I had to do further courses in doctrine, moral theology and history for the General Ordination Examination, the Theology School having exempted me from the Biblical papers.

Alongside all this was Arthur's training which was nothing if not very practical. There was a large doll, called Pocahontas, which he used for baptism practice. He advised us to look carefully at the names proposed for baptism to make sure that the initials did not spell anything that could become an embarrassment. I was caught out over this at the first baptism I took, for having scrutinized the names and made sure that Denis Owen Brown did not seem to present any problem, at the last moment the parents added George so that the child was DOG Brown. In addition to instruction about the sacrament of penance, he would make specimen confessions, kneeling down beside us and making sure that we dealt adequately with what had been said and did not ramble. We were taught that, as priests, our day should be carefully regulated. It should begin with meditation and Mass, then breakfast, after which one should deal with the post. The rest of the morning should be spent in study and sermon preparation until an early lunch. After lunch one should go to sleep for an hour, preferably in bed, getting up at about 2pm and going out visiting. A cup of tea would be followed by Evensong in church and a period of private prayer before supper. After supper, one should go to whatever parish clubs or meetings might be taking place. There should be one day off a week, kept completely clear.

Arthur was very keen on the Boy Scout Movement as offering a real pastoral opportunity in parish work. Vocations to the priesthood could be encouraged and nurtured within it and when I arrived at the House there were several men there who had been scouts at St Mary's, Somers Town. A House troop had been formed, I think the 14th Oxford, and I joined it as a Rover Scout, gaining skills which I found useful after my ordination. Much later, when I was a Fellow of Exeter, I ran a troop for a short time in one of the South Oxford parishes but it was not something I was particularly good at and, frankly, I did not enjoy the camp we had. However, I continue to believe in the value of scouting in a parish.

Arthur was a strict disciplinarian. He was very conscious of the reputation the House had acquired under Dr Mitchell's predecessor, Bown, of being excessively High Church and papalist, and of the difficulties that there had been with the then Bishop of Oxford, Charles Gore. Accordingly, we adhered strictly to the liturgical formularies of the Church of England. Later there had been unjustifiable allegations of excessive drinking and homosexual behaviour. Under Arthur, if there was any question of misdemeanours in either of these areas, the person concerned was removed within 48 hours. Both Arthur and Freddy Hood were most strict about homosexual behaviour, not only because of the traditional teaching of the Church but also because they saw it as damaging to proper relations within friendship. Arthur once said to me that the House was always being criticized for one thing or another and he was determined that there should be no grounds for it. In this he was successful as far as morals were concerned, though there were always those who disliked his strict discipline. For myself, it was a happy time and I owe a great deal to Arthur's training, particularly as it followed on so well from the teaching I had received from Freddy Hood.

During the three years prior to going to St Stephen's House, I got to know Sister Mary Ruth and the community at St Thomas's Convent and had become involved somewhat in her programme of social work with the unemployed and the local tramps. Through this connection I came to know Father Trevor Jalland, the Vicar of St Thomas's, and was asked by him to help on Sundays as subdeacon at the High Mass. This was valuable liturgical formation, at a practical level like Arthur's at the House, and I was grateful for the experience.

As I was now a graduate, I was invited by Leslie Cross to join the senior canon law seminar run by Claude Jenkins, the Regius Professor of Ecclesiastical History and Canon of Christ Church. It met at his house next door to the cathedral. We were working on the considerable corpus of law known as the African Canons, a collection which had developed in the fourth and fifth centuries owing to the frequency of their plenary councils and the legislation generated subsequently. In addition to myself and my friend John Sutters, the other members of the seminar were all very senior in the university. They were SL Greenslade, Chaplain of St John's, RLP Milburn, Chaplain of Worcester, RC Mortimer, Clerical Student of Christ Church, and FL Cross of Pusey House. As we worked, eventually they all moved to other posts: Greenslade to be Canon Professor at Durham, Milburn to be Dean of Worcester Cathedral, Mortimer to be Professor of Moral and Pastoral Theology at Oxford and Canon of Christ Church, and Cross to be Lady Margaret Professor of Divinity and also Canon of Christ Church. These last two gained preferments that enabled them to stay in the seminar. I had it in mind in due course to work for the Bachelor of Divinity degree but how and when I did this would depend on my degree of success in the Theology Schools.

In 1938 it was decided that someone needed to go and look at the manuscripts of the canons in the Vatican Library and so, in December of that year, I went with Cross to Rome. The political situation in Italy made this visit not an altogether pleasant experience. Cross had decided that we would save money by taking tickets to the Italian frontier and buy further necessary tickets on the train from there on. This scheme proved disastrous. We gave the conductor rather a large banknote but he did not have any change. By the time we arrived at the station where we were to get off, he had not reappeared with our change. Cross eventually tracked the conductor down but he denied any knowledge of us, let alone that we had paid him for our tickets. After some vigorous argument, the train departed with him on board and us on the platform in the care of the police. As a result, we had to pay a second time for our fare.

We had decided to spend a few days at Sorrento before going to Rome and this short break was generally pleasant except that we were not made to feel very welcome in the hotel. We were able to visit Capri, which was lovely and warm, and I remember having a picnic there in the open air one day in the middle of December. When we arrived in Rome we had to register with the police because we were due to stay rather more than the few days the rules allowed. This was not very easy to accomplish and we were treated with great suspicion. At the Vatican we had to copy and sign a formal request to the Pope before we were allowed to see the library, but eventually we were permitted to see the manuscripts we wanted and were able to do our work. We had some time available to see a little of Rome but I did not really enjoy it.

However, I was most impressed by the church of San Clemente and the catacombs. We were also able to attend a public audience with Pope Pius XI, who was by then an old man near the end of his life. I remember he was carried in on the *sedia gestatoria* by the uniformed *palifrenieri*, from which he walked with some difficulty to his throne. We could see his lips moving but it was some seconds before he was able to speak. Nevertheless, he gave me the impression of great moral strength and I am very glad to have had the experience of seeing him. When our work was finished, Cross remained in Rome for a few days longer, but I left for home, spending the night in Paris on the way. The weather had now changed from the balmy days in Sorrento and it was exceptionally cold. I could not stay out in the streets very long and had to keep going into shops to warm up. On the ferry it was essential to go below deck in order to keep warm and I was glad to find it milder in England. I did not see Rome again until after I became Bishop of Chichester, and although I have always been kindly received and welcomed, particularly at the English College, my liking for the city has not greatly increased. I much prefer Paris and Vienna. It was interesting, however, to have seen something of both Germany and Italy under Fascist rule. It left me in no doubt about the rightness of the war when it came.

4

Southampton

When I first raised the possibility of ordination with my parish priest at Waltham, Mr Holme, he suggested, quite properly, that I should go to see the Bishop of Lincoln to take the matter further. The bishop at the time was Frederick Cyril Nugent Hicks, known as 'Bumbo', who had been translated from Gibraltar. Some years later, I discovered the background to this rather surprising appointment. Cyril Norwood, who had been headmaster of Harrow, told me that he and some other Harrovians had approached the prime minister, Ramsay Macdonald, about Hicks, a fellow Harrovian, whom they felt was being wearied by all the travelling involved in occupying the see of Gibraltar. The prime minister had promised to see what he could do but they were all somewhat taken aback when it was announced that Hicks was to go to Lincoln, a large and demanding diocese.

Mrs Hicks was a powerful lady who was known as 'the Lincoln handicap'. Stories about her were legion, not least among the ordinands at the theological college in Lincoln. One of them told me about an occasion he witnessed when the Bishop's preaching in the cathedral had become rather rambling. Mrs Hicks summoned one of the vergers and told him to go and tell the Bishop to stop. The verger approached the pulpit with some hesitation and said, 'My Lord, Mrs Hicks says that you are to stop,' whereupon he stopped.

I went to Lincoln to see the bishop, told him I was considering ordination and asked his advice as to what I should do. He said that, as I was born in Lincolnshire and been at school in Lincolnshire, I should go to another diocese for ordination. In the light of this, I told Arthur Couratin that I was free to seek a title anywhere. Within a few months he had a letter from the Vicar of St Luke's, Southampton, saying that he would want a curate in the summer. John Sutters and I were sent down to Southampton to be looked at and I was chosen, largely on the assumption that as Sutters had the better degree, I was the less likely to be taken away early to an academic post. The vicar, Harold Douglass

Caesar, told me that I should be paid £210 a year, a princely sum which would go up by £10 each year until £230, at which level it would stop. I was further told that I had to find my own accommodation and I was given a list of suitable places to try. Nearby, I found lodgings where I would have two seemingly very pleasant rooms, the use of a bathroom and meals provided – all at reasonable cost. I made a provisional booking with the landlady, subject to my acceptance by the bishop which appeared to be taken for granted.

Father Caesar informed the Bishop of Winchester that he had found a potential new curate and in due course I was summoned to see the great man, Cyril Garbett, and take the deacons' examination. This consisted of two papers about which I recall very little, save that in the second there was a misprint in one of the questions. It was explained that the question which read, 'Discuss the view that the distinction between national and revealed religion is no longer tenable' should have read 'natural' rather than national. At some point during that day I must have met the bishop but I have no recollection of seeing him until the ordination retreat. I evidently passed the examination and must have seemed satisfactory to the bishop as I heard nothing more until I was told the date and time to appear at Winchester for ordination. Within a few years, this whole procedure was to become much more complex and formalized.

On Sunday, 28 May, I assisted as subdeacon for the last time at High Mass at St Thomas's and then went round to Pusey House to make my various farewells. I had a beer at the Union with an undergraduate friend from Wadham, Ian Crombie, then Richard Southern joined me at St Stephen's House for lunch. The diary I was keeping at the time records that after lunch we walked round the garden until 2.30pm discussing St Thomas Aquinas and Jolliffe's book on English Constitutional History, of which Dick approved. I then went to Exeter for tea with Paul Kingdon, with whom I had remained on good terms in spite of having declined to be taught by him. I then returned to St Stephen's House for the Ignatian-style, pre-ordination retreat conducted by Arthur, which began at 5.30pm with Evening Prayer. This included a private interview with Arthur on the Monday evening, at which one was given advice about planning and making a confession covering one's whole life, and the necessary reorganization of one's rule of life and prayer once ordained. Time was to be spent on these two areas during the next two days, and on the Tuesday evening I went to make my full confession to Freddy Hood. The following day, I spoke to Arthur of my thoughts towards a rule of life and we discussed them and wrote down the resulting rule together. In another instance of his wisdom and practicality, he advised me to leave the formulation of a rule about reading and division of time until I had been in the parish for a week or two. The purpose and effect of the whole retreat was to create in me a determination at my ordination to devote myself wholly to God's will and to serve him to the best of my ability wherever I might be called.

On Thursday, my parents arrived with the car to take me down to Southampton. On arriving at the lodgings I had booked, I was met by the landlady who informed me that she was leaving the following Monday. I was not to be alarmed, she said, as she had let me to her successor along with the house. We had no time to discuss this slightly alarming development as we had to go on to Winchester where I was to stay with Mrs Hoskyns, the widow of an Archdeacon of Chichester, for the diocesan ordination retreat. It was here my parents left me.

The retreat programme began on Saturday when I went to the Bishop's Chapel at Wolvesey to attend Matins and a celebration of Holy Communion. This was followed at 10.30am by an interview with the bishop's chaplain, who talked to me about the youth work in the diocese. Garbett's chaplain at the time was Gerald Ellison, who was about to leave to go into the Navy, and was eventually succeeded by one of my fellow-ordinands, Peter Hamilton. Ellison was later to become Bishop of Willesden, then Chester and finally Bishop of London and he was a great help to me when I was at Chichester. At noon there was a rehearsal at the cathedral, and after lunch I went to call on Canon Brabant, who for a time became my confessor. I was then able to rejoin my parents. They, in the meantime, had sought out the bishop's former secretary, Mr Speake, with whom my father had lodged during his brief time as a tyro journalist in Farnham. This reunion gave great pleasure to my father after so many years. Speake had recently retired as secretary to the bishop and was living at St Cross Hospital. He assured them that I had thus far made a good impression. After tea and Evensong in the cathedral, I returned to Wolvesey for the legal ceremonies of the Declaration of Assent and the oaths of Allegiance and Canonical Obedience. The diocesan registrar, Sir Henry Dashwood, had written to me some time before to say that he would not be present but nevertheless asking me to send him a fee of five guineas to arrange for the administration of the oaths. After that we said Compline and listened to the Bishop's charge. This, I remember, consisted chiefly of an exposition of the oaths we had just taken and warning us that we must not ourselves ask for any preferment or get anyone else to do so for us, and that canonical obedience meant that we must follow the bishop's directions. In the course of all this, the vicar of one of the parishes in the New Forest gave us some addresses, but we kept being told that the real spiritual guidance would come from the assistant bishop, Bishop Karney, a retired South African bishop, who was recovering from an accident. Eventually he appeared and, frankly, all I can remember him saying was: 'While I have been lying in bed in hospital thinking what I should say to you, one thing has been borne in on me, namely that we are in a very real sense "fellow workers with Christ".' At some stage on the Saturday, Bishop Garbett took us individually for a walk round his garden. I cannot remember what prompted him to talk to me about St Theresa of Lisieux during that walk, but he described her as 'a very remarkable young woman'. He also said, 'You will have been taught at your theological college to be in church early every morning and you must remember that if you are going to do this you must be in bed reasonably early the night before. When I was Vicar of Portsea, I had a rule that the curates must all be in the Vicarage not later than 10.30pm.'

On Sunday, 4 June I put on my clerical clothes for the first time, walked down to Wolvesey at 9.30am, whence we went in procession to the cathedral for the ordination at 10am. Father Caesar had been asked by the bishop to preach but of his sermon I can only remember his injunction, 'Be good'. The service was over by about noon. My parents left immediately for home and I had a little breakfast with Mrs Hoskyns, who gave me a photograph of the High Altar of the cathedral, which I still have. Father Caesar then drove me to Southampton where we went first to the church to listen to the catechizing of the children. At Evensong I read the lessons and 'read myself in', making the Declaration of Assent in before the assembled congregation. My diary records that the next morning I went to the local branch of the Midland Bank to transfer my account from Oxford and deposit my Letters of Orders, licence to the curacy and signed Declaration of Assent with them for safekeeping. My parents had arranged an account for me at the Midland Bank in Oxford when I went up in 1933 and I have remained with the bank ever since. The rest of the Monday was my first day's work in the parish.

St Luke's, Southampton, was in those days a parish of about 8,000 people, chiefly working class but with a large congregation which included people from other parts of the town. The focus of the parish was at the bottom of the Avenue, going downhill to the railway, the vicarage being in the Avenue itself and the church lower down, a little way off to the left. Father Caesar's predecessor, Dr Trevaskis, had been appointed before the First World War. He was a remarkable character whose biography, written by his curate, Beaumont James, is well worth reading both for interest and amusement. In perhaps the most curious story, James relates how on the death of the first Mrs Trevaskis, he was summoned up to the vicarage where he found the vicar kneeling at the death bed. Dr Trevaskis indicated that they should go out and so they walked together in the rain up to the top of the Avenue, stopped briefly at the house of one of the churchwardens, all in silence, and then returned to the vicarage. James writes: 'We reached the gate, and I had to leave him. Suddenly the extraordinary nature of the man flashed out. "James" he said, and I waited upon his words. "I have made up my mind not to allow any woman to marry me for five years".' He married again exactly five years later. He was a great preacher whose sermons were advertised in the *Southampton Echo* on Saturday evenings, and such was his popularity that a cobbled area along the road leading down to the church was specially laid so that visitors' cars could be parked. Both he and his successors would have been horrified to know that the church is now a Sikh Temple, having been sold to the Sikh community by the Church Commissioners at the instigation of a later bishop.

Many stories not in the biography were passed on to me by an elderly lady, Miss Frances Mitchell, with whom I became friendly through shared historical interests. She had, at one time, been at Glastonbury and knew something of the archaeological excavations conducted there in the 1920s. It was good for a bachelor curate of an academic mien to have someone like Miss Mitchell to go and talk with from time to time. Miss Mitchell told me that, at one stage during the First World War, a prominent local baker was a member of the con- gregation of St Luke's. There were increasing complaints about the quality of his bread and this came to a head when a child died and it was discovered that the last thing he had eaten was a piece of the baker's bread. On the following Sunday, Dr Trevaskis preached on the text, 'Our soul loatheth this light bread' (Numbers 21.5). On being rebuked afterwards, Trevaskis said the text he had wanted to preach on was, 'And he hanged the chief baker' (Genesis 40.22)!

In addition to myself, there was another curate, John Burt, who was six months my senior. Father Caesar seemed always to have had two curates and I heard a good deal about them as they had all been at St Stephen's House. One of them, Billy Favell, I knew in Oxford as Vicar of St Paul's, and I met him later, first as Vicar of St Paul's, Brighton, and then of St Thomas's, Hove. John Burt had been trained at Mirfield and was the first curate not from St Stephen's House. Quite unnecessarily, he had something of an inferiority complex as a result. The parish was divided for pastoral care between the two of us. Each of us had a list of sick people for visiting and had to report on them at the weekly staff meeting. I was responsible for the Sunday School and for preparing the girls for confirmation. There was a fine layman, Mr Loughran, who had had much to do with the Sunday School and during my first few weeks, time was spent with him in working out a syllabus, which did not seem to have existed till then. I had devoted time over recent years to the study of catechetical teaching, and during university vacations had acquired some experience helping Mr Holme with the Sunday School at Waltham. At Southampton we had 200 children in the Sunday School when I joined the parish.

Father Caesar was a fine and sympathetic incumbent to work under. He had been an evangelical but some time before he came to St Luke's had moved to an Anglo-Catholic outlook. He advised me once I was priested to join the Federation of Catholic Priests, which I did, and have remained a member ever since. With the help of his first two curates, George Fawkes and Billy Favell, he had made it the leading Anglo-Catholic parish in the diocese of Winchester. Although Bishop Garbett may not have altogether agreed with everything he did, he was able to recognize and appreciate a hard-working, devoted priest. He was well respected by Arthur Couratin, who was always ready to send him curates, though at the point John Burt joined the staff there was no one at the House ready for ordination.

The weekly staff meeting was held at the vicarage on Friday mornings and we always stayed for lunch with Father Caesar and his family. Mrs Caesar was a delightful, sensitive and devoted lady who was at early Mass in church every morning. They had four children, two adult boys, John and Hugh, a daughter Muriel, who was a children's nurse, and a younger boy, Anthony, a chorister at Winchester. Anthony

Caesar was eventually ordained and had a distinguished career in the Advisory Council for the Church's Ministry, as a chaplain to the Queen, and then at Winchester Cathedral. Father Caesar senior had succeeded Trevaskis in the early 1920s and remained at St Luke's until he retired. During his long ministry there he became an Honorary Canon of Winchester and was elected to represent the clergy of the diocese as a Proctor in Convocation.

From the time of my ordination until the end of August, I tried to follow the pattern of life that Arthur had recommended. In the afternoon I went out visiting, going from door to door in the streets allocated to me and by the end of August had covered most of my part of the parish. I was, on the whole, very well received and there were only two or three houses into which I was not invited. At one, they did not want to see me because they went to a church in another parish. At another house, the people were taken off to an asylum the following week. A Roman Catholic family said they wished their own priest would come and visit them and were very welcoming to me. I was surprised to find one house with no hot and cold water or sanitation indoors in the middle of Southampton.

My colleague, John Burt, went away for his summer holiday on 29 July and came back on 26 August. As I was so recent an arrival, I was not expecting much in the way of holiday myself but Father Caesar said I could go away on 28 August for three weeks, so I went first to Oxford, intending to stay there for a week before going home to Waltham. As I came out of Mass at St Thomas' on Sunday, I was met by the news that war had been declared and when I arrived at Pusey House there was a message that I should ring Southampton. I telephoned Father Caesar who told me he had assumed that, as a territorial army chaplain, he would not be called up but he had received orders to report to Devonport the following Saturday and, therefore, I must return by Friday. I took the next train to Grimsby and enjoyed a few days with my parents and was back in the parish by Thursday evening. There was a meeting in the vicarage on Friday morning to discuss the situation. John Burt and I were both still in deacon's orders so there was an immediate problem about Mass the coming Sunday. The situation seemed to have been saved for the time being by the fact that a priest, Father Wright, whom John Burt had known in Leeds had arrived. He was on his way out to South Africa but was held up at Southampton by the war. He agreed to look after the parish – at least until he was able to continue his journey. Father Caesar was able to depart for Devonport that evening knowing that he had left a priest in charge of the parish.

The next six weeks proved to be something of a nightmare – Father Wright turned out to be eccentric and unreliable. We could not obtain any sort of timetable from him as to what we were to do under his direction in the parish. He would preach for forty minutes at Evensong on Sunday and then break off, saying, 'I may continue this next week.' This meant we did not know until the following Saturday whether we would have to preach or not, which, as we were supposed to preach only once a month and to send the sermon to one of the bishop's chaplains for examination, created some difficulty. Gradually, troops began to assemble on the common in Southampton and he spent a lot of time with them. One morning, as we were waiting for him to come and say Mass, Mrs Caesar arrived and said that Wright had suffered an accident the night before and would not be able to be with us. He had become involved with the troops in a game which consisted in throwing bottles, one had smashed and he had cut his hand rather seriously. It was a relief when after six weeks, he was able to get a passage and leave us for South Africa. We never heard anything more of him. After his departure, we were put under the care of Father Roe, Vicar of St Augustine's, and, in the Advent, John Burt was ordained priest so that eased the problem of the daily Masses, though I have to say his punctuality was not much better than Father Wright's.

Meanwhile, my lodgings had changed as my second landlady had left and, like her predecessor, was proposing to let me along with the house. I did not wish to go through this again. John Burt said there was a vacancy in the house where he lived, so I decided to move there. This turned out to be a mistake and after a couple of months I moved yet again, this time into the house of the verger, Jack Richardson, and his wife, Gladys. I liked them both and was happy there but after the air raids at the end of the year, they decided to leave Southampton. As Gladys worked for Herbert Samuels, she was able to transfer to their shop in Salisbury and they moved there. I then lodged in the house of the mother of one of my confirmation candidates and stayed there happily until I left Southampton. I wonder whether any other curate has ever had four different lodgings and five different landladies in the space of two years?

On 2 March, Father Caesar was released from the army and permitted to return to the parish. He was once again in post and able, after my ordination to the priesthood, to assist at my first Mass. During this first year of my curacy, I only saw the bishop twice and experienced his apparent coldness which I think was really shyness. I remember taking some of our children to be confirmed by him at a church in South-ampton and all he said to me was, 'Your vicar still away?' Before that, I had been at a gathering of junior clergy at Wolvesey and found myself standing next to him at the buffet lunch. Thinking hard of something to say to break the silence I said, 'I was very sorry to hear of Mr Speake's death.' To which he simply replied, 'Yes', and that was that. Later, I came to understand that he had no small talk but could be completely relied on when there was any problem.

My failure to achieve more than a second class in the theology school meant that if I was ever to do any higher academic theology I would have to take the Bachelor of Divinity Qualifying Examination. In my final year at St Stephen's House, I took this examination and passed it. I then turned to Kenneth Kirk for advice on a subject for research for a Bachelor of Divinity dissertation and he suggested that I might look into the canonization of saints and how papal control of the process originated and developed. This resonated with my nascent interest in canon law, and so after I was ordained I began as much research as my time in the parish allowed. Realistically, time was in short supply, but such as there was enabled me to make the acquaintance of Canon Goodman who was in charge of the library at Winchester Cathedral. He took a kindly and encouraging interest in this young curate and made the resources of the library available to me.

I have no recollection of any diocesan retreat before my ordination to the priesthood, but I did go to the retreat organized by Arthur Couratin at St Stephen's House. My parents were again able to come to Winchester for the occasion, and as an ordination present they gave me a white, Latin-shape chasuble made by Messrs Grossé, which I wore for my first Mass. I still have it and, indeed, wore it for the 50th anni-versary of my ordination in 1990. My ordination as priest was on 19 May, the anniversary of my baptism, and I said my first Mass at 6.30am on the following Monday in St Luke's, with Jack Richardson serving. Also present was a splendid lady called Miss Petty who was sacristan at St Luke's. She kept us all in order and we were all very fond of her.

The evacuation of schools took place almost immediately upon the declaration of war and it had happened before I was back in South-ampton after my brief holiday. I was left with virtually no children in the Sunday School, but gradually families began to drift back. By the middle of 1940 this became a sizeable problem as the schools remained closed. We had not only to provide for Sunday School but I also found myself having to run a day school and cope with the problem of the ignorance of primary school pupils. When there was a second evacuation after the air raids, we were more prepared and were able to cater for the children until the schools reopened.

From early June 1940, we began to have air raid warnings most nights, but there was no damage until August, and once again during the Battle of Britain when the docks and the buildings surrounding them were hit. We watched many of the air battles but experienced no serious bombing of the town itself until November. I had joined the Air Raid Precautions (ARP) Service shortly after arriving in Southampton and was attached to a post at the bottom of the Avenue. On Saturday, 17 November, 1940, there were very heavy raids all night from about 7pm continuing through to Sunday night. Parachute bombs were dropped and there was much damage. The following Wednesday there were incendiary bombs and a local school was burned. There was another long raid on Saturday, 23 November, in the course of which the southwest corner of the church was hit. How the Bishop heard about this I do not know, but he rang up Father Caesar at about 8am and said that he was coming to preach in Southampton that morning and wished to visit us first. He arrived at about 10.30am as people were assembling for the 11am Mass and he spoke to the congregation before going on to his other engagement. The local ARP authorities wanted to pull down the substantial pillar that was left isolated at the west end of the church on the grounds it was dangerous. Father Caesar, who knew that it had separate solid foundations, protested and asked them to wait until the architect who lived in another part of the town could be summoned but they refused. While we were in church after the bishop had gone, we had the amusement of watching them try to pull it down with a lorry and a rope. It took most of the rest of the day and Father Caesar was vindicated. There was an odd sequel to this incident a couple of years later when I was attending an ARP lecture in Oxford. The speaker had come to tell us about problems to be expected during an air raid and, as an example of the sort of difficulties one might meet, he cited a church in Southampton that had been hit during a raid, leaving a pinnacle hanging from the tower in a dangerous fashion. He told us that the authorities had wanted to pull it down immediately but the vicar of the church had tried to prevent this until he had consulted the Church Commissioners architect in London. I was, of course, uniquely able to give the correct version of the story, but have always remembered the incident as an example of how things can be distorted to people's discredit by inaccurate repetition.

There were smaller raids during the following December weekends, and I have often wondered why the Luftwaffe then stopped. During the worst period, soon after the sirens sounded we would see planes flying round the lines of the Test and the Itchen and dropping incendiaries to make a marker ring of fire around the town so that the bombers could criss-cross it dropping their bombs. While a raid lasted, there was little one could do but sit in the shelter, though I felt happier on the occasions when I had to ride my bicycle to take messages down to headquarters at the Civic Centre. By the beginning of December, people began to trek northwards out of the town every afternoon, and I am sure that if the raids had continued the place would have been deserted. As it was, we pulled ourselves together and although we heard bombers going over our heads to Coventry and other places and saw in the distance fires in Portsmouth, there was no further damage to us on a similar scale.

The clergy of the rural deanery had set up a small committee to co-ordinate our ARP work. Jack Vyse, the curate of St Mary's, and I were the joint secretaries. There were many complaints about the inadequacy of rest centres after the raids, including the centres not being opened promptly enough. When we failed to get anything done locally, it was decided that Jack and I should go to see the Bishop. We were able to get an immediate appointment and we both went up to Wolvesey. Garbett listened carefully to what we had to say, asked a few questions and then said, 'I am going to Southampton on Tuesday. I shall go and see the mayor and say that unless this situation is improved I shall ask a question in the House of Lords.' Needless to say, there was an immediate improvement but it did not make us very popular with the mayor, who complained about me to Father Caesar.

By the beginning of 1941, things had quietened down somewhat and we began to pull the congregation together again. Some had been killed in the raids and some families had left the district, but there was a solid nucleus remaining and I had been able to restore a much smaller Sunday School. I was, therefore, somewhat disturbed in March to receive a letter from Freddy Hood inviting me to join him on the staff of Pusey House. He explained that following the death of Darwell Stone, Leslie Cross had been asked to take on the editorship of the *Lexicon of Patristic Greek*. He felt that he could only do this new work if he was relieved of some of the responsibility for the library. Although things were quieter now in the parish, I was very uncertain whether it would be right for me to leave Southampton at that stage and was inclined to refuse. I went to the vicarage to talk the letter over with Father Caesar. He asked me if this was the sort of thing I had hoped to do if we been living in normal times. I replied that it was. However, I went on to qualify, this was because I had only achieved a second in the schools and so assumed that an academic future was unlikely. I had put a return to Oxford out of my mind, for the time being, at any rate. His advice was that I should definitely accept Freddy's offer, but should first go and talk to the Bishop. This led to another visit to Wolvesey, this time with some trepidation.

The Bishop sat me down in a comfortable chair in his study and listened while I explained all that had happened and the dilemma in which I found myself. He then asked, 'What does your vicar say?' I told him what Father Caesar had advised and without hesitation he said, 'I agree. You should go.' I returned to Southampton and told Father Caesar what the Bishop had said and, with his agreement, wrote and accepted the Pusey House appointment. I made the proviso, however, that I should be free to go back to the parish during the vacations. This I did, though after I became a chaplain to the cathedral in Oxford I had to be there for Christmas and Easter.

I have thought about this time in my life many times since then and have never ceased to be grateful to my two superiors for giving a young man such clear and definite direction in a difficult situation. In the circumstances, they could both very well have said that it was my duty to stay, or, more difficult still, have left it up to me to decide. I remembered their clear direction some years later when one of the dons at St John's told me of the circumstances surrounding the appointment of their new chaplain. They had wanted Hugh Montefiore, who at that time was on the staff of Westcott House where Ken Carey was principal. Montefiore had said when he was appointed that he would stay for a definite period of years and felt that he could not go back on that undertaking. St John's, being very anxious to have him and thinking that being Fellow of an Oxford College was superior to being simply on the staff of a theological college, approached Carey directly and asked if he would release him. The reply was, 'I leave it to his own conscience.' Of course, Montefiore refused the offer. In similar circumstances, when asked for advice by a young man about his future, particularly if he was under my authority, I have always tried to be clear and definite and not simply leave him to his own devices.

So, my two-year curacy was an unusual one in many ways. In the extraordinary circumstances of those early war years, amidst the rubble and devastation of the air raids, I had much to do and a great deal to learn. I very much enjoyed the Sunday School work and regret that I was not able to develop my plans for a syllabus. I made some very good friends in that short time. I owe much to Reg Brombie, a Church Army Officer in the deanery, who had mainly attached himself to us at St Luke's. He taught me a good deal about the social needs of the area and how to approach them. It was a stressful time, however, as I discovered early on when I became ill and took myself to the doctor. He said I was suffering from nervous exhaustion and must try to have at least a week's rest. In April 1941, I saw him again and he advised a further two weeks' leave after Easter. Shortly after moving to Oxford, I finally collapsed through exhaustion. I had just not realized the strain put on me during those two years in Southampton. This time taking the doctor's advice, I went away for three enjoyable weeks, staying with the parents of my old friend Tom Parker in Bidford on Avon. In retrospect, the Southampton years were the loneliest period of my life and I am particularly grateful to Father Caesar and to his family for seeing me through them. I am glad to be able still to see Anthony from time to time.

5

Return to Oxford

Going back to Oxford was like going home. Back at Pusey House I found myself working with my old friends Freddy Hood, Leslie Cross and Tom Parker. Humphrey Beevor had left to go into the Navy. I was fairly soon reunited with the OUCU as its senior secretary, with Bob Mortimer as chairman. It was very active among those undergraduates who remained in Oxford, meeting every Friday evening in the large drawing room of Bob Mortimer's house at Christ Church. There was usually a large assembly, mostly sitting on the floor. We had quite a number of visiting speakers and once a term there was a corporate Communion in St Mary's, very well attended.

After a while I received two additional appointments, which were both quite unexpected. The first was as the chaplain to the cathedral through circumstances I have described earlier. When Professor NP Williams died in 1943, I was asked to assist as a singing chaplain at the Vespers of the Dead sung in Christ Church before his funeral. This led to my being asked to be a chaplain – the Christ Church term for a minor canon in the cathedral – on the understanding that my duties at Pusey House took precedence.

At the cathedral one learned to be tactful with the Dean, John Lowe, and the canons, especially Herbert Danby, the evangelical Professor of Hebrew. I had already a very good relationship with Thomas Armstrong, the organist, through my membership of the Bach Choir. On my first Sunday on duty I went up a whole tone while singing the Litany and Tom suggested that I go to Arthur Cranmer for some singing lessons. Arthur became a good friend from whom I learned a great deal about music generally, and singing in particular, and with whom I remained in touch until his death. He urged me to read Richard Capell's book on Schubert's songs. He also insisted that I was a tenor and so having already moved from second to first bass in the Bach Choir, I now moved to second tenor. We were rare birds indeed as there were few tenors left in Oxford because of the war. Indeed, Tom told a story of a visit to Cairo for some musical event where a young officer came up to him at breakfast one morning and said, 'You may not remember me but I was a tenor in the Bach Choir.' To which Tom replied, 'Yes, we've still got the other one.'

The other unexpected appointment was as temporary chaplain of St John's College, just across the road from Pusey House. Stanley Greenslade had been appointed to one of the professorships at Durham. The college, having failed to lure Hugh Montefiore away from Cambridge, decided not to replace him until after the war and, apparently with some trepidation on account of my churchmanship, asked me if I would fill in. After my first celebration of the Holy Communion in the chapel, someone asked WC Costin, one of the senior fellows, how things had gone, to which he replied, 'Oh very well. You see he's a gentleman.' Costin told me that he had been raised a Presbyterian but that when he became a fellow of St John's he decided that as he was living in a predominantly Anglican community he ought to join the Church of England. This he did, was confirmed and became a regular communicant.

I was made a member of the Senior Common Room at St John's and entered into the world of a most interesting collection of people. The President was Cyril Norwood, formerly headmaster of Harrow, and now also president of the Modern Churchmen's Union. He always preached at the first Evensong of the academic year and I recall one occasion when he said that there had been two remarkable prophecies made in the nineteenth century about the twentieth, both of which were being fulfilled. One was made by some American chaplain who had said that the nineteenth century had been one of material progress and the twentieth would be one of spiritual progress. The other was by Bismarck who had said that in the twentieth century the most important factor would be that England and America spoke the same language. As we came out of chapel the senior fellow, AL Poole, whispered to me, 'If the President was going to quote Bismarck, I think a better one would have been, "You can do everything with a bayonet but sit on it."'

I became particularly friendly with Poole, a medieval historian who gave the Ford Lecture while I was there. He was a rather sad figure, having lost two children at an early age, and he was not on very close terms with his wife. After Norwood retired he was elected President. Costin was Senior Tutor, one of those bachelor fellows so important to the life of a college. He had been an undergraduate at St John's, lived in college and embodied the traditions of the place. He was a keen supporter of the chapel and became President after Poole. Edwin Slade, the law tutor, was a close friend of Costin, and they had gone abroad for many holidays together. Mabbot the philosophy tutor was younger than the others. He succeeded Costin as President. There were also several undergraduates who became friends, and I particularly recall Donald Bullough, alas now dead, whom I baptized and presented for confirmation, and who became a very distinguished medieval historian and professor at St Andrew's. I am still in touch with Philip Bowcock who is my daughter Alice's godfather.

After NP Williams' funeral there was much discussion led by the Warden of Keble, Dr Kidd, as to who should succeed him as Lady Margaret Professor. I cannot remember the details but the election to the professorship lay in the hands of quite a large body of clerics, not all of whom were resident in Oxford. There seemed to be a fairly general feeling among those who were resident that Leslie Cross was the right person. Just as it looked as though this was going to go through without difficulty we suddenly learned that the Archbishop of Canterbury, William Temple, had proposed another candidate, someone with whom he had had dealings formerly at Queen's. There was much annoyance at this and although the archbishop had the right to make a proposal it was thought improper for someone outside the resident members of the faculty to do so. In the event, the outside candidate received few votes and Leslie was elected. This meant a move from Pusey House to Priory House in Christ Church, where his sisters came to look after him. In holding the chair, he was not particularly prominent as a lecturer but he did great and important work on the *Lexicon of Patristic Greek* and in encouraging and helping other scholars. He arranged learned meetings and founded and guided the Oxford Patristic Conferences. In his little book on religion and science, published as one of a series to commemorate the centenary of the Oxford Movement in 1933, he says that it had been his good fortune to be connected with three places of religious and useful learning in Oxford. From the first he learned his science, from the second his theology and from the third his religion. He does not give the names but I know that the three places were Balliol, Ripon Hall and Pusey House.

My first literary effort was the result of an old member of Brigg Grammar School having established an annual prize for an historical essay. As I mentioned earlier, I entered for it and wrote on the conflicting political theories which led up to the Reform Bill of 1832. I enjoyed writing the essay and it won the prize. It had no further life as a piece of work but I still have it in the pile of stuff which has survived from my school days. My next effort did achieve publication. It was called 'The Augustinian tradition in the religious life' and it was published in the *Church Quarterly Review* in 1937. It originated in my undergraduate study of St Augustine as part of the history school. I discovered a confusion about the origins of what is called 'The Rule of St Augustine' and its connection with that followed by the Canons Regular of St Augustine. I do remember that, at the time, I was wondering whether I had a call to the religious life and to found an Augustinian community modelled on the Dominicans whose own rule was modelled on the Augustinian. I talked this project over with a member of the Society of Retreat Conductors while in retreat at one of their houses and was wisely advised that perhaps I should consider joining one of the established communities first, before thinking of founding my own. The thought stayed with me for some time but had disappeared by the time of my ordination.

My return to Oxford enabled me to resume serious work on the subject Kenneth Kirk had suggested for my Bachelor of Divinity degree, namely papal authority in the canonization of saints. I had begun tentatively in Southampton by looking at the lives of saints in the centuries immediately before papal canonization became established and it was much easier to develop this with the resources available in Oxford. I was able to complete this work and submit a dissertation with the title, 'Canonization and authority in the Western Church'. It was one of the features of the Bachelor of Divinity degree in those days that it was not done under supervision or with limit of time but with a *viva voce* examination. Mine took place in the chapter house at Christ Church and my two examiners were Professor Claude Jenkins and Professor Christopher Cheney. The first I knew well already and the second later became a real friend. I was awarded the degree and the thesis was subsequently published by the Oxford University Press in 1948. It was suggested to me that I should enter for the Alexander Prize of the Royal Historical Society, which I did, entering what became chapter 5 of the book. I won the prize and Sir Maurice Powicke suggested that I join the Royal Historical Society and he later proposed me for election as a Fellow. When, in 1955, a commission was set up to consider the Calendar of Saints in the Church of England and how new names might be added, I was the natural choice for secretary to the commission because of the work I had done and published in the field. Eric Milner-White, the Dean of York, was Chairman and the other members were the Bishop of Leicester, Ronald Williams, and Max Warren, Secretary of the Church Missionary Society. We consulted EC Ratcliffe several times and I remember him commenting on Archbishop Geoffrey Fisher's opposition to the invocation of saints: 'He thinks why go to the ushers when you can go straight to the Headmaster!' We urged great caution in calling people saints.

This commission was one of several such bodies set up in preparation for the 1958 Lambeth Conference, and its report was taken up as a basis for discussion by a conference committee on the commemoration of saints and heroes of the Anglican Communion. This body agreed with our contention that a distinction should be drawn between those who displayed heroic sanctity such as inspired veneration by the people of God and those who are more appropriately called 'worthies'. It seemed to us that in the modern Anglican Communion only two names fell into the former category, namely Bishop Edward King and a lay catechist in southern Rhodesia called Bernard Mizeki, who was martyred in a rebellion in 1896 and was clearly the object of considerable veneration in southern Africa. We recognized that there might also be other martyrs who deserved recognition in local calendars. The distinction we made was very much blurred when the Church of England revised its calendar in 1997 in the run-up to the *Common Worship* project. I suspect our report had been consigned to history and was not dug out and read by the revisers. A lot of names were added of people who were simply distinguished or significant in church history. When I was Bishop of Chichester I revised the diocesan calendar with the help of my then chaplain, Jeremy Haselock. We included many who subsequently found their way into the *Common Worship* calendar but we made a clear distinction between them and those who were being added to the calendar of saints. I remember discussing with Bishop Lloyd Morell whether to include George Bell. Lloyd, who had worked closely with him and knew him well, was quite clear that although he was a distinguished church leader who had done much for the cause of Christian unity and for the Church in Germany he was not properly to be called a saint.

As the war drew to an end, the Church of England gave new attention to finding its role in the country in the post-war situation. Society was clearly going to be very different and radical changes in attitudes to pastoral ministry and mission were required. I became involved with some people of an Anglo-Catholic outlook who were part of these discussions. I was asked to contribute to a *Quarterly Journal of Reconstruction* published for the London School of Economics and in 1945 wrote a substantial piece entitled 'Reconstruction in the Church of England' for their second volume. Two years before, I had been member of a group under the chairmanship of Dr VA Demant which had produced a book entitled *Thy Household the Church*. I contributed a chapter called 'The discipline of the Church, canon law and the ecclesiastical courts'. In the course of this, I mentioned the fee charged to a prebendary of St Paul's on his resignation. Sir Henry Dashwood, the registrar, wrote to ask me which prebendary this was, with the obvious implication that I was wrong. It was a friend of mine, Prebendary Merritt, who told me that he had been charged the fee, so I supplied the name but heard nothing more.

Pusey House was a centre for Catholic churchmen concerned about the future of the Church of England and its identity, which was much under discussion at that time. Among our frequent visitors was Dom Gregory Dix, a monk of Nashdom Abbey, the main Benedictine community for men in the Church of England. He was a close friend of the Bishop of Oxford, Kenneth Kirk. Both Dix and Kirk, along with many others, were worried about the developments taking place in the Church of South India, which they thought raised serious questions about its allegiance to the apostolic ministry as the Anglican Communion had received it. They believed that in its move towards union with non-episcopal groups of Christians in India it was being encouraged by some English Anglicans to provide a precedent for what might eventually come to pass in England. When I came to write my biography of Bishop Kirk, I dealt more fully with this and explained how these developments were regarded by him and those who thought like him as a threat to the Catholic doctrine of the ministry. He and they were also concerned about their impact on the 1948 Lambeth Conference. I learned much from Dom Gregory for which I am grateful, particularly for showing me the weakness of Liberal Anglicanism and for stressing the importance of constant reference to the Early Fathers. I also saw how in his brilliance, he could exaggerate what he was arguing in ways which irritated rather than persuaded opponents. This has been a common failing, it seems to me, among many of the chief spokesmen of the Catholic Movement in the Church of England.

Other regular visitors to Pusey House at this time included Bishop Arthur Foley Winnington Ingram. For many years as Bishop of London, he had established a pattern of a visit to Oxford at the end of October each year. He would go first to Radley College, a nearby public school, on the Saturday, stay the night there and preach in chapel on the Sunday morning. After lunch a group of sixth formers would walk with him into Oxford where he stayed at Keble, preached at the University Church at 8.30pm and then presided at a meeting in support of the Universities' Mission to Central Africa. In his retirement, the Radley visit was dropped and Freddy invited him to preach at Pusey House on a Sunday morning. When saying farewell, Freddy asked if he would like to come again the next year, to which Winnington Ingram replied, 'I had been wondering whether the time had come to drop my Sunday evening visit to St Mary's and when I said this to Milford [the vicar at the time] he said he thought that it had. So I shall come to you on Sunday morning instead.' That meant that we had him each October for the next few years. One such visit happened to be shortly after the death of William Temple in 1944. His sermon was almost entirely composed of reminiscences, but I am not sure that his memory by then can have been wholly accurate. He recalled that when he was Bishop of Stepney, he used frequently to go to Lambeth Palace to take the young William out for walk. On one such occasion he was told that William was with his father in the library. On opening the library door, he saw William sitting in a high-backed chair and his father, Archbishop Frederick Temple, putting the waste paper basket with great solemnity on the boy's head, rehearsing for the coronation of Edward VII. On handing William over for his walk, Temple senior apparently said, 'Don't steal his heart away from his old father.' Winnington Ingram had three baths a day: a cold bath in the morning and before going to bed at night, and a hot bath before dinner. I found him a loveable and interesting person.

One who came to live at Pusey House for a time was the cricketing commentator EW Swanton. He was an old friend of Freddy's who invited him to Oxford when Swanton was released from the prisoner-of-war camp where he had been incarcerated after the fall of Singapore.

He stayed in Oxford for several years and I got to know him well. He was a great authority on the game and became the cricketing correspondent of the *Daily Telegraph*, as well as writing on soccer and rugby. He once played for a cricket side organized by Robert Runcie in a match at Canterbury and I remember the former archbishop ringing me up after Swanton's death in 2000 to ask for my memories of him at Pusey House for an obituary. I kept in touch with Swanton until his death and visited him at his home at Sandwich in Kent.

Early in 1945 things began to change at Oxford and some of the temporary wartime arrangements could be dismantled. Leslie Cross's departure to the Lady Margaret Professorship meant that I was now in sole charge of the library and so had to supervise the removal of the books that had been stored in the chapel during the war. This led to a general re-cataloguing and the examination of the large section of Dr Pusey's library which was still stored in the cellar. I was still very much occupied with St John's College in my temporary capacity as interim chaplain. With the ending of the war, the governing body of St John's decided that they could now go ahead with the appointment of a new chaplain-fellow. I do not think there was ever any question of my being considered for the permanent appointment and they chose an Exeter contemporary of mine, Geoffrey Lampe. He had yet to be demobbed from the army so there was some delay before he could take up the post but eventually he arrived, thereby I was released and able to devote my time fully to Pusey House. With some undergraduate help I managed to clear the chapel and begin the rearrangement of the library. There was a great deal to do, so Freddy appointed Rees Phillips as an additional Librarian to work with me.

The Bishop of Oxford asked me to become secretary of the Diocesan Ordination Candidates Fund. This was not just a matter of dealing with financial arrangements but involved much negotiation with the Church's Advisory Council for Training for the Ministry (CACTM) about the sponsorship of ordinands. Bishop Kirk was clear and insistent that the final responsibility and ultimate decision as to whether or not a man should be ordained rested with the bishop and he often pressed ahead with men of whom CACTM disapproved. I had to keep the peace between Bishop Kirk and CACTM, although I generally found myself in agreement with the Bishop. When, many years later, I became a bishop myself, I maintained successfully the episcopal right to sponsor candidates even when they were not recommended by a selection conference. Such conferences are as capable of making mistakes in identifying candidates as bishops but the local bishop often has the greater knowledge and experience of individuals. I deplore the current and increasing tendency to have the Church run on management principles. This must be resisted and the personal responsibility of the bishop protected.

During this period I first became acquainted with the Old Catholic Church, with which I was subsequently to have many dealings. Lambeth Palace asked us to accommodate a Dutch Old Catholic priest, Canon BA Van Kleef, who had come to England to make preparations for a formal visit by the Archbishop of Utrecht the following year. I had read JM Neale's book, *The Jansenist Church of Holland,* so I knew a little of what to expect when it came to making conversation and entertaining our guest. He became a great friend. As arranged, the following year he came again with Archbishop Rinkel, whom I was able to get invited to preach in the cathedral. In 1948, as a result of these contacts, I was asked to attend the first Old Catholic International Congress to be held after the war.

I became aware that the governing body of Exeter was looking for a Chaplain-Fellow and that both Tom Parker and I were being considered. The post had been vacant for some time as early on in the war the college had appointed Paul Kingdon to its living of Great Somerford. He had become increasingly difficult and objectionable and the Rector (now Barber) told me that the limit had been reached when he preached a sermon in chapel which contained an attack on the organ scholar. He had always been singularly lacking in tact but the limits of a tolerant community had been reached. Kingdon had charge of the college library and in that capacity had written to the brother of an undergraduate who had been killed in the war. The letter said that when the brother went down he had in his possession certain books from the library and would he please return them. It went on to say that there was a fine for keeping books out of the library for more than three weeks and that as the period in question now amounted to six months he would be glad to receive a cheque for the appropriate amount. The letter ended, 'May I say how much we sympathize with you on your brother's death.'

Eventually it was I who was elected to replace Kingdon, which made me feel rather embarrassed in my relations with Tom. He was, however, typically very good about it and I was greatly relieved when later he was elected a fellow of University College. I think that the choice between us may have been influenced by my membership of the medieval history group meeting under the chairmanship of Sir Maurice Powicke. I came to know him and his wife well and used often to go to see them in the evening. Accordingly, he knew me well socially as well as academically while he did not really know Tom. A recommendation from the Regius Professor of Modern History for someone who was to teach history may well have carried weight.

6

The Old Catholics

My interest in the Old Catholics and my first involvement in ecumenical work began at this time, inspired, as I have said, by my contacts with BA Van Kleef at Pusey House. I knew something of the origins of the Dutch Old Catholic Church, of which he was a member, and its history. Through conversation with Van Kleef I discovered that after the first Vatican Council, Roman Catholics in Germany and Switzerland who were unable to accept some of the conciliar decrees and decisions had organized themselves into a dissident Church and appealed to the Old Catholic Archbishop of Utrecht for help and ongoing legitimacy. As a result, Old Catholic Churches were formed in those countries and elsewhere. In the United States a group of Polish Roman Catholics later separated and formed the Polish National Church which then, in turn, formed a branch in Poland itself. All are now united in the Union of Utrecht, of which the Archbishop of Utrecht is president. Initially the Dutch Old Catholics were the most conservative of the whole movement. For two centuries they kept to the liturgy and discipline of 1723, the year of their definitive split with Rome. Canon Van Kleef told me that when he wanted to marry he had to leave Holland and join the German Old Catholics in order to be allowed to do so. This conservative line had begun to soften by the time I went to the Netherlands.

It was through Canon Van Kleef that I was invited to attend the Old Catholic Congress which took place in Hilversum in August 1948, at much the same time as the Lambeth Conference in England. At his invitation, I made the journey to the Netherlands in advance of the beginning of the Congress and stayed with his family at Culemborg. At that time after the war it was necessary in the Netherlands to register at a police station on arrival and then go to a food office for a ration card. Early on Tuesday, 17 August we left by train for Hilversum, which, for me, had hitherto been just a name on the wireless tuning dial. There we were met by Van Kleef's son and his wife and taken for a brief motor tour around north Holland. I remember particularly that at Egmont, where Van Kleef had been parish priest for 12 years, I was told that, of its population of 2,700, 2000 were Old Catholics. I fear this is no longer the case. In the evening there was the official welcome to the congress and entertainment was provided by the choir and youth club of the Hilversum church. I stayed as a guest of the Van Vliet family. Peggy Van Vliet became very much involved in ecumenical exchange and in 1967 was a founder member of the International Ecumenical Fellowship.

On the following morning the Archbishop of Utrecht, Andreas Rinkel, celebrated a Mass and present were the Bishop of Haarlem, Bishop Jasinski of the Polish National Church in the USA, Bishop Steinwachs from Germany and Bishop Kury from Switzerland. Bishop Sturtevant of Fond du Lac represented the Archbishop of Canterbury. Germanos, the Orthodox Archbishop of Edessa was also there. That evening there was a great dinner which lasted from 6.45pm until 11pm, with speeches between each course. The best of these speeches, in my opinion, was made by a French priest from Switzerland, Fr Cousy, who spoke of the Gallican movement in the French Church at that time. The sessions on the Thursday were addressed by theologians whom I came to know well during the following years: Urs Kury, who followed his father as a bishop in Switzerland, Dr Maan of Utrecht, Dr Kuppers of Bonn and Professor Rutti of Bern. Afterwards, we had a meeting of the Anglican–Old Catholic friendship society, the Society of St Willibrord, at which the Bishop of Edinburgh, who had by now arrived from the Lambeth Conference, was able to take the chair.

The next morning I was subdeacon at a Requiem celebrated by Bishop Lagerwey of Deventer. The final business session was in the afternoon and in the evening we all went to the Grand Theatre for a performance of a specially written oratorio, *The Song of Unity*, with words by Bishop Lagerwey and music composed by a local organist. This was followed by a series of speeches by the leaders of the foreign delegations. The Bishop of Edinburgh spoke very well but Bishop Steinwachs talked at great length about the misery and sufferings of the German Church. When he was persuaded to sit down, Van Kleef said, 'I must remind Herr Bishof Steinwachs that other people as well as Germans suffered in the war.' Professor Rutti, who was sitting next to me said to me, 'A German should not speak so long in Holland', and I understood that Bishop Kury said to Steinwachs afterwards, 'You could have won over the whole of the Dutch people with one word: "sorry", but that word you can never say.'

There was a sequel to all this a few days later when I attended a dinner arranged by the Dutch students association. Again, the various foreign delegations were present and again there were speeches, but this time the German speech was made by Professor Küppers who said, 'When we knew that we were to come to Holland we were very anxious about how we should be received and I would like to say that you Dutch have taught us Germans what forgiveness really means.'

After I returned to Culemborg, Canon Van Kleef said to me that on the following Sunday there was to be the opening service of the first general assembly of the World Council of Churches in Amsterdam. He had a ticket and, as he was not very keen on the occasion, invited me to go in his place, so I attended sitting among the Old Catholic delegates. It was an interesting but not very moving occasion, more like a meeting in a public hall with some hymns than a service. The procession, I noted, seemed to be without any order and the speech of Dr John Mott, one of the founding fathers, without dignity.

I have written rather fully about this congress as it was the first meeting after the war between German Old Catholics and those from other countries and as it was held in Holland, which had been overrun so early by the Nazi forces, it had a special interest. I have attended several such congresses since in Switzerland, Germany and Austria but there has not been another quite like it. I was invited to speak to one such gathering in Vienna to explain the Anglican–Methodist Conversations and was grateful on that occasion to have my view supported by the Metropolitan of Thyatira. I have also spoken on theological questions between our churches at the regular Old Catholic Theologians Conference. At one of these meetings in Switzerland, I had an interesting experience relating to translation into different languages. I had written my lecture in German and asked my host, who was a Swiss German, to check it. He looked it over and suggested a number of changes, some of which, I must say, I was not very happy with. When a German Old Catholic priest whom I knew well arrived, I asked him if he would check it and to my pleasure he proceeded to change back almost all the alterations to my original version, an illustration of how much Swiss German can differ from that spoken in Germany.

Over the years I have made a number of friends among the Old

Catholics in Switzerland, Germany, Austria and the USA. When eventually I became a bishop, I was determined to continue the tradition of Old Catholic participation in Anglican episcopal ordinations. As will be recounted later, two Old Catholic bishops participated in the laying-on of hands when I was consecrated and the protocol they signed is appended to this memoir. One of them, Marinus Kok, I met on my first visit to the Netherlands when he was a young priest. He was consecrated co-adjutor bishop of Utrecht by Archbishop Rinkel and was soon after elected as his successor. The huge number of contacts I made stood me in good stead when Archbishop Coggan asked me to oversee his personal ecumenical relations with the Union of Utrecht. I was greatly moved when the Old Catholic faculty at Bern University awarded me an Honorary Doctorate of Divinity in 1987, mainly for my Bampton Lectures. Sadly, the Old Catholic Churches have suffered the same disaster as the Anglican Communion over the ordination of women, and to my knowledge only the Polish National Church remains opposed to women priests and faithful to the original Old Catholic principles of order.

7

Fellow of Exeter

I had effectively been rather detached from the life of Exeter College since 1938 and returning in 1946, found the composition of the governing body and the senior common room somewhat changed. The Rector, RR Marrett, had died and had been replaced by EA Barber. CT Atkinson, who had been my tutor, had retired but was still regularly in college on Sunday evenings and still teaching, a little for the college but much more for St Catherine's. RM Dawkins had retired from his professorship of Greek but still lived in college. He had been succeeded by John Mavrogordato who was later followed by Constantine Trypanis. There was now, for the first, time a fellow in Politics, Herbert Nicholas, and this caused offence to the traditional-minded Atkinson who had wanted a second full-time historian. He tried to cold-shoulder Nicholas whom the rest of us liked. Atkinson's own successor was Greig Barr, who had come straight from the army, and it pleased Atkinson that he was a Magdalen man. He and I divided the history teaching between us and I took on the politics from Kneale for the time being. Nevill Coghill was the senior fellow. Dacre Balsdon, who been in the civil service and away for most of the war, returned at the same time as I arrived and he resumed the office of Sub-Rector. As he had intended, this post was taken over by Greig fairly soon. It quickly became plain that without any office of responsibility, Dacre would be intolerable to live with, so Kneale was persuaded to give up the position of senior tutor and Dacre was appointed. Four or five of us were designated moral tutors and the undergraduates divided between us. I had my own group but as chaplain I made a point of seeing each freshman for a few minutes within the first 48 hours of their arrival, partly to find out whether they were attached to any Church and also to make plain that, whatever their religious position, I would be happy to see them at any time. Bob Mortimer had told me that much of the chaplain's work could be done by hanging about in the lodge to chat with undergraduates as they went in and out of college. I felt it useful to have a regular 'At Home' after chapel on Sunday evenings.

As chaplain, I was naturally involved in the provision of music for chapel services. We had two undergraduates, known as choral exhibitioners, whose duty it was to sing in the choir with some volunteers and a group of boys who were paid by the college. Finding suitable boys for the choir became more and more of a problem and, from time to time, I was accused of taking boys away from their parish church. My connection with Christ Church led to an arrangement with the cathedral choir, by which we took a kind of second eleven from there, boys who had tried for the cathedral choir but not been chosen. This worked very successfully and the example was soon followed by Worcester College. The duty of the choir was to sing Evensong on Sundays and Wednesdays during term, under the direction of the organ scholar. During my time we had a good selection of such scholars. The only problem I encountered with music was in the 1960s with the introduction of new hymns. A number of my friends, including Cheslyn Jones, belonged to the Twentieth-Century Light Church Music Group and they published a small collection of new tunes for various favourite hymns, as well as some altogether new hymns. I introduced some of these into chapel services but although they seemed to appeal to a number of the undergraduates, they were not very acceptable to the musicians or to some of the fellows.

One of the difficulties I discovered in being a college chaplain is that a large part of the congregation is constantly changing. Roughly a third would leave in late June and a substantial number of freshmen would arrive each October. In addition, I came to realize that undergraduate fashions changed about every five or six years. Consequently, one was always improvising and trying to keep open to new ideas and new outlooks. It was not always easy to reconcile this desire to remain fresh and lively with the wishes of the governing body. Initially, I had to work with a chapel committee of fellows, with some of whom I had occasional difficulty. An example of this was when Dacre complained about a sermon I had preached. Fortunately, I had kept the full text of what I had said and showed it to the then Regius Professor of Divinity, Henry Chadwick, who said he could see nothing wrong with it. Later, I was able to have some undergraduates added to the committee. Things were much easier when Dacre decided that he did not wish to serve on it any more. Not since the chaplaincy of NP Williams had there been a daily Mass but with Dacre's departure from the committee I was able to start one which continued until I left.

The first five or six years after the war were a strange period in the university. At first, a high proportion of the men in college had served in the forces and thus had much more experience of life than I had, for example, when I came up as an undergraduate. These men were sometimes only with us for a couple of years or so, while they completed courses begun earlier but cut short by going into the forces. Others, having seen active service, were allowed to do shortened courses. Many of the men in those first three years were enthusiastic and committed Christians, and societies such as the OUCU were crowded. They were also accustomed to a much more mature social life, of which one had to take account. A chaplain was wise if he knew when it was prudent to leave a party. Then a generation of men arrived who had not actually served in the war but had come from two years' compulsory national service and were, again, older than the traditional undergraduate. Some of these had taken advantage of the opportunities available in the armed services to learn other languages, particularly Russian. Among these were some who became distinguished in their field, or even celebrities. One of my pupils, Alan Bennett, showed great promise as a medieval historian and after graduating was elected a research fellow at Magdalen to conduct research on the court of Richard II. He had always been prominent in entertainments in the junior common room and his association with three other undergraduates of Oxford and Cambridge in the revue *Beyond the Fringe* led him, as is now well known, into a non-academic career. I sometimes wonder if any of my sermons provided him with material for his famous sketch, 'Esau was an hairy man, but I am a smooth man'. He and I have kept in touch over the years and it gave me great pleasure when my son became involved as assistant director of *The Madness of George III* at the National Theatre. Another undergraduate of that period to become a household name is Ned Sherrin, who started as a lawyer. Many of the men of that time were good supporters of the chapel.

One of the most remarkable of these men was Brian Brindley. When he came up from Stowe for a scholarship examination, he proved himself enormously able and we had no hesitation in electing him. As history tutor, I taught him for two terms and although his brilliance showed through in his essays, he did not work hard enough to ensure the First his abilities merited. In spite of his poor showing in the schools, he persuaded the college to allow him to stay on for a further two years to read Law. During that time, he was elected president of the junior common room and ran the most successful Commemoration Ball in living memory. At the end of the two years, he left without taking schools. Perhaps two years later, I received a letter from him, asking if he might come and see me. When he arrived, it was to tell me that he had been resisting a vocation to the priesthood but could do so no longer. We talked for a long time and, forming a fresh opinion of him, I tried to arrange for him to go to St Stephen's House, thinking that the disciplined life there would be good for him. Arthur, however, was adamant that he would not have him and so he went instead to Ely Theological College, which was in its last years.

Brian was ordained in the diocese of Oxford to a title at Ascot. I encountered him again when I addressed the diocesan conference on the Anglican–Methodist Conversations then in progress. He spoke against the proposals in such offensive terms that he was rebuked from the chair by Bishop Carpenter. His hard work in the parish of Holy Trinity, Reading, resulted in the amazing transformation of the interior of a very undistinguished church building and the establishment of a rich liturgical life in a working-class district of the town. As a proctor for Oxford diocese, he made a significant and valuable contribution to the work of the General Synod, becoming chairman of its influential business sub-committee. Though his own unvarying custom was to use the Roman Missal whenever he celebrated Mass, he had an important influence on the Eucharist in *The Alternative Service Book 1980*. He contributed at the eleventh hour of the revision stage a reworking of Eucharistic Prayer III from the Roman Missal which, remarkably, he persuaded the evangelicals in Synod to accept. I remember the work of that Revision Committee was very long and drawn out, partly because of the large number of proposed amendments it had to deal with, and partly through the sheer numbers of people who wished to attend and make their point in person. Brian's work in his parish and on Synod was recognized by the Bishop of Oxford, who made him an honorary canon of Christ Church.

Brian's synodical career and parish ministry came to a tragic end in 1989. He was lured into an indiscreet conversation in a railway carriage by a young journalist with a concealed tape-recorder. His largely fanciful revelations regarding his sexuality were splashed across the

Sunday newspapers and two evangelical members of Synod created such a fuss that the matter was further publicized and he had to resign his benefice. He had a small flat in Brighton to which he withdrew. I did what I could to rescue him and found him a job in our diocesan office where he did extremely good work as secretary to both the Diocesan Advisory Committee and Pastoral Committee. In this capacity he was much liked by the clergy and the parishes with which he had to deal. Alas, Brian was one of those so upset by the decision to allow the ordination of women to the priesthood that he left the Church of England and became a Roman Catholic. A typical Brian gesture was to take the name Leo on being received, in homage to the pope who had declared Anglican Orders null and void. I was happy to allow him to continue to work for the diocese of Chichester but after a year of poor health and disillusionment with the Church of his baptism, he resigned. He continued to live in Brighton until he died while celebrating his 70th birthday at the Athenaeum. I remember well the exotic character of his rooms in college but was never invited to the Brighton house which, I hear, was equally remarkable.

In the 1950s, the college filled up with younger men, and in the shadow of the nuclear bomb one became aware of their increasing desire for security and certainty. With some, this took the form of an attachment to Biblical fundamentalism and adherence to the Inter-Collegiate Christian Union, OICCU. This organization, at times, established a group opposed to the chapel. Twice I succeeded in getting the college OICCU to cooperate with the SCM, the OUCU and other religious groups. Each time, after a year, this compact was broken up by the arrival of a freshman who had been involved with the equivalent in his school of the OICCU and who regarded working with others as quite wrong. More than once, by dint of patient teaching, I would bring a young man to acceptance of the Christian faith only to have him captured by the OICCU and told that my teaching was not true Christianity. This could be particularly annoying when, a little later, he gave up Christianity altogether. From time to time there would be a university mission conducted by some Christian leader such as William Temple, George Cockin, Stephen Neill or Michael Ramsey. The following year, the OICCU would hold a rival mission of its own, which they expected us to support but not play any part in. These difficulties did not prevent some of us at senior level from discussing and praying together and we formed a Catholic-Evangelical group. When Michael

Harper and I got to know one another, we invited John Stott to join us and we had very fruitful meetings which resulted in a joint pamphlet that we hoped would encourage similar groups to meet. I became very friendly with John Stott and much admire him. Personal relations are vital in this area.

At the opposite end of the spectrum were the Roman Catholics, where papal infallibility gave a similar sense of security. I had a problem with one of the choral exhibitioners who came back from two years in the RAF and told the Rector that he had become a Roman Catholic. He had seen the Roman Catholic chaplain, Valentine Elwes, who had told him that it was all right to continue in the choir as a paid musician. I thought I had better see Mgr Elwes myself and he confirmed that he considered it quite all right for the man to continue membership of the choir but added, 'He will not be taking any part in the worship and we do not think that there is any danger to his faith.' When I demurred and said that I was not happy about having someone in the choir who was not taking part in the worship, he said he hoped there would not be any question of religious persecution. When I reported this conversation to the Rector, he agreed with my view and we settled the matter by relieving the man of the obligation to sing and giving him the equivalent of the exhibition from another fund. On another occasion I became quite close friends with an ordinand who stayed on after the end of one Michaelmas term for ten days and served me at the altar each morning. At the beginning of the next term he came to tell me that during all that time he had been receiving instruction from Mgr Elwes and was going to be a Roman Catholic. Happily this sort of secretive behaviour would not now be necessary, and, indeed, before I left Oxford I had the privilege and joy of preaching at two Masses in the Roman Catholic chaplaincy. Michael Hollings was an altogether different style of chaplain from Valentine Elwes and we were able to do a great deal together. I find that people born in the second half of the twentieth century do not always realize how much things have changed since the Second Vatican Council.

Amongst my recreations, opera continued to be important. I found several undergraduates in college who were as keen on Wagner as I was and we were able to drive up to London several times to see *The Ring*. As I drove, we could return to Oxford the same evening and I could let them into college with my key. I was also glad to see the cycle on further separate occasions during those years with both Tom

Armstrong and Sidney Watson. I remember Tom saying to me while we had a drink before *Götterdammerung*, 'Watch Flagstad. You will see her come to the front of the stage, lift up her arms and then the most glorious volume of sound comes out.' Sidney said something similar about Nielson. They were great occasions. One of the greatest operatic experiences I have known was the first production of *Peter Grimes* at Sadlers Wells in 1945. I did not see the first night but I saw it soon afterwards and can still remember the thrill of what seemed the opening of a new era in English music. I have since seen most of Britten's other operas and liked them but none has reached the level of *Peter Grimes*. I think that when it was first put on at Covent Garden it suffered somewhat from the size of the stage and the production did not convey the sense the brooding music does of a small enclosed community.

Exeter had three Professorial Fellows. RM Dawkins was in post when I arrived and continued to live in college after his retirement, to the great joy of the senior common room community. He had been educated at King's College, London, and during the First World War had been a naval officer. He had command of a ship in the Mediterranean which cruised among the very Greek islands with which he was especially acquainted through his academic studies. He became the first Bywater and Sotheby Professor of Modern and Byzantine Greek. He had a close knowledge of the monasteries on Mount Athos, where he had stayed several times. He told us of an incident which he felt admirably illustrated the theoretical outlook of the Greek monks. One evening, a discussion had developed about the version of the psalms used at vespers. Was it the Septuagint or some other translation? Various reasons were advanced for one or the other and for what another translation might be. At last, Dawkins himself had said, 'There is an easy way of settling this. Let us get a copy of the service book and a copy of the Septuagint and compare them.' At this there was deathly silence. His scientific method had put an end to what was developing into a fascinating discussion. He had an interesting array of friends who would come and stay with him in college and whom we all enjoyed meeting. Among them I remember particularly the travel writer Patrick Leigh Fermor. I always had the impression that Dawkins' Greek links were not the kind of which his colleagues, Barber and Dacre, entirely approved.

He was very fond of an owl which used to appear frequently in the college garden and it was remarked that for some days after he died the owl came every evening to sit on the back of the chair in the garden which he usually occupied. He had many funny stories about a previous Rector, LR Farnell, whom he had found rather pompous. He welcomed my arrival as a fairly orthodox and traditional priest who encouraged the use of the Authorised Version for the lessons at Evensong.

A second Professorial Fellow was the Professor of Spanish, Entwistle, who was the kind of person one respected but never came to know at all well. I knew his successor, Peter Russell, much better and liked him. The third professorial fellow, who had joined Exeter shortly before me, was Sir Cyril Hinshelwood, Dr Lee's Professor of Physical Chemistry. He had been a fellow of Trinity where he was a colleague and friend of Kenneth Kirk, who had been the chaplain there before he moved to Christ Church. He told me that, from time to time, Kirk would announce a choir practice for those who stayed behind after Evensong, having previously arranged with the members of the rugby club that they would sit tight at each end of the pews so as to make it difficult for others to get out. Of course, there were drinks in the chaplain's rooms after the service for members of the club. As a scientist, Hinshelwood was distinctly annoyed by the superior attitude about Classics adopted by Barber and Dacre. He was rumoured to speak 12 languages himself and was president of the Classical Association. He, Derek Hall and I became great friends and I was touched that after he retired he left instructions that I was to take his funeral. He had been very regular at Evensong on Sundays.

Hinshelwood had a great dislike of authority, especially in the shape of the registrar and the police, the origin of which I never discovered. We shared an opposition to capital punishment and when in the Craig and Bentley case, Craig was only sent to prison as he was under 18, although he had fired the gun, whereas Bentley was condemned to death, we both signed the unsuccessful petition for appeal. Some years later, when I met Bentley's sister, I was able to tell her this and was glad when I read the terms in which judges later condemned Lord Goddard's judgement and handling of the case. The Craig and Bentley case made me think more deeply than I had before about capital punishment so when the Report of the Royal Commission was published, I obtained a copy and studied it. I was not surprised that the chairman of the Royal Commission, Sir Ernest Gowers, followed up the report with a book of his own, advocating the abolition of the death penalty. It seemed to me that if one seriously examined the three traditionally acknowledged purposes of punishment – reform, deterrence and retribution – they could not justify capital punishment. Reform obviously did not apply and there was no conclusive evidence for deterrence. Indeed, Albert Pierrepoint, for many years the official executioner, said, 'I do not believe that any one of the hundreds of executions I carried out has in any way acted as a deterrent against future murder. Capital punishment, in my view, achieves nothing except revenge.' That only left retribution, which Archbishop Fisher and a number of eminent judges thought a sufficiently strong ground to continue the practice. It seemed to me, however, that there were a number of good arguments against retribution as justification, not least the fallibility of the judicial process. One has only to consider the number of cases in which the verdict has later been shown to be wrong. Another argument emerged from the report of the Royal Commission, which said, 'The ambition that prompts five applications a week for the post of hangman, and the craving that draws a crowd to the prison where a notorious murderer is to be executed, reveals psychological qualities of a sort that no state would wish to foster in its citizens.' I became a firm opponent of capital punishment and have remained such. Later, as Bishop of Chichester, I had to consider the matter again when the question arose in Parliament. I wrote to all the Sussex MPs making clear my views and was glad when most of them agreed with me. In the House of Commons, Ted Heath and William Whitelaw spoke against capital punishment and I was relieved when the debate led to its abolition. Although some politicians have expressed themselves in favour of the restoration of the death penalty, our membership of the European Community now makes that impossible.

My closest friends in college were Greig Barr and Derek Hall. Greig was Sub-Rector and until he married he and I shared the history teaching. Derek was younger than me. After my mother died he, my father and I went for a long holiday together, driving almost all round France. When Greig married, Derek succeeded him as Sub-Rector. Later he, too, married and when I left Oxford had just been elected President of Corpus. Sadly, he died at an early age soon after. His widow still lives in Oxford and remains a friend.

After the war, I was able to resume my friendship with Richard Southern, now a fellow of Balliol and married to a woman named

Sheila. He had been released from the army but had developed a chest infection which turned out to be tuberculosis, and he was, for a time, in the King Edward VII Hospital at Midhurst. I was able to visit him there and to take books for him to read. I remember one of them was *The Life and Letters of Dean Church*, which I was pleased to learn he found as interesting as I did. It is a very important book. He was kind enough to say that I was his best provider of books. I think it must have been shortly after this that he suggested me to the senior historian at Christ's Hospital as suitable to examine the history 'Grecians'. This was an experience I much enjoyed and it resulted in at least one of them coming to Exeter as an undergraduate.

I was very pleased when Dick and Sheila Southern asked me to be a godfather to their second son, Peter, who later became headmaster of Christ's Hospital. Some years later, I asked Dick to be godfather to our first child, Sarah, and he was very good and caring in this role. When he was president of St John's, he arranged for Sarah's wedding in St John's Chapel. After I had become Bishop of Chichester, Dick wrote to ask if I could help in the confirmation of Peter's second son, Nicholas, who had inherited his grandfather's deafness. He was at a special school in Sussex and I was glad to be able to help. Nicholas was prepared for confirmation largely by his grandfather who was able to communicate with him more easily than I and many others could. I confirmed him in St John's Chapel. Dick's own increasing deafness, though otherwise very sad, was useful in that context. I remained in close touch with Dick and Sheila until we left Oxford, and I always visited them when I returned, once dining with Dick at High Table at St John's. Although we talked about it often, I was never able to get him to come down to Chichester. He died in 2001, and Sheila two years later. I miss them both very much.

Among other former members of Exeter resident in Oxford who used to come for dinner quite often were JRR Tolkien and my great friend Hugo Dyson. I did not have much contact with Tolkien. I had not read *The Hobbit* at that stage and it was not until the first volume of *The Lord of the Rings* was published that I realized how much of an author he was. It was much talked about in common room so I bought a copy and read it. I was gripped and waited anxiously for the second volume. In the meantime, I happened to visit Bob Mortimer and his family who were camping in the country and found that they were also waiting anxiously to know what had become of Gandalf! As far as I remember, the third volume was not so long delayed. Ever since, I have been a firm fan of Tolkien and have now read most of this other books, as well as having read *The Lord of the Rings* aloud more than once to my wife and children. Much later, when I was Bishop of Chichester, the BBC radio dramatization was issued on cassette tapes. I bought a set, and my chaplain, Jeremy Haselock, and I listened to it all the way through over a period as we drove around the diocese. Not everyone was quite so enthusiastic. Hugo Dyson did not much like Frodo and the hobbits and once, when I had persuaded him to come and talk to the College Church Society, said that he thought CS Lewis's *Narnia* books distinctly superior. Hugo was quite a noisy talker, as were both Tolkien and Nevill Coghill. When all three of them dined in college together, it could be quite difficult for the rest of us to hear one another, especially on one occasion when to add to the tumult they had Lord David Cecil as a guest. Hugo and his wife were most hospitable and I remember a very enjoyable Christmas dinner with them when one year I was unable to leave Oxford and go home.

Another old member of the college who visited us from time to time was the Reverend Philip Clayton, known universally as 'Tubby'. He took a First in the theology schools in 1910 and was ordained to a title at St Mary's Portsea during Cyril Garbett's incumbency. He became well known as an army chaplain in the First World War, during which time he founded Toc H. In 1947, he was responsible for encouraging a number of young American students to come and work for Toc H under the auspices of an American diplomat, John Gilbert Winant, who had been America's war-time ambassador to Britain. The first such students arrived in 1948 and were named Winant Volunteers. By 1959, the scheme had grown into an exchange programme with the British students known as Clayton Volunteers. Tubby Clayton was quite elderly by the time I knew him but still a very lively and enthusiastic priest and Vicar of All Hallows by the Tower.

During his few years as Sub-Rector, Derek Hall was landed with one of the most difficult situations that can arise in the small world of college politics. Some years before it was expected, Barber, the Rector, suddenly announced his retirement. The choice of time was never explained but it came while Dacre was out of the country on sabbatical leave in Rome. Derek had to take charge of the college and conduct the election of a successor. Among the fellows, Nevill Coghill and Constantine Trypanis both favoured Dacre, but all the rest of us were quite clear that he was, frankly, so overbearing that he was the last person we wanted. Derek had to write a difficult letter and tell him this. In response, Dacre wrote back that on the occasion of Marrett's death, he and Barber had come to an agreement that Barber should become Rector and Dacre would succeed him in due course. Whether or not that was true, a private compact could not bind the governing body and so we had to go ahead with our own discussion. We initially asked Hinshelwood and Kneale if they would be interested but both demurred. We did not consider Neville Coghill very suitable even if he were prepared to consider it, which in the event, he wasn't. We were in a dilemma which made our relationship with Dacre even more difficult as we would have to look outside the college for a suitable candidate. In the end we approached Kenneth Wheare who was a Professorial Fellow of All Souls and had previously done some teaching for Exeter when he was a Fellow of Oriel. He accepted and I am sure we had made a good decision. He and his wife made the Rector's lodgings very much a social centre for everybody. However, when Dacre came back from Rome there was a very tense situation. He had convinced himself that he had not been chosen because he was not married. For some time he would hardly speak to those of us who were married and whom he believed had been influenced by our wives against him. It was a very difficult time.

When I was appointed to the chaplain-fellowship my full title was 'Fellow, Chaplain and Lecturer in Theology and Medieval History'. For the first few years, I was expected to spend 16 hours a week in teaching or lecturing. I was allowed to set against this total two hours a week as chaplaincy work. The history tutorials took up much more time than the theology. This was because of the large number of men reading history. I had to cover English history to 1484 in two terms, and then deal with the smaller number of men doing Stubbs' *Charters* as the first period for constitutional history. I also taught those doing the first and third periods of European history, one or two of those doing a medieval special subject – mainly St Augustine, and, of course, the political thought course with the three set books, Aristotle's *Politics*, Hobbes' *Leviathan*, and Rousseau's *Du Contrat Social*, which had to be read in French. As far as lecturing was concerned, I began by giving a course on the period III of European history and then took up the St Augustine special subject and lectured for a time on the letters of St Augustine. I acquired the title of University Lecturer in Canon Law so I started a series of lectures in the history of canon law. There were always a few people interested in these, but I remember above all a man called Peters who later became notorious in ecclesiastical circles in England, Wales and central Africa for representing himself with academic qualifications which he did not possess. He had attached himself to Magdalen but was recognized one day by Cuthbert Simpson, the Dean of Christ Church, who had encountered him in Canada. In spite of this, he got himself somehow accepted elsewhere in the University. When he came to my lectures, he brought with him a manuscript of cases in a sixteenth-century archdeacon's court which he said he had been lent by the diocesan registrar. I fear I did not enquire into this and I have wondered since what became of it. Kathleen Major knew about his activities and spoke to me about him. He disappeared into Wales but rapidly got himself into trouble with the Church there. The last I heard of him was over some trouble in Africa.

The Rousseau set book came up in a curious way during one of the three years when I was one of the examiners. In the schools, the European history periods were examined in two papers in chronological order and in the year in question, one was to be done on Friday afternoon and the other on Saturday morning. As many of the periods overlapped, some candidates were doing Paper One of their subject while others were doing the same paper as Paper Two of theirs. On that particular Friday, the first examiner to arrive at the schools was handed the wrong bunch of papers and put them out without checking them. I was the senior examiner that afternoon and arrived a few minutes afterwards, naturally assuming that everything was in order. It was not long after the exam began that people came up to me and said that, instead of the paper they had anticipated, they had been given the one they were expecting the next morning. I had to think quickly what to do and so I said, 'I understand that some of you have been given the paper you were expecting tomorrow morning. I suggest that you do the best you can with it and the examiners will make allowances in due course.' There was just one candidate who handed in his script after the statutory half hour, having written on it, 'I am a man who depends very much on last minute revision. If I had been able to revise for this paper, I should have attempted questions two and five and I hope I may be asked about these in the *viva*.' About four weeks later, he came up for his *viva* and was duly asked about the questions he had specified but, in spite of having had four weeks in which to mug something up,

he was not able to say anything satisfactory about them. We sent him
out and conferred together as to what we should do. Some were in
favour of ploughing him at once but most of us felt that in view of the
mistake in the handing out of the papers, we should give him another
chance. We had him back in and one of the other examiners tried him
on the political science paper, saying, 'Will you look at the Rousseau
passages on the paper and begin by translating the first of them for me.'
After some feeble attempts, the candidate said, 'I'm afraid I read the
book in English.' The examiner tried again to see if he could translate
anything asking, 'What about the words *"contrat social"*?' The student
replied, 'I don't know the meaning of the word *"contrat".*' That, of
course, was the end of him.

The other major difficulty I had when examining was more alarming. I should explain that there were usually over 300 candidates, the
exam took place in the sixth and seventh weeks of the Trinity term and
the scripts poured in for marking while one was still teaching, so that it
was not until after the end of term that one was able to settle down to
marking them. Among the papers I was marking was the Stubbs paper
on constitutional history, which always started with two questions
containing short passages from Stubbs for comment. I had locked the
scripts away in a drawer as they arrived and when I came eventually to
mark this paper I found one script which began, 'Paper 2, question 2'.
What on earth had become of Paper 1? I hunted through all the other
scripts I had and there was no sign of it so I telephoned the chairman
of the examiners and told him what had happened. He consulted all
the other examiners but there was no sign of the missing script, so we
got in touch with the schools to see whether anyone remembered a
paper being left on any of the desks, but without success. There was
nothing for it but to tell the Junior Proctor who had overall responsibility for the examinations and he said that we must wait until the
day appointed for the *viva* and then tell the candidate to go and see
him. About three weeks later this duly happened. The Proctor saw him
and asked how he thought he had done in the exam to which he
replied, 'Not too badly.' However, he went on to reveal that he had
disliked the constitutional history paper and had felt so dissatisfied
with what he had written that he had torn up his answer to Question 1
and not handed it in. That was an immense relief but even more so
when his tutor, who happened also to be one of the examiners, told us
that he was the son of a judge and that his grandfather was Lord

Goddard, the Lord Chief Justice of the day, who had a reputation for unbridled severity.

There were also happier occasions during the exacting period of examining. I remember one when a man was having a *viva* for a possible first and the chairman decided to take him up on his military history special subject. The following dialogue ensued:

> *Chairman*: 'Can you think of any battle in the eighteenth century which caused a marked change in methods of fighting?'
> *Candidate*: (after thinking for some time) 'No sir, I can't.'
> *Chairman*: 'What about the Battle of Mollwitz?'
> *Candidate*: 'Mollwitz sir, why Mollwitz?'
> *Chairman*: 'Wasn't that the occasion when the Prussian musketeers for the first time fired five rounds to the minute?'
> *Candidate*: 'I don't believe it, sir. I have a Prussian musket of that period and I can't make it fire more than three rounds.'

Needless to say he got his first.

When, later, I examined in the theology school, the three years I did so were devoid of any such incidents. Sadly, not so was the week in which I was chairman of the examiners for the theology preliminary. My mother was ill and I had been told she had cancer, but she was still at home. We had by then moved into Grimsby and Grove House had been sold. She seemed rather worse that week and I was clear that I must go home as soon as possible. However, I could not easily leave Oxford because of the examination and the *viva* which was to be on the Friday. I planned to be home on the Saturday and I spoke to her on the telephone on the Friday night but by the time I got home she had died. This was the first great bereavement I had suffered. My father's parents had died some years before, and my maternal grandfather during the war, but I did not miss them as I did my mother. Her funeral was in Waltham parish church and she is buried in the cemetery there. The priest who ministered to her in her last days was Canon Marsden, Vicar of Grimsby, whom I came to know well later when he was Archdeacon of Lindsey and based in Lincoln. I was grateful for all that he did for her and that he came and prayed with me as she lay in her coffin.

I remember that at Marsden's own funeral the hymn, 'Jesu, the very thought of thee' was sung to the tune St Botolph, composed by the then organist of Lincoln Cathedral, Gordon Slater. Dick Milford, who was Chancellor, said to me, 'I wonder what angel descended on him to write that tune.' Slater was organist at Lincoln for a great many years and was not really a very inspiring musician. Dr Ken Andrews, who was organist at New College, had known Slater many years before. Once, when driving down from Durham, Andrews had stopped at Lincoln and gone up to the organ loft during Evensong. The time came for the anthem which was by William Byrd, and Slater went down to conduct it. When he came back he said, 'Andrews, you will have to go a long way to hear Byrd sung like that.' Andrews' comment to me was, 'I was regretfully constrained to agree with him.' Andrews was a very big man, and when he died in the organ loft at Trinity, where he happened to be playing, there was great difficulty in getting his body down.

On my return to Oxford I found that Claude Jenkins' seminar on the African Canons was still running and I was able to rejoin it. While I was in Southampton, Greenslade had left for Durham and Bob Mortimer had become Professor of Moral and Pastoral Theology but was still in the seminar, as was Leslie Cross, now at Christ Church. Milburn was still at Worcester for a few more years and I used to meet him also at a regular lunch on Saturdays during term. This was a luncheon club to which I was elected soon after I went to Exeter. The 'Saturday Lunch' had been founded by NP Williams and Ronnie Knox. It was comprised of six or seven members, including John Kelly and Graham Midgeley of St Edmund Hall, Eric Mascall, and the Bishop of Dorchester, Gerald 'Puffles' Allen, who had been a fellow of Wadham. One of his Wadham colleagues had known Dr Routh, the celebrated president of Magdalen, who had known a lady who had seen King Charles II exercising his spaniels in Magdalen Grove.

The Saturday lunch, the Bach Choir practice and the Jenkins seminar on Thursday afternoon were three very enjoyable points in the week during term. For the seminar we met for tea in Jenkins' house next door to the cathedral and continued until 6pm. Conversation over tea was very discursive and diverting. It was once said that between them, Jenkins and Lowther Clarke knew everything that was worth knowing. Jenkins' knowledge appeared to embrace every field. I happened to arrive a little late one day, having been to one of the symphony concerts in the Sheldonian. Jenkins asked what had been played and when I said that the concert had included Schubert's Ninth Symphony he spoke very knowledgeably about it and its history. Jenkins divided his vacations between Malvern Wells and Tunbridge Wells, where there were particular second-hand bookshops which, as he was on close terms with the proprietors, he visited regularly. When we arrived for the first seminar of each term, we would find the hall of his house filled with packing cases containing the books he had bought, usually a very miscellaneous collection. During the subsequent weeks they disappeared into various parts of the house, some gradually piled up on the stairs and, it was said, in the bath. On his death several crates of books were found which had never been unpacked. He was well known in Blackwell's and was soon informed of any substantial purchase of second-hand books there. A story circulated that on one occasion, when he had been informed of a new purchase, he arrived rather late to inspect it, apologizing that his housekeeper had just died. 'I left her in the chair,' he said, 'and she will be there when I get back.' Whether he ever had another housekeeper, I rather doubt. He was senior librarian of the Union Society and attended the Thursday debates regularly, always dining with the committee beforehand. The Principal of St Edmund Hall told me once that Jenkins visited him on a certain day in every year with a substantial gift for their scholarship fund, having satisfied himself that the Hall was less well provided with scholarships than most other colleges. A similar concern for the poorer foundations in the university became evident from his will, in which he left the first choice from among the 30,000 books of his library to one of the women's colleges. To wealthy Christ Church he left a sum of money sufficient to provide snuff for the common room.

As a preacher he was always well worth hearing. For some reason, he always chose to do residence in the ninth week of the summer term, that is, the week after the end of full-term, and the small boys of the Dragon School always attended Matins in the cathedral on that Sunday. I happened to be on duty in the cathedral on one such Sunday and heard him preach. His text was, 'Who hath despised the day of small things?' (Zechariah 4.10) and, as I recall, the sermon began thus: 'Sixty years ago, a small boy took a large piece of paper, called foolscap because if you look at the watermark on it you will see that it is a fool's cap, and began to write a story. The story was about a man and a tiger. It was not clear which of the two was the hero but that did not matter because by page five they had been united when the tiger ate the man.' There followed a lurid description, much enjoyed by the boys, of the precise details of the tiger's meal. Ultimately, it was revealed that the small boy was Arthur Conan Doyle and the story his first attempt at writing. At the beginning of the following Michaelmas term, I noticed he was to preach the University Sermon in St Mary's, so I went to hear it. To my surprise, he gave out the same text and I waited with interest for a repeat of the tiger story, but the sermon began: 'Seven hundred and twenty years ago, Walter de Merton added a codicil to his will . . .' and proceeded with an account of some significant incident in the history of the university.

Before coming to Christ Church as Regius Professor of Ecclesiastical History, Jenkins had been for many years in charge of Lambeth Palace Library, and subsequently also a residentiary canon of Canterbury. At Lambeth he had been adviser to the archbishop on many technical matters involving scholarly, historical knowledge, both in regard to such things as the coronation – he had attended three – and to details of the archbishop's powers of dispensation. This was one of the various subjects mentioned at tea on Thursday and I discovered that his knowledge embraced not only those dispensations still in regular use but also some lesser-known ones. One such was the authority for a bishop to ordain a man deacon and priest at the same service. Fortunately I remembered this years later, when I had to re-ordain a man whose orders were doubtful and it was convenient to be able to ordain him deacon and priest at the same service. Jenkins left very little in print but, for the historian, there are some useful articles concerning the controversy over episcopal consecrations in the sixteenth century.

Shortly after moving back to Exeter, I came into contact with a south Oxford parish, South Hinksey, and with a member of the congregation who was in charge of the Scouts there. He was more concerned with the activities for the younger boys and was anxious to find someone to deal with the older ones, so for a time I became Group Scout Master. I cannot claim that this was the most successful thing I ever did, but somehow I managed to run a summer camp on the hills just above Gloucester. I was involved with leading the South Hinksey Scouts for about two years before deciding that, important as I believe scouting to be for a parish, it was not something to which I, personally, was called. In this extended experiment, I had the assistance of a more expert student from St Stephen's House, Ernest Chown, with whom I was to have further dealings later when he was at St Andrew's, Worthing.

I decided to follow the example of some other college chaplains and encourage members of my chapel congregation to do some voluntary work together in parishes during the vacation. I had the help of my friends at Lincoln Cathedral for the start of this who suggested that we go to a parish in the south of Lincolnshire, near Bourne, and work in the surrounding four or five parishes. We made our headquarters in the parish hall of Edenham and for two weeks the group did various jobs, such as clearing a churchyard, listing gravestones preparatory to removal and such other such jobs in other nearby parishes as needed doing. About 20 undergraduates were in this first party. We all enjoyed the fortnight and thought the work worth doing. It was clearly much appreciated. The next year we went to a parish in the St Albans diocese, which did not seem as good as the previous year and we were looking around for somewhere to go in the following year when a fresh suggestion was made. In that year, Derek Hall had become sub-rector and so to give him some relief as law tutor, the college appointed a young law lecturer, Peter Glazebrook, who had been at Pembroke and similarly involved in vacation jobs. The chaplain of Pembroke, Colin Morris, had a friend who was the rector of Spennithorn in Wensleydale, Joe Jory, who one day was rung up by the Leeds police to say that they had a youth in custody who was being sent to Borstal. The boy had no relations and on being asked whether there was any adult whom he would like to see had mentioned Joe's name. Joe spent some time with him and through his conversations with the young man came to think it would help such youths if they could have contact with other young men of similar age but more stable background. Joe got in touch with Colin and out of that came into being the first Oxford–Borstal camp. Peter Glazebrook had taken part in this experiment and suggested that we at Exeter might do something similar and we were glad to fall in with that. The Yorkshire end of the organization was in the hands of Joe Jory, assisted by a retired police superintendent and Frank Theakston, the brewer. The scheme had the support of Lady Masham, her husband and her father-in-law, Lord Swinton. We were linked with Everthorpe, which had been built as a prison and was the only closed Borstal.

We started with 20 undergraduates but in subsequent years it was slightly fewer. In addition, there were Peter, myself and Michael Hollings, the Roman Catholic chaplain, and Leslie Houlden from Trinity. We all travelled up to Yorkshire on the Saturday after the Trinity term and spent the weekend with the Theaksons at Masham, where the Exeter party was said to drink more beer than any other college. On the Monday morning we went to the field where we were to camp, and at midday were joined by 20 Borstal boys from Everthorpe and one of the wardens. Together, they all put up the small tents in which they were to sleep and a big marquee. The undergraduates and Borstal boys paired off in groups of four and lived and worked together for the whole of the camp. On Tuesday and Wednesday, they did jobs for people in the neighbourhood and on Thursday there was a cricket match – one year, I remember, against Ampleforth College. On Friday each group set off for a two-day hike on a route specified by Frank Theakston, and returned in time for supper on the Saturday. On Sunday morning we all went to church, the Roman Catholics to Mass at their nearest church or on the camp site, and the rest of us to parish Communion at Masham. The service was conducted by one of us and I recall, one year, Lord Swinton said it was the first time he had been able to understand what it was all about. The following day we all went back to the Borstal at Everthorpe and the Oxford contingent stayed there for five days. It was quite an experience to be locked in prison and live on Borstal food. I was disturbed at finding boys as young as 15 there. The scheme was such a success that we repeated it every year for the remainder of the time I was at Oxford. Other colleges gradually established links with other Borstals and eventually there were five colleges involved. The Borstal authorities considered it well worthwhile and I think it supports the view that much good can be done to young people by persons of the same age, being closer to them. I count these camps as one of the most valuable things in which I have been involved. Frank Theakston sadly died during one of our camps and was buried at Masham. The brewery was then taken over by Scottish and Newcastle Brewery but they kept the name Theakston. One of Frank's sons was so sad at this that he started another brewery in Masham under the name of the Black Sheep, which was very successful. I understand Scottish and Newcastle have now handed Theakston's back to the family but keep an interest in it.

In 1949, Bob Mortimer was appointed Bishop of Exeter and became Visitor of the College, which gave me great pleasure. He asked me to become one of his examining chaplains, giving me a connection with the diocese of Exeter which I enjoyed. In 1950, the diocese observed, with great celebration, the 900th anniversary of the removal of the see from Crediton to Exeter. I came down for the main service in the cathedral and stayed with the Mortimers along with Sir Harry Vaisey, the Chancellor of the diocese, whom we both knew well. Geoffrey Fisher preached and I gained the distinct impression that he was not enjoying himself. He was not happy with the new bishop's distinctive liturgical style, and later complained to Bob about the red episcopal gloves he saw him wearing at the service. He did not tarry in Exeter after the service but hurried back to Lambeth. That evening after dinner, Bob, Harry and I enjoyed ourselves by arranging the bishops of the current bench in first and second eleven cricket teams according to our opinions of them.

Another consequence of Bob's appointment to the see of Exeter was that I was invited to take his place as one of the two proctors in Convocation for the clergy of the University. I think that it was NP Williams who got this system accepted. On a parallel with the parliamentary university seats, there were two proctors in the Canterbury convocation for each of the universities of Oxford and Cambridge and one for the other southern universities, all becoming also *ex-officio* members of the Church Assembly. At Oxford, by agreement, one was to represent the Catholic-minded clergy and the other the rest of the clerics. The first to occupy these positions were Williams himself and LB Cross, of Jesus College. When Williams died, Bob Mortimer had succeeded him and now I was to follow Bob and, in so doing, became the youngest member of convocation. Later, I was to add to that distinction by being the first member to be congratulated on his engagement by the prolocutor during a session.

By now I had come to know well the Dean of Lincoln, Bishop Colin Dunlop, and I think he may have recommended me to Bishop Maurice Harland, for in 1952 I received an invitation to accept appointment as one of his examining chaplains and a little later to be made a canon and prebendary of Lincoln Minster. I had the pleasure of succeeding Michael Ramsey in the stall of Caister. When I became Dean of Worcester, Bishop Kenneth Riches asked me to keep the stall, as did his successors, until the cathedral statutes were revised in 2000 when I felt it proper to resign. I always enjoyed my visits to Lincoln for my annual prebendal sermon which, whenever it was possible, I combined with attendance at the annual meeting of the Lincoln Record Society. This was always an enjoyable occasion, with the council meeting in the morning, a good lunch to follow, and the annual general meeting (AGM) in the afternoon. Sir Frank Stenton was president when I first became a member, and was followed by Christopher Hill, Mayor of Lincoln, and then by Kathleen Major, all of whom were very good friends. Kathleen was secretary when I joined the society. When, at each AGM, it came to election of officers, the president would say with regard to the post of secretary, 'The question is whether the society shall continue,' and then propose Kathleen's name as the only possibility of ensuring this. However, she eventually went to Oxford as a reader and was succeeded by Joan Varley, who certainly ensured the continuance of the society. Kathleen had a house in Lincoln, to which she retired after she had ceased to be Principal of St Hilda's, and she used to invite my wife and I and the children to tea every year, an event which we all enjoyed.

After the death of NP Williams, Trevor Jalland was asked by Mrs Williams to sort out the books and papers left in Priory House preparatory to writing a biography. He asked me to help him and it was an interesting job, but before we had got very far Trevor was appointed to a post in the theology department at Exeter University. He felt that the new post would involve him too deeply for him to continue with the biography so I was asked to take it on. This brought me into closer contact with the Williams family and I became a close friend of Mrs Williams and, among their children, of Gelda. Writing this biography was not as simple a task as it first seemed as Williams was a man of very distinctive character, and I was afraid of offending the family by being too outspoken. Happily, Mrs Williams realized the difficulty and solved the problem by writing an introduction of personal reminiscences, for which I was very grateful. Trevor Jalland married Beatrice Hamilton Thompson. I was best man at the wedding in Durham Cathedral, and stayed with Michael Ramsey. I remember vividly the preacher, Egbert de Gray Lucas, Archdeacon of Durham, speaking in his sermon, unfortunately, as it seemed to me, of 'the rough and tumble of married life'!

In the course of my research for the Williams biography, I came across evidence of rather more involvement on his part in the foundation and early years of the Society of Ss Peter and Paul than I had realized before. As the society was important in the history of the Catholic Movement, particularly between 1910 and 1930, I thought it right to give some space to this. Williams was involved right at the beginning with Maurice Child, Sam Gurney and Ronald Knox, and he continued his association with the founding group after Knox had become a Roman Catholic. He wrote one of the tracts, 'Serving better to Godliness', which advocated clerical celibacy. His gift as a cartoonist was used to poke fun at a number of contemporary episcopal utterances and I decided to reproduce some of these amusing pictures in the biography. I think I was right to do so, though some said, wrongly, as it turned out, that it diminished Williams' standing as a scholar and theologian. I also reprinted some of his sermons, including the long one preached at Geoffrey Fisher's consecration. However, it was not possible to use what I consider one of his major contributions namely the essay on 'The Theology of the Catholic Revival', published by the SPCK in 1933 in *Northern Catholicism*. That title caused a certain amount of criticism and indeed ridicule but the book itself is important. My biography was published by the SPCK in 1954.

In that same year, I was asked by Kathleen Major to work with Professor Walter Holtzmann of the University of Bonn on a volume for the Lincoln Record Society. This was a collection of Papal Decretals relating to the diocese of Lincoln in the twelfth century. I contributed an English translation of the documents and an introduction on canon law and its administration in the period covered by the volume. I much appreciated the honour of collaborating with Holtzmann and our work was published as volume 47 of the Lincoln Record Society in 1954.

In 1948 the Archbishop of Canterbury, Geoffrey Fisher, asked me to write a new history of the Convocations as discussions were beginning about their future. As I read for this project, I realized that, in the past, there had been some argument about their nature and origins, whether they were just bodies brought into being by the king to ensure the grant of taxation by the clergy and what was the relation of a convocation to a provincial synod. I decided, therefore, that my first task must be to study something of the history of provincial synods. The best available material seemed to concern France so having looked at the printed records from Narbonne, Sens and Bourges, I went to France in September 1948 to see what else survived. I visited all the dioceses of the old province of Sens and some of Bourges and saw material in the Bibliothèque and Archives Nationales. The results of this research I later incorporated in the first two chapters of my book, *Counsel and Consent*. I then started to examine all the English medieval episcopal registers and cathedral registers which were not in print, beginning with Winchester and Salisbury. I was surprised and pleased to discover in one of the Winchester registers clear evidence of the distinction between a provincial synod and convocation. This I described in an article for the *Journal of Ecclesiastical History* and enlarged upon later in my book.

In 1950 I went to Lichfield. As I wanted to consult the chapter acts, I had some preliminary correspondence with the Dean and one of the canons. The Dean, who was FA Iremonger , the biographer of William Temple, sent me a pamphlet that one of his predecessors had written about Convocation and said that I should return it on my visit. When I was there I asked the canon with whom I was staying what would be the best time to call and return the pamphlet. The Dean took a late dinner, he informed me, and would be at liberty after that so I called at the deanery at about 9pm. The housekeeper, who answered the door, seemed rather hesitant and went to consult her employer. Eventually, she returned and showed me into a room where I could see a tall figure standing. The Dean beckoned me in, received the pamphlet I had brought, put it on a bookshelf and pointed to a chair beside his desk. I sat down and there was silence. After a time I thought I had better leave so I stood up. The Dean said, 'Mr Kemp, let me give you some advice. Do not call on busy people without first making an appointment. Several people have been to see me today without appointments and as a result I have an hour's work to do this evening.' At that point I left. The next day was Sunday and as I was sitting in a stall waiting for the Sung Eucharist, Iremonger approached me and said, 'I should be interested to hear about what you are doing. Can you come for a drink after the service?' I did and no-one could have been nicer.

At Norwich I found the registers were kept in what had been the Bishop's private chapel. I was intrigued to find there not only the medieval registers, but also the later records including the registrar's notes of summoning the clergy to elections throughout the eighteenth century. His clerk must have gone round delivering the summons to vote in person and making notes as he went. Against one incumbent he had written, 'Non compos mentis.'

By 1960 I had seen all the surviving medieval episcopal registers and all the other related material, and so turned my mind to thinking how this could all be incorporated in a new edition of Wilkins' *Concilia* for the fourteenth and fifteenth centuries. David Wilkins' *Concilia Magnae Britanniae et Hiberniae* had been published in 1737 and was the standard collection of conciliar records for the Church of the British Isles and I had been invited to take over responsibility for updating the fourteenth- and fifteenth-century part of this compilation from Billy Pantin and Ernest Jacob. Pantin was a fellow and history tutor at Oriel and Jacob was Chichele Professor of History and a fellow of All Souls.

By now Kenneth Wheare, who had been Gladstone Professor of Government and Public Administration, had become Rector of Exeter and he suggested that I should consider applying for the Bampton lectureship, which I did and was appointed. So, such material as I had by then collected, I summarized and delivered as the 1960 Bampton Lectures under the title 'Counsel and Consent', and published in 1961. I continued to collect material for the new edition of Wilkins but my other commitments made this very difficult. After I went to Worcester Cathedral it became even more difficult to find time for this work and when I became a bishop, virtually impossible. I was very glad to learn recently that a new edition of the convocation records has been undertaken by Dr Gerald Bray for the Church of England Record Society, and I have been happy to make all that I had available to him.

There were other literary projects in which I became involved as events in the Church of England unfolded. For example, after John Robinson's *Honest to God* was published in 1963, Michael Ramsey asked a number of people, of whom I was one, to spend a day with him at Lambeth to discuss the issues it raised. Among our group were several other people from Oxford and we decided to get together afterwards with one or two others to carry on the discussion among ourselves. The meetings were held in my rooms at Exeter and I acted as chairman. We concluded that some of the issues raised really centred on human nature and the doctrine of the Fall and we eventually brought together a book containing some of the papers we had discussed. It was called *Man, Fallen and Free* and published in 1969. I edited the collection and contributed a chapter on 'Augustinianism'.

At some stage during the 1950s, a new young fellow of Exeter aroused my interest in watercolours and I started a small collection, visiting picture shops and galleries wherever I happened to be. On one occasion, when returning from Scotland, I stopped in Moffat and enquired in an antique shop if they had any watercolours. They had none but directed me to a dealer in Carlisle which happened to be my next port of call as I was on my way to stay with the Dean. In Carlisle I found the man's house, which was stuffed with fine furniture, and he produced two watercolours. One was of a white horse, which he said I could have for ten shillings. The other was a landscape which I could have for a pound. The landscape was by Sam Bough (1822–78), of whom they thought rather highly locally but who was not much known outside Carlisle, where he was born, and Glasgow, where he worked for many years. I bought them both and when back in Oxford and had an occasion to be at a meeting with John Betjeman, I asked him if he knew anything of Sam Bough. Yes, he did and there was a biography. I went straight to the Bodleian and ordered it. Imagine my excitement when reading it I came across an exact description of the picture I had bought: *Naworth Castle, Wind and Rain*. This kindled an interest in Sam Bough and over the next few years, I concentrated on him as the prices of more well-known water colourists were rising beyond my reach. By the time I retired, I had acquired some 30 watercolours and sketches and one oil by Sam Bough. As retirement involved scaling down into a smaller house, I sold a number of them very profitably but I have kept *Naworth Castle* and the best two or three of the others. Sam Bough seems now to be much better known.

I greatly enjoyed singing with the Bach Choir, as I had done before I was ordained, and I felt privileged to be asked to join the committee under the chairmanship of Norrington, President of Trinity. When Thomas Armstrong left Oxford to become Principal of the Royal Academy of Music we appointed Sidney Watson, who succeeded him at Christ Church, as our conductor. Two concerts stand out most clearly in my mind. One was a performance of Elgar's *The Dream of Gerontius*, in which Kathleen Ferrier sang the angel, and sang it most movingly. I can still picture her in the Sheldonian, standing there and singing without a note of music in front of her. The other was the first performance in Oxford of Vaughan Williams' Fifth Symphony, which he conducted himself. He was not a good conductor but the orchestra loved him and it was a tremendous performance. The second half of the programme consisted of Elgar's First Symphony which Sidney conducted, and coming after the Vaughan Williams it seemed almost vulgar, not the impression it has ever made on me since. Vaughan Williams was often at our concerts. I remember Sir Hugh Allen, who had conducted the Oxford Bach Choir in years past, commenting on how easily the choir seemed to learn the *Sea Symphony*. When it was first performed in Oxford, Vaughan Williams had to spend a fortnight in Allen's house, simplifying the score for the amateur orchestra. Another regular attender at Bach Choir concerts was *The Times* music critic, Frank Howes, and I remember his face lighting up on one occasion when the orchestra played the Brahms *Academic Festival Overture*, as the choir rose to its feet and he realized that we were going to sing *Gaudeamus Igitur*. On two occasions, we sang with Sir Thomas

Beecham as conductor, once in Oxford and a repeat performance of the same programme in the Festival Hall. He rehearsed us in Oxford and was very satisfied with the way Armstrong had prepared the choir. A good deal of the time allocated for the rehearsal seemed to be taken up with a discussion with his wife over the time of the concert and what he should wear. It is not easy to say where his secret lay but I think that it was in his eyes and the way in which, through the force of a magical personality, he kept one attentive at all times. Sir Adrian Boult was a quite different but equally inspiring conductor with a manner quite unlike that of Beecham. He was a very quiet conductor, employing the minimum of gesture, but, again, attracting our complete attention. I sang under him in both Oxford and Worcester. I will always remain grateful for the experience of singing under two such distinguished musicians.

A fellow member of the Bach Choir and also of the committee of the OUCU was Patricia Kirk, third daughter of Kenneth, Bishop of Oxford. Through the various things I was doing for the bishop, I had got to know his family quite well but with our shared interests, Pat and I saw quite a lot of one another. She would come back to my rooms at Exeter after choir practices and this led to a deepening of our relationship. In 1952 we became engaged. It was our wish to be married in the cathedral and the Dean and Chapter were happy that this should happen. They were clear, however, that their permission was given because I had been chaplain of the cathedral and not because Patricia was the Bishop's daughter. The relationship between the Bishop of Oxford and his cathedral has always been unusual, as a poem by Bishop Stubbs illustrates. He had been an undergraduate at Christ Church and was amused when having become Bishop of Oxford he was invited to speak as a visitor. He declined in the following words:

Though to dinner, dear Censor, you kindly invite us,
I cannot your Visitor be;
For *incorporatus, annexus, unitus,*
You can't make a stranger of me.
The Chapter and Dean must go to the Queen
If they would their Visitor see;
the Fidei Defensor might visit the Censor
If he should invite her to tea
But I'm the old man of the See, dear Strong,
you cannot eliminate me.

In the House I'm at home, as the Pope is at Rome,
How can you exist without me?
However you treat me you cannot unseat me
I am the old man of the See.
I'm W Oxon DD CG
You cannot disintegrate me;
Yes I am the old man of the See.

The Bishop of Oxford, as such, is treated as a guest in his own cathedral. We were, however, able to be married there on 7 April 1953 by Patricia's father. Bob Mortimer preached. My father and Kythé Waldram were able to come from Grimsby. Patricia's mother had died some years previously, but her oldest sister Hilary was there and her other sister, Joan, was bridesmaid along with Hester Buchanan-Riddell. Arthur Couratin was my best man and our health was proposed by Willy Scott, Pat's uncle and godfather. Between them, they managed things so expeditiously that we were away by 5pm. We spent the first night at Devizes and the rest of our honeymoon at Salcombe. On our return we moved into the house we had bought in North Oxford, 11 Davenant Road, where we stayed until we left Oxford in 1969. All our children where born during this time: our first daughter, Sarah, in January of the following year, Katharine, our second, in September 1955, the third, Alice, in May 1959, the fourth, Harriet, in February 1961, and our son, Edward, in October 1965. Sarah was baptized by Kenneth Kirk in Exeter Chapel and Katharine at Wolvercote Church by the Vicar, Michael Ottaway. Alice was baptized by Arthur Couratin, again in Exeter Chapel, using a new form of service just devised by the Liturgical Commission, of which he was a member. The service was so new it was not yet formally authorized for use. Harriet was baptized by Harry Carpenter and Edward by me, both in Exeter Chapel. They all now have children of their own, so we also have nine grandchildren.

Kenneth Kirk, my father-in-law, died suddenly in June 1954. The family were anxious that I should write his biography, which I was happy to do. I found the research a good deal easier to do than I had when writing the NP Williams life. I took the opportunity to put on record much of the public debates and private discussions concerning the Church of South India which had taken place in the previous seven years. This background was to be very helpful in the Anglican–Methodist Conversations which were soon to begin. The Kirk book was published in 1959 by Hodder and Stoughton and the process brought me into contact with one of the publisher's senior commissioning editors, Leonard Cutts, who had been a close friend of Kirk's.

Peter Kirk, Pat's brother, was an MP and became leader of the first Conservative group in the European Parliament after the Heath administration had taken us into the European Community in 1973. From early on he had been very committed to European integration, and said to me one day how much he regretted that the Church of England had not said anything officially in support of the movement towards European unity. I talked this over with John Kelly, Principal of St Edmund Hall, who at that time was my fellow proctor in Convocation, and we agreed that I should propose a motion which he would second. I therefore proposed something in roughly the following words: 'That this house expresses the hope that the British government will be willing to make such sacrifices of national sovereignty as may be necessary to ensure European unity.' There was a good debate in which the motion was opposed by Geoffrey Fisher, who said he was in favour of the responsible use of our sovereignty but opposed to any sacrifice of it. Bob Mortimer spoke against him and eventually the motion was carried. So far as I am aware, it remains the only official expression of Church of England opinion on the subject.

I discovered that a former member of Exeter College had been Father Charles Lowder, parish priest of St Peter's, London Docks. He had been an undergraduate when John Henry Newman was Vicar of St Mary's and attended his sermons. He was deeply influenced by them, particularly by Newman's call to spiritual discipline. After ordination he served curacies in two small country parishes, Walton-cum-Street in Somerset and Tetbury in Gloucestershire, where the inhabitants remembered he held services in church every day whether or not there was anyone there, and that he visited them frequently. After a time at St Barnabas, Pimlico, he went to be an assistant at St George's in the East where there were ritual riots and much opposition to Christian ministry. He was placed in charge of a mission where, in 1866, he built a permanent church and founded the parish of St Peter's, London Docks. Lowder's ministry there is one of the great things in the history of the Catholic Revival and his life was a great inspiration to me. He saw ritual as an essential part of his pastoral and evangelistic strategy but, again, there were riots and he had to be protected by the congregation against men who wanted to throw him into the river. It is thought that many of the riots were stirred up in part by the owners of the brothels in the parish. Lowder established himself firmly in the affections of his people by his devotion and diligence, and particularly by his activity during the cholera epidemic which severely afflicted that part of London. Lord Halifax and Dr Pusey came down to help, and the latter found that he could communicate best with some of the parishioners in Hebrew. With five other like-minded priests, Lowder founded the Society of the Holy Cross (SSC) as a body of clergy devoted to ministry to the poor, and to extending Catholic faith and practice in the Church of England. I saw it as important to renew the connection between the college and Lowder's work and so made contact with the parish, visited it and was invited to preach there. For several years I was able to send collections from the chapel to help with parish projects, and once I went with the parishioners on their annual pilgrimage to Lowder's grave at Chislehurst. London's docklands have changed greatly in recent years, but St Peter's remains as a thriving parish and I know that the story of Father Lowder and of his successor Father Wainwright, who is said never to have slept a night out of the parish, is still remembered.

In addition to teaching history and some theology, I also dealt with the political science paper, and this led me to think further about politics than I had done hitherto. I think that during most of my early life, I just followed the example of my parents and voted Conservative. In the pre-war period I was attracted by some Socialist writers and joined the Socialist Book Club. I remained in that for a time but came to see it as essentially a Marxist-inspired body and the Socialist party itself dominated by Marxism. As I read, it became quite clear to me that Marxism and Christianity were basically incompatible.

When I was elected to Convocation and realized that I was going to have to stay in London fairly often, I began to look for a club. Freddy Hood and others were keen to propose me for the Athenaeum but I felt that to join that august institution would be to declare an ambition that I thought wrong. Bishop Kirk proposed me for the National Club, of which I became a member for a while, but a friend, Sam Gurney, suggested the National Liberal Club and as I had, at that time, several friends who were active Liberals, I became interested and joined the club as a political member. When I became Bishop of Chichester I received an invitation from the Athenaeum to become a member but the letter did not say anything about the subscription and, as I suspected it might be rather large, I had to reply that I could not definitely accept until I discovered what my financial position as a bishop was going to be. I heard nothing more from them. Many of my friends are members and a group of them gave me and my wife an enjoyable luncheon there to celebrate my 90th birthday.

Sam Gurney was a member of both the National Liberal Club and the Athenaeum. He slept at the one and ate at the other. I first met him when he was living at Pusey House for a time. He had a house in the country somewhere near Shrivenham and when our children were quite young, he invited us all to tea. I remember the occasion well because it was the first time any of the children had seen a dumb waiter, which was in the middle of the tea table. As I have mentioned earlier in connection with NP Williams, Sam was one of the founders of the Society of Ss Peter and Paul. When he was staying with us at Pusey House, we were always amused at the amount of correspondence that came for him from 'The Metropolitan Drinking Fountain and Cattle Trough Association', of which I think he was chairman. Sam proposed me for the National Liberal Club in 1949 and James Schuster, vice-principal of St Stephen's House, seconded me. During my first year I was approached several times by an elderly member in clerical garb who asked me if I was there as a Methodist. I gathered that there were at that time several Methodist members and some committees of the Methodist Conference used to meet there.

After a few years, I came to know the chairman, Leonard Smith, well. When he found I was in London for a night he would always invite me to join him and a few others at breakfast, which was often an amusing start to the day. One of the people with us was never satisfied that the toast had been done enough. Through these meetings I became aware of the financial difficulties the club was going through and the unsuccessful attempts to meet them. Eventually, the club was saved by a Liberal businessman, Sir Lawrence Robson, but at the cost of selling the upper floors, which included the library and the bedrooms, to the Royal Horseguards Hotel next door. The club continued to have the right to 20 rooms at standard hotel rate, which rather reduced its usefulness to me, but I was keen to remain a member. I was surprised to be invited to become a trustee, and still more surprised and hon-oured when some years later I was elected President. Although, since my retirement, I do not go to London so often, I still find the club very enjoyable and have made a number of friends there. I was glad that the formation of the Liberal Democratic Party did not lead the club to change its name and though I have always been a political member my interest in Liberalism has grown over the years. In the House of Lords I often voted with the Liberal Democratic Party, though I did not think it right as a bishop to join the party in the Lords. The bishops are all invited to the cross-bench meetings and I often went to those. I have regarded TH Green as the fundamental author for Liberalism.

When I got to Chichester, through my Liberal connections I was invited by Sir Cyril Smith to preach at Rochdale on the centenary of the Rochdale Pioneers. When thinking about the sermon, I happened to pass a public house called the Richard Cobden and noticed that it was a 'Free House' so I used that as a text. At the tea party afterwards, Cyril Smith made a speech of thanks to those who had helped with the centenary celebrations and I was somewhat taken aback when he said, 'And now I come to the bishop and I will say straight away that he was not my first choice.' He went on to say that he had invited Michael Ramsey, who declined because he had recently preached at Westminster Abbey for the centenary of the Liberal Party and could not do a similar sermon, so I had been suggested. Cyril was a member of the National Liberal Club and I once came down in the lift with him. There was only just room for me but not for anyone else as he was so large.

Gabriel le Bras, the *doyen* of canon law studies, to whom I have referred earlier, came to Oxford in the 1950s as a Visiting Fellow of All Souls. I went to his lectures and was able to meet him. He was a most entertaining and intelligent person, and, as I gathered from Ernest Jacob, took quite a lot of money from the fellows of All Souls at bridge. Later, I visited him several times in Paris, at his flat in the Place du Pantheon, where, among other things, we talked about music and he played the piano. He was a very entertaining person as well as a distinguished scholar. During one of my visits I learned he was going to the Quai d'Orsay to advise the French government about those whom the Vatican was proposing to appoint to bishoprics. He told me that this was a courtesy consultation on the part of the Vatican but in the case of the dioceses of Strasbourg and Metz, the provisions of the Concordat made with Germany when it had annexed Alsace-Lorraine had been continued when that region was returned to France so there the consultation was by right.

Le Bras was Dean of the Faculty of Law at the Sorbonne. In 1965, I was honoured to be asked to contribute to the *Festschrift* the Sorbonne put together in his honour. I wrote about 'The Canterbury Provincial

Chapter and the Collegiality of Bishops in the Middle Ages'. Most provinces had one diocese which is next in seniority to the metropolitical one, and of which the bishop is sometimes called 'Dean of the Province' but I have not discovered any other which has the elaborate provincial organization of Canterbury. The Bishop of London is Dean of the Province and when the archbishop summons the other bishops to a provincial synod or otherwise communicates with them formally, he does it through the Bishop of London. If London were to be vacant he would use the Bishop of Winchester, who is variously called Chancellor or Sub-Dean. On at least one occasion when both London and Winchester were vacant, the Bishop of Lincoln was used and he was sometimes referred to as chancellor. The Bishop of Salisbury is precentor, presumably because of the hegemony of the Sarum Rite by the late medieval period, the Bishop of Rochester Cross-Bearer, and the Bishop of Worcester Chaplain.

In June 1958, I received a letter from Maurice Harland, now the Bishop of Durham, asking if I would accept the Lightfoot Professorship of Divinity, being vacated by Stanley Greenslade, who was going to Cambridge as Dixie Professor. The chair carried with it a residentiary canonry at Durham Cathedral. This was in many ways an attractive proposition, and I was flattered to be asked but it raised a number of problems in my mind. By that time I had become much involved in the Canterbury Convocation and was secretary of the canon law steering committee. I had already been asked by Geoffrey Fisher to write the official history of the Convocation and was busy collecting material. I was also a member of the Standing Committee of the Lower House, and I felt that my membership of that house was important for my understanding of its history. There would be no guarantee that I would become a member of the York Convocation if I went to Durham. I had also to think carefully about my family. My wife had just had a miscarriage and we were very uncertain about changing to another doctor, and the two elder girls were at a stage when a change of school would not be desirable. In addition to all that, I had formed an unfavourable impression of Durham as a place to live, finding it, as it was at that time, an unattractive and very cold city. Dick Southern, whom I consulted, was inclined to advise acceptance. I talked to the Bishop of Oxford, who was clearly uncertain, but just said that I should ask the opinion of the Archbishop of Canterbury. I therefore wrote both to him and to Michael Ramsey at York and had replies from them both on the same morning. Michael said that he had been very happy as a canon professor at Durham and urged me to accept. Geoffrey was quite clear in urging me to refuse. He wrote:

> This is a serious choice that you have to make; in ordinary circumstances I should be very happy to see you at Durham but if I may give my own opinion quite bluntly, I think it would be at this juncture such a disaster for the process of canon law revision in the Convocation of Canterbury that I certainly could not encourage you to accept and feel really bound to discourage you ... The death of Canon Smethurst was a terrible loss: if you went too I do not know how we should get on at all ... I am sure you appreciate all this and need only add that if you decline I shall feel profoundly thankful. I do not want to press you too hard but I think you would thus serve the best interests of the Church.

By the same post I received a private letter from a friend of mine, Michael Adie, later Bishop of Guildford, who was one of the Archbishop's staff at Lambeth. He had sight of the archbishop's correspondence and said he had experience of the considerable moral pressure the archbishop could exert if he was anxious to have or to retain the services of any man whom he valued. If a decision had to be made against the archbishop's expressed wish, it often had to be made in the face of this pressure. I was grateful for this insight into Fisher's way of working but a real dilemma remained. Naturally, I discussed the matter fully with my wife and, thinking it over carefully together, I decided that I must refuse. My commitment in so many various ways to the Canterbury Convocation and my sad experience of Durham as a place should make me stay where I was. In writing to Maurice, I recommended in my place Christopher Evans, a New Testament scholar who was chaplain of Corpus. He was appointed and, I think, was academically much more suited to the professorship than I would have been. For my part, I remained in Oxford.

Geoffrey Fisher, who, as I have said, played some part in influencing my decision to stay put in Oxford, had been an undergraduate – a classical scholar – at Exeter, where he had read Mods, Greats and Theology, his tutors being Farnell, Marrett, AWF Blunt, later Bishop of Bradford, and NP Williams. After being headmaster of Repton, then successively Bishop of Chester and London, he was made Archbishop of Canterbury on the sudden death of William Temple. Naturally enough, in view of his association with the college, he was soon after elected an honorary fellow. It was inevitable that I should be brought into contact with him, but after I was elected to Convocation, this relationship became close. He began to consult me in 1949 about some matter concerning Calendar Reform, and this led in the early 1950s to him frequently contacting me about points of canon law. When I consulted him with regard to the canon professorship at Durham, I had just, as his letter indicates, succeeded Canon Smethurst on his death as secretary of the canon law steering committee. Fisher was chairman of this and so I had constant dealings with him until his retirement in 1961. He was an excellent person to work for in many ways but he could be infuriating and difficult. I have mentioned the affair of Bob Mortimer's episcopal gloves. I, too, had a run-in with him over an issue of churchmanship.

In 1859, the present college chapel had been consecrated by Bishop Wilberforce, the Bishop of Oxford, in the presence of the Visitor, Bishop Philpotts of Exeter. In 1959 we celebrated the centenary of this event, and Fisher came for the weekend and preached at Evensong. He was at Holy Communion on the Sunday morning, which was celebrated by the Bishop of Oxford, Harry Carpenter, who had no hesitation about using a little Communion manual which I had prepared, as many chaplains were doing at the time. The only change in the 1662 *Book of Common Prayer* order that I had made was to put the Prayer of Humble Access after the Comfortable Words, before the beginning of the Eucharistic Prayer. Fisher said nothing to me or to Harry at the time, but after he had got back to Lambeth he wrote a long letter to me criticizing this change on the grounds that the resolution the bishops had passed after the rejection of the *Revised Prayer Book* in 1928 said that from the Offertory onwards either the 1662 form or the 1928 form must be used unaltered. We had some little correspondence about this but he obviously felt very strongly in a legalistic way.

In 1972, in an obituary of Geoffrey, I wrote:

> Fisher will probably be remembered for three things which he did as archbishop. First, his university sermon at Cambridge in 1946 which opened a new stage in relationships between the Church of England and the Free Churches, and led ultimately to the scheme for Anglican–Methodist union which Fisher helped to defeat in 1969 and 1972. In spite of that particular outcome, the Cambridge sermon has a secure place in modern English Church history. The second is his part in the coronation of Queen Elizabeth II in 1953, which he did as much as anyone to make a great

spiritual as well as national occasion. The third is the journey which he undertook to Jerusalem in 1960 and then to Istanbul, where he visited the Ecumenical Patriarch, and then to Rome where he visited the Pope, being the first Archbishop of Canterbury to do so since the end of the fourteenth century. Very few men but Fisher could have taken that last initiative at that time. It was a necessary preparation for the more official visit of Archbishop Ramsey to Pope Paul VI. Fisher will also be remembered by many ordinary people, for he had a remarkable gift for recalling individuals and making them feel that they were of importance to him and drawing out real affection. He was in some ways a country pastor at heart and always looked back to his upbringing in a country parish. As a person to work for and with, he was infuriating, unpredictable and disarming.

There is one thing to be added which shows that Fisher never ceased to be a headmaster. After Bishop John Robinson, fairly recently appointed Bishop of Woolwich, had given evidence in the *Lady Chatterley's Lover* case, he was summoned to Lambeth. He was shown up to the study, where Fisher said, 'Sit down Woolwich. Now that you are a housemaster you must remember that you must have a sense of responsibility.'

Michael Ramsey, with whom I also worked closely, was a very different kind of person from Geoffrey Fisher. I met him first when he was Professor of Divinity at Durham and a canon of that cathedral. We were both appointed to the conversations with the Scandinavian Lutheran Churches at a meeting in Denmark in 1947. I rapidly got tired of hearing about Luther at this gathering and I recall being told that at a similar meeting, after hearing 'Luther sagt' ad nauseam, Fr Gabriel Hebert SSM had burst out, 'Was Luther crucified for you, did Luther die for you!' After the meeting Michael and I travelled back to England on the same ship, we sat together on the deck late into the evening and he was more inclined to conversation then than on any later occasion that I can remember.

The next time I saw him was when he came to take a university mission at Oxford. He was in his element speaking in the Sheldonian Theatre and I still have a vivid mental picture of him there. During a later mission, after he had become a bishop, I persuaded him to come to Exeter College one evening and he seemed to enjoy sitting in an undergraduate room, with men on the floor all round him, and answering questions. The answers were not glib ones but thoughtful and never avoiding difficulties. I think people felt that he had faced, and perhaps did still face, problems of belief. Certainly of the missions that I remember from my time at Oxford, as both an undergraduate and a don, his two were the most impressive and inspiring.

As a member of Convocation I came into contact with him from time to time over matters which affected both provinces, and on issues such as the Church courts to which I have referred earlier I several times consulted him as I felt that he had a more independent mind than Geoffrey Fisher. Later, there was the rather dramatic change when Fisher retired and Michael took over, with Donald Coggan succeeding him at York. I was asked to go and meet them both at Lambeth one evening as they wanted to find out how much of what they had inherited from Fisher could be scrapped. I had to explain that the canon law revision and the synodical government proposals had gone too far to be shelved. I took the opportunity to say that I had been asked by the BBC to give a talk about the Church and State on the Third Programme and wondered whether it would be right to do so in view of my position in relation to the canon law revision committee. Donald said he thought I should not but Michael said, 'I don't see why he should not. There has been too much of people not being able to say what they think because of the official positions they hold!'

Michael Ramsey, as Archbishop of Canterbury, was after 1961 to have a significant part in shaping the direction my life took. In the meantime, having turned down in 1958 the Durham chair and canonry which once was his, I was to remain in Oxford for a further 11 years. Much of my time not taken up with teaching, academic research and the pastoral care of those in college during this period, was given over to canon law reform with which I had become deeply involved, and to Convocation and the evolution of new synodical procedures for the governance of the Church of England. It is to these areas I now turn.

8

Convocation and Canon Law Reform

The first problem that arose in Convocation after I became a member concerned the recognition of those ordained in the Church of South India (CSI). This Church had come into being in 1947 as a result of the union of four dioceses of the Anglican Church of India with the Methodists of the region and the United Church, itself a product of an earlier scheme which had brought Dutch Reformed, Congregational and Presbyterian bodies together. Controversially, the clergy of all participating bodies were united into one ministry by mutual recognition and not episcopal ordination. Episcopacy was part of the scheme, achieved by incorporation into the historic Anglican episcopate, but existing ministers at the date of union were not to be re-ordained. The Lambeth Conference in 1948 had been divided on the subject, giving the scheme only a qualified approval, and there had been a similar division in the two Convocations. In 1950, Gregory Dix proposed that a decision be postponed for five years. This was accepted but within a short time a joint committee was set up to prepare for a determination of the matter in 1955. The two chairmen were Michael Ramsey for York and George Bell for Canterbury and I was appointed a member. We had good discussions and decided unanimously to recommend that those who had been episcopally ordained in the Church of South India should be recognized but that, should they come to minister in England, they should limit their activities consistently to one or other of the Church of England or the Free Churches so as to avoid confusion.

When 1955 came, there was a complication. In those days, Convocation was dissolved at the same time as Parliament and the unexpected dissolution of Parliament meant that, with the general election, there had to be fresh elections to Convocation. The regular meeting of Convocation had to be postponed and, as its normal meeting place was not available on the new date, it met at Lambeth. The unexpected election presented a particular problem for me as I had been nominated by the archbishop to preach the Latin sermon at the opening service in St Paul's Cathedral. In addition, George Bell had asked me to second our report. There would have been no difficulty had not LB Cross decided not to stand again. His supporters had put forward Bishop Geoffrey Allen, the Principal of Ripon Hall, to the annoyance of some of the electors who thought that they should always be represented by a fellow of a college. In retaliation, they proposed Christopher Evans, then chaplain and a fellow of Corpus. For the first time, there was to be a contested election and although it was probable that I should be one of the two returned, as indeed I was, I could not be sure until very near the date of the meeting. This gave me very little time to prepare either the sermon or the speech in support of George Bell's motion. Not being a classicist, I was helped with the Latin sermon by Leslie Styler, chaplain of Brasenose. This was the last time that the Convocation sermon was preached in Latin.

George Bell presented our report in full synod. He dealt with the restrictions on functioning in this country which we had proposed and left me to present the theological arguments for accepting the South Indian bishops and their ordinations. As was usual at that time, the two houses then separated and I was left to pilot the proposals through the Lower House. There was some opposition within Convocation both from a group of Anglo-Catholics led by Canon Brierly, Vicar of Wolverhampton, and from the representative of the Modern Churchman's Union. Outside, the opposition was stirred up by the *Church Times* whose editor, Rosamund Essex, was very difficult. As our recommendations had the backing of Michael Ramsey, we had assumed that the *Church Times* would at least be neutral or mildly favourable, so it was an unexpected disappointment when it turned out to be definitely hostile. Stephen Langton, the vicar of St Mary's, Bourne Street, and I were worried about the effect of this on the Catholic constituency, so we arranged to go and see Rosamund Essex in case there were any helpful explanations we could give. She received us on a Tuesday and throughout the time we were with her, she was passing proofs of the edition due out on the Friday. She began by saying that it was not her business to have a policy on these matters but she had a duty simply to reflect what she understood to be public opinion. In the end, she said she would reconsider the matter in the light of what we had said and we went away thinking that we had persuaded her to take a more favourable view. We were thus very cast down when Friday's edition not only continued its opposition but increased its hostility. She must have been passing these proofs while we spoke to her. In the event, our report was accepted. Behind the scenes, I had agreed with Douglas Horsefield, a prominent Evangelical and a friend of mine, that we would jointly see this report through and so we did. I found myself unpopular with some of the more rigid Catholics in Convocation for the line I had taken, but my old boss from Southampton days, Harold Caesar, approached me after the debate to support me and said, 'Remember that politics is the art of the possible', for which I was grateful. Geoffrey Fisher was very pleased with the outcome and grateful to me and I suspect that my involvement influenced his decision the following year to invite me to be a member of the Anglican–Methodist Conversations.

Meanwhile, I had to deal with another subject – that of nullity of marriage. The Matrimonial Causes Acts 1937 and 1950 had introduced into English law new causes for nullity of marriage which gave rise to some concern in the Church and so the two archbishops set up a commission to review the matter. Archbishop Fisher was somewhat sensitive about the issue of nullity as he had come rather unstuck in an exchange with Lord Merriman, the president of the Probate, Admiralty and Divorce Divisions. In an aside in an after-dinner speech, he had remarked that 'Our judges have not the slightest idea of what the law of nullity really is' and implied that Lord Merriman was not well-informed on the variety of grounds for nullity. Lord Merriman responded with an attack upon the archbishop at a dinner of the Scottish Law Agents and poured scorn on Fisher's suggestion that the Church might set up its own courts to pronounce decrees of nullity. The spat was ended amicably and Fisher apologized but it was clear that work needed to be done. The commission was a large one, presided over by JWC Wand, then Bishop of London. Apart from some argument in full session about the phrase 'indissolubility of marriage', to which the Bishop of Rochester, Christopher Chavasse, strongly objected, most of the work was done by the four lawyers on the commission working with me, usually in my rooms at Exeter. They were all Queen's Counsel with practice in the matrimonial courts: William Latey, Noel Middleton, Harry Phillimore and Jack Simon. Harry and Jack went on to become senior judges and remained close friends and I took the wedding of one of Harry's daughters.

There was no problem about most of the content of the two Acts, so our discussions really centred on the introduction of 'wilful refusal to consummate' as a ground for nullity. This seemed to be in conflict with the principle that nullity meant the annulment of a marriage already in existence for reasons which, had they been known at the time of contracting the marriage, would have prevented it from taking place. We suggested that 'wilful refusal to consummate' could be regarded as evidence of incapacity, and this was accepted by the commission. Much time was spent in discussing Fisher's suggestion that the Church might set up its own matrimonial courts to consider other issues arising for which nullity might be argued. Stephen Langton was very keen on this but in the end we decided against any extension which 'could leave the validity of a marriage dependent upon private stipulations or mental reservations of the parties'. We pointed out that to set up central ecclesiastical courts would be a major expense if they were to be expertly staffed, and there would be problems if such courts reviewed the decisions of civil courts. We also rejected the suggestion that individual bishops, taking such legal advice as they might deem appropriate, could decide on whether the proposed marriage of a divorced person should take place in church or not. The report of the commission was presented to the Canterbury Convocation in the autumn session of 1955 and I had again to second it and see it through the Lower House.

With our last recommendation, on the discretion of an individual bishop to allow a second marriage in church, I reluctantly agreed and continued to agree until I had been a bishop for five or six years. I then became concerned about the number of instances brought to my attention in which it seemed obvious that circumstances did exist which, if they had been known at the time of the marriage, would have prevented it from taking place, but had not been relied on in relation to the divorce. I discussed this very thoroughly with my two suffragans, and we decided that if we thought it right, after careful investigation and recommendation by the incumbent, we would agree that he might conduct the new marriage in church.

In the course of the many changes in Church administration made in the 1840s, the High Court of Delegates as the appeal court from the Court of Arches and the corresponding court in York was replaced by the Judicial Committee of the Privy Council. This became, in effect, the supreme court in ecclesiastical cases. When the ritual prosecutions began to take place, many priests refused to recognize the authority of the Privy Council because they regarded it as a lay court rather than a Church court and one which based its procedure on the common law rather than canon law. Some priests were sent to prison for refusing to obey decisions from such a court. A different procedure was proposed when the report of Archbishop Garbett's Canon Law Commission was published in 1947 but there was opposition from some quarters and Fisher decided to deal with it himself. Instead of having a commission to report on the whole subject, he appointed one under Mr Justice Lloyd-Jacob to look at the ordinary courts and left the issue of a final court of appeal to the Church and State commission under Sir Walter Moberly. Each body had the difficulty of dealing with its remit without knowing what the other was going to say. In the event, the proposals did not emerge too badly but they did not satisfy Fisher. When the Moberly Commission's report came to be debated in the Church Assembly, he persuaded Canon GWO Addleshaw to propose an amendment restoring the Privy Council as the final court of appeal.

I remember that at 2.30 one afternoon we started a debate which was to end at 5pm. One or two evangelical laymen supported retaining the Privy Council, but the majority, led by George Bell, was clearly opposed to it. At 4.30, Fisher said from the chair, 'I don't suppose that Canon Addleshaw will want the whole of the remaining half hour to reply so I will say what I think.' He then delivered a debating speech in support of the Privy Council option. After five minutes, as it became clear what he was doing, people began to shout 'No', and before long he had the whole assembly shouting at him. I have never seen anything like it. The Addleshaw amendment was, of course, rejected and the report of the Moberly Commission accepted. But that was not the end of the matter.

A committee under the chairmanship of Dr Wand, Bishop of London, was set up to draft a measure for the synod. I was a member and it included Sir Thomas Barnes, previously treasury solicitor, who had been lent to us to advise on the reform of the canon law, Sir Alan Ellis, counsel to the Speaker, and a Conservative MP, Sir Griffiths Williams. These three, though they did not try positively to restore the Privy Council, advised that we would not get anything through Parliament unless we adopted something like it. At this point, Wand resigned. He had accepted the chairmanship on the assumption that the Privy Council issue had been settled by the Church Assembly vote. I recall going to Bishop Auckland to consult Michael Ramsey, then

Bishop of Durham, who took the same view as Wand and urged me to stand firm. We were given a new chairman in George Armitage Chase, Bishop of Ripon, who, in the end, steered us to a compromise which satisfied the lawyers. The court of appeal in matters of doctrine, ritual and ceremonial, known as 'reserved' cases, was to consist of two lay judges and three bishops and there was provision that, in the case of further dispute, the Queen could appoint a special commission of three law lords who were Anglicans, and two bishops, all from the House of Lords.

Since this arrangement was implemented there have been two appeals to the Court of Ecclesiastical Causes Reserved and on each occasion I have been one of the bishops sitting to hear the case. The first concerned a picture in a side chapel of St Michael and All Angels, Great Torrington, in Devon. It lasted for one day and was quickly settled. It was really a faculty matter and only came before us on a technicality. The other was of greater moment and concerned the Henry Moore altar which had been installed at St Stephen's, Walbrook. The Chancellor of London diocese had caused it to be referred to us because of a nineteenth-century judgement declaring stone altars illegal on doctrinal grounds. This was properly our concern, though we felt it was also necessary for us to say something about the aesthetic question. We sat for three days in the court room of the Judicial Committee of the Privy Council in Downing Street. The two lay judges and my two fellow bishops – Woollcombe of Oxford and Saye of Rochester – were all quite happy with the aesthetic issue concerning the suitability of Henry Moore's altar in that building. I was not so sure but not clear enough in my own mind to dissent. I went along with them, partly because, after some discussion, they left the doctrinal part of the judgment to me to write. We were not bound by the nineteenth-century precedent, my fellow judges all agreed with my acceptance of counsel's argument, so in writing the judgment I was able to free the Church from the precedent about stone altars and to establish the legitimacy of using sacrificial language about the Eucharist. In neither case did anyone invoke the further provision.

Before the war, a commission under the chairmanship of Arch-bishop Garbett had been appointed to revise the canon law of the Church of England which stood, with but minor changes, much as it had been framed in 1604. With the war intervening, the publication of the report of the commission was long delayed and it did not appear until 1947, so it fell to Geoffrey Fisher to decide what to do with its findings and suggestions. In the view of Fisher's successor, Michael Ramsey, advantage should have been taken of the general readiness of people for revision of many things. It was a new era in which to revive the Cecil Church and State Commission of the immediate pre-war period. This would have provided an opportunity to initiate a major review of the relations between Church and State and within that framework review the various matters that needed reform and set canon law revision in a wider context. In the mind of others, liturgical revision had an equal, if not higher, claim on the energies of the Church. Instead, Fisher decided that canon law reform on its own was the way to proceed. He was unwilling to take up the recommendations of Garbett's commission wholesale and instead began a process of, frankly, piecemeal revision which occupied much of the time of the Convocations and the Church Assembly for the next 20 years.

At a fairly early stage it was realized that constant contact with the Home Office would be needed and, also, as many of the changes proposed involved the existing law, measures passed by the Church Assembly would be required which, of course, would bring the laity into the whole process of revision both at the Church Assembly stage and in Parliament. Relations with the Home Office were facilitated when Fisher was able to persuade the government to lend us the services of a former treasury solicitor, Sir Thomas Barnes. He kept a close eye on what was proposed and told us what would and what would not be acceptable. He was assisted by Sir Alan Ellis, counsel to the Speaker. Barnes took a fairly strict view of anything affecting the laity, and also kept an eagle eye on any proposed changes in such matters as the marriage law. As a result of his advice, some of the proposals of the Garbett Commission had to be dropped.

One matter which caused a great deal of trouble concerned the seal of the confessional, in other words, the rule that a priest must not disclose any matter told to him in the course of confession. It had been assumed that, as this was referred to in the old canons, there would be no difficulty about incorporating it in the revision, but we were told that the current law of evidence only allowed such a privilege in the case of lawyers and doctors. While it was felt that most judges would not allow questions on such matters to be pressed, there was no legal protection for a priest who refused to break the seal. To secure this protection, a change in the law would be needed and this was unlikely to be acceptable. Argument about this went on for some time and a number of articles about the matter were published. A special committee consisting of members of both Houses of Parliament was set up to advise us on this and other matters and we were urged to drop it. The revision committee decided to accept this advice but that we should repeat the old canon as an appendix. I had to tell the standing committee of the Lower House what was proposed and they declined to accept it. Fisher was at Canterbury, about to go to Japan, and I had to ring him up and tell him what had happened. He was very angry and said he would deal with it on his return. In fact, he got back only very shortly before the meeting of Convocation. When it had assembled, I was sitting in my place waiting for things to begin when I was summoned to see the Prolocutor. He had learned that Archbishop Fisher was proposing to prevent the Lower House from discussing the subject by referring it to the Upper House as soon as it had been introduced. Would I go with him to see the Archbishop straight away? The opening of Convocation was delayed as we spent 20 minutes with Fisher, but he was adamant and said that he must have a meeting with the standing committee. He took the view that the Lower House Standing Committee should concern itself simply with the arrangement of the agenda and not try to alter its content. He was not able to meet us until October.

When I arrived at Lambeth Palace, I was met by the chaplain, at that time Michael Adie, who told me that the Archbishop was very worked up about the whole thing and he wondered what would happen. We all sat down in the conference room and Fisher came in. We waited and then he said, 'I want to take my full share of responsibility for what happened in Convocation. I was much more tired than I realized after my visit to Japan, and my wife tells me that as I get older I talk too much so I have told my chaplain that if I diverge from the subject he is to shout out "Agenda".' We then settled down to a rational discussion of the problem and the standing committee accepted what had been proposed. Fisher was capable of being charming when he had had time to think a matter over and decided to take a different view.

Another issue which caused difficulty was the proposal to legalize the use of Eucharistic vestments. After much debate, this had been passed by a large majority in the Church Assembly, but there was much evangelical opposition and some of this was known to have support in the House of Commons. The parliamentary committee to which I have referred told us that, in their view, there was a real possibility of the proposal being rejected. After the meeting I walked down the steps to the front door with Fisher, who was determined to press ahead. I said that I feared a very difficult confrontation of Church and State if the House of Commons rejected something which had been passed by the Assembly with a large majority. Fisher said, 'Oh no. We shall simply say, "This is an area that you will not allow us to deal with for the present" and go along as we have done.' I do not think he always understood the strength of feeling in the Church over these issues. As it happened, the measure was passed by the Commons and a potential crisis averted. The other matter causing us some difficulty was the proposed canon preventing the marriage in church of the unbaptized. Sir Thomas Barnes said that this would require an Act of Parliament, which we were unlikely to get, and in the end we felt it was not worth having a fight about.

I was invited to give the 1956 Lichfield Divinity Lectures, which I did under the title, 'An introduction to the canon law of the Church of England'. They were published in 1957. *Inter alia*, I discussed the contrast between canon law and common law and put in a plea that, in relation to the revision of the canons, proper attention should be paid to the place and nature of custom in canon law. The Garbett Commission had referred to the lack of any body of canon lawyers to maintain interest in the subject and encourage knowledge of its principles and customs. Therefore, Chancellor Garth Moore and I decided to gather some people together to fill this gap, and started a canon law revision group which met alternately in Oxford and Cambridge, at my college and at Garth's, which was Corpus. We succeeded in gathering a number of lawyers, historians and others and met regularly for several years. A year or two after we had stopped, Chancellor Graham Routledge and others convened a conference at Cambridge which formed the Ecclesiastical Law Society, which meets frequently and publishes a valuable journal. I was surprised and honoured to be invited to become its first President. In 1998, the Society presented me with a *Festschrift* in my honour, *English Canon Law, Essays in Honour of Bishop Eric Kemp*, of which I am very proud.

As I have mentioned, the need to proceed by measure in the Church Assembly and have certain parts of our work ratified by Parliament brought about the involvement of laity in canon law revision which had hitherto been the province of clergy in Convocation. This had major consequences for the future government of the Church of England. Convocation procedure perhaps needs some explanation. Convocation was, and still is, divided into two houses: bishops constituting the Upper House under the chairmanship of the archbishop of the province, and a Lower House of clergy chaired by their prolocutor. The two Convocations were somewhat different in operation, probably because of the smaller number of bishops in the North, where the York Convocation did most of its business in full synod, with both Houses sitting together. In the Canterbury Convocation, each house informed the other of what it had done and if they disagreed there could be complicated interchange, more or less as happens now in Parliament between the Commons and the Lords. The first reform, therefore, to be achieved was for all debates in both Convocations to take place in full synod. This was not difficult to bring about. Far trickier was to secure joint meetings of the two Convocations, as the York Lower House much feared being swallowed up by Canterbury Convocation. The York Convocation was very much smaller than that of Canterbury and as its two Houses generally met together it was very conscious of itself. Joint meetings were eventually achieved but at the cost of joint decisions occasionally being referred back to the individual Convocations. Some of the revised canons required alterations in existing Church Assembly measures and some new measures as they involved changes in the law. The involvement of the Church Assembly necessarily brought the laity into areas which had hitherto been the prerogative of the clergy, namely doctrine and worship. For a time, there were separate meetings of the Assembly's House of Laity to consider and vote on what the Convocations had done. The laity's views, suggestions and disagreements often resulted in the need for further meetings of the Convocations. This going to and fro was a very time-consuming and cumbrous way of proceeding, and led to a desire that some way be found for the Convocations and House of Laity to sit together, possibly being combined as they were in the Assembly. The chief difficulties lay in the fear of Convocation that it might lose control of doctrine and worship and that York might lose its much-prized independence. A commission under John Lowe, Dean of Christ Church, proposed that Houses of Laity be attached to each of the Convocations but this did not find general acceptance.

As I have mentioned earlier, in 1960 I delivered the Bampton Lectures in which I brought together much of the work that I had been doing on the history of the Convocations. The lectures were published in 1961 under the title of *Counsel and Consent*. In the last chapter, called 'Parliament, laity and provinces', I had not simply discussed the problems arising from the revision of the canon law, but had done so in the framework of a wider consideration of the place of the laity in Church government and the general principles involved. In reviewing these issues, I made some proposals for the reform of diocesan and provincial organization. These suggestions formed the basis of the eventual Synodical Government Measure. A committee under Lord Hodson put forward proposals similar to those I had suggested and these were agreed by the Convocations. They were then embodied in a measure which I piloted through the Church Assembly.

For some reason I do not understand, after the Synodical Government Measure was passed, I was not brought into any further discussions and the principles which I had laid down were largely ignored when the procedures and standing orders for the new Synod were drawn up. I still think that if what I had proposed had been taken into consideration, as a whole at least some of the criticisms so frequently made now about the Synod might have been avoided. At the time, I shared the concern of the York Lower House that there was a danger of gravely reducing the input of the clergy on matters of doctrine and liturgy. These are, after all, subjects on which they are supposed to have professional knowledge from their training and experience. What we feared has, I think, come about. I accepted then the view that the laity have a right to a voice in these matters and I am still of that opinion, but this principle could have been safeguarded through the rules of synodical procedure. As I have said, I had no part in framing these rules but had I been consulted, I would have suggested that any measure concerning doctrine or worship should first be debated in the Houses of Bishops and Clergy. Only after they had expressed their views clearly should the matter be referred to the laity for debate. This would have ensured that the 'professional' view was clear and could be one of the factors for the laity to take into consideration. In devising synodical procedure, I think too much influence was allowed to David Carey, the archbishop's principal registrar and legal secretary, and John Guillum Scott, who became Synod's first Secretary General, and one or two members of the House of Laity who had little appreciation or understanding of either doctrine or Church history.

Geoffrey Fisher had by this time officially retired but, as is well known, he made it quite clear that he proposed to continue to concern himself with the central affairs of the Church. Canon John Satterthwaite, later Bishop of Fulham and Gibraltar and then the first bishop of the new diocese of Gibraltar in Europe, who was then at Lambeth as Chaplain for Ecumenical Affairs, told me that Fisher had even asked him to provide him with a desk in his office for his use when in London. This he declined to do so Fisher had to conduct his correspondence from his retirement house, Trent Rectory.

In the week before the crucial meeting of the Church Assembly at which the Synodical Government Measure was to be debated, Fisher published an article in the *Church Times* criticizing some aspects of the proposals. I, perhaps unwisely, referred to it in my speech and the result was a flood of letters from him. These continued for some time until there came a Tuesday morning when I received a letter which seemed to sign off on the subject and I heaved a sigh of relief. I had breathed too soon, for on the Saturday came another letter starting up on the Anglican–Methodist Scheme. This correspondence continued for some considerable time. He used to come to Oxford to stay with one of his sons, who was headmaster of St Edward's School. On one occasion, I was summoned there to be taken through the little book I had written about the Convocations, rather as if it were a school essay, and I think that Harry Carpenter had a similar experience. Both Robert Stopford, Bishop of London, and Oliver Tomkins, Bishop of Bristol, wrote to me about letters they were receiving from Fisher, and I believe that Michael Ramsey suffered intolerably. There was a layman called Hathaway Tucker who had been at school and Exeter with Fisher and Tucker used to go and stay with him every year at Trent Rectory. He generally came on to Oxford afterwards and would tell me what had been said. On one occasion, the door was opened by Lady Fisher who, having welcomed him, said, 'Now Hathaway, while you are here you must remember that you must not mention Harold Wilson, Rhodesia or Anglican–Methodism!' I was told that in the last years, the family did their best to prevent him from posting letters.

Michael Ramsey, on the other hand, found the change to synodical government rather a relief as it meant that he did not have to be in the chair all the time. He was not a good chairman of Church Assembly if the business did not greatly interest him. Robert Beloe, the lay secretary, and I found this also to be the case with the canon law steering committee as, unlike Fisher, Ramsey had little interest in canon law. We worked out a plan for handling committee meetings by which Robert and I sat either side of him. Robert looked after the agenda and so kept the meeting moving, while I had prepared a series of resolutions which, at the appropriate moment, I prompted Michael to put. Others, I know, found similar stratagems to help him through the detail of committee business with which he had little personal interest.

There was another matter in which I became involved later which has not turned out altogether to the good. Owen Chadwick's biography of Michael Ramsey (Clarendon Press, 1990) has some interesting things to say about the appointment of bishops, not least my own appointment to Chichester, and Ramsey's own views on the system within which he had to operate. Archbishop Coggan, succeeding Ramsey, managed to persuade Prime Minister Jim Callaghan to agree to a discussion about the Crown appointments system in so far as it related to diocesan bishops and I was invited to become a member of the small group brought together for this purpose. We met the Prime Minister's secretary, Sir Philip Allen, and it was agreed there should be a Crown Appointments Commission representing the Church which would have the right to propose two names to the Prime Minister, who would then present one of them to the Queen. He should not originate them himself, but could reject both and ask for others. He could, however, only present to the Queen a name originating from the Commission. Callaghan secured the agreement of the other party leaders and since then the procedure has been carefully followed. Under Margaret Thatcher, however, there were suggestions in the press that, on occasion, she was producing names of her own for bishoprics. I discussed this with Philip Allen, by now Lord Allen of Abbeydale, and he confirmed my understanding that the Prime Minister can only put forward a name coming from the commission. What we did not settle in our initial discussions with Callaghan was how the permanent members of the Appointments Commission were themselves to be appointed. When the scheme went before General Synod, it decided that it should itself elect the permanent members from among its number. This was to my mind an unsatisfactory arrangement as the membership of the Commission in any given quinquennium reflects the contemporary state of parties within the synod and thus there is not the freedom which existed when the Prime Minister himself made the choice.

In both the case of lay involvement in doctrine and worship issues and the appointment of bishops what seemed a right change at the time has turned out not to be for the good of the Church and I must feel, with regret, some degree of responsibility for this.

9

Worcester

By 1968 I was beginning to feel that it would not be right for me to remain as chaplain at Exeter College for very much longer. I would certainly have been happy to go on teaching and lecturing but the work of a college chaplain involves a degree of improvisation and constant adaptation to changing undergraduate outlooks. I truly felt my usefulness as a college chaplain had come to an end and I was running out of ideas. Some colleges had taken the decision to divide the chaplaincy from the fellowship, keeping the latter as a purely academic post but, for financial reasons, I could not see Exeter doing this. I was also becoming rather fed up with developments in university politics which seemed to take up far too much of the time of the governing bodies. I had already refused the canon-professorship at Durham but had nothing else in view when, in 1969, the offer of the Deanery of Worcester came as a complete surprise. I was aware that Bobby Milburn had gone there from Worcester College, and had heard that he was leaving to become Master of the Temple, but I had never been to Worcester and knew nothing about it. I had little or nothing with which to make a decision. The position was the more difficult because the Prime Minister's patronage secretary, Sir John Hewitt, told me that I must not, on any account, go anywhere near Worcester or talk to any of the people there until I had accepted. I was in a dilemma. As a family we were happily settled, my wife had just started an agreeable job at the Bodleian, and all our children were well established at schools in Oxford. I went to see Hewitt, who gave me the impression that the Bishop of Worcester, Mervyn Charles-Edwards, had suggested my name, and I later discovered this to be so. He also told me that he had mentioned to the Prime Minister that I might have reservations on financial grounds as a dean's stipend would be considerably lower than my academic salary. Harold Wilson had said, 'Offer it and try.' On the positive side, the move would mean I could remain a member of Convocation and continue with that work.

I spoke to the Bishop of Oxford and he was clearly doubtful. He asked me if I had had any discussion with the archbishop, which I had not and now rather wished I had. I did, however, talk to my wife's cousin, Bill van Straubenzee MP, who was strongly in favour of my accepting, and to one or two friends in Oxford whose views were rather mixed. Pat and I considered our finances carefully and decided that, by one means or another, we could afford it. So in the end I accepted, assuming that this would be my last ecclesiastical appointment. I was somewhat embarrassed by the number of letters I received once the appointment was announced, some from diocesan bishops, expressing surprise that I should be going to a deanery and not to a diocese. I was installed in Worcester Cathedral on Ascension Day, 1969, though we did not move until the end of the year. Amazing though it is to recall, we had no clear idea of where we were going to live as the deanery was to be altered, nor did we have any real conception of what we were going to. We moved with, among other things, 12 guinea pigs belonging to the children.

We were sad to leave the house in Davenant Road, it had been a comfortable family home and we were fond of it. For a while we thought of letting it but, of course, we had no idea how long it would be before we might come back to Oxford. I also had in mind the problems we had after my father died and left me the property where he and my mother had lived in Grimsby. I had had to deal at long distance with complaints from tenants, demands for reductions in rent and the like – all very tiresome. These factors, combined with my changed financial situation on moving to Worcester, led us to the decision to sell Davenant Road and find a house somewhere in Yorkshire which we could use as a holiday home, and possibly as an eventual retirement house.

The Deanery, when we eventually moved in, was a pleasant, large house in which we made ourselves reasonably comfortable. We had some initial problems when we asked to have the large dining room divided so that the kitchen next to it would be big enough for family meals. There was complaint that some society had always had its meetings in the dining room, and also that passers-by would now be able to see my wife cooking in the kitchen. It also seemed to be a problem that we had a dog. Not in living memory had there been a dog in the Close, only cats. It was hardly the most welcoming place, but after the first year as far as domestic arrangements were concerned, we were very happy there. It was a convenient place for entertaining and building a sense of community. Worcester maintained a twice-yearly custom of roll call, when the members of the foundation – the chapter, the minor canons, the men and boys of the choir and the vergers – had to appear in the Chapter House at an early hour in the morning and answer to their names. My wife and I decided that this was a tiresome ceremony on its own so we arranged for everyone to breakfast at the Deanery afterwards and this transformed the event in a way that was much appreciated.

Taking up the Deanery of Worcester was not without its challenges. I did not go with any preconceived notions of how a cathedral should be run, save the belief that all cathedrals are somewhat different from each other and any policy for a particular cathedral should be developed in relation to the unique circumstances and environment in which it is set. As Worcester Cathedral was essentially a city-centre church as well as the mother church of the diocese, it became clear to me that the services we provided should be comprehensive, catering to a wide range of people. I was also clear that a definite Catholic basis was the most adaptable for this. One thing seemed to me to be essential, namely that the chapter should worship together in the offices and at the Eucharist each day. When I arrived at Worcester I found this was not the case. There was a distinct lack of a sense of spiritual community in the chapter, and I went on to find such a sense more associated with the minor canons and with some of the committed laymen working for the foundation.

The Residentiary Canons of Worcester, as well as the Dean, were all appointed by the Crown, with the result that there was little unity or coherence of outlook among them. The senior canon at the time of my appointment was Canon Claude Armstrong, who was 80 years old and about to retire. He had made a number of preparations for his retirement, including a cathedral house at a reduced rent, and he hoped to be made librarian so that he could still count as a member of the chapter. This did not come about as I was happy to take on the responsibility of the cathedral library at Worcester as it is one of the most important of such libraries. It has a fine collection of manuscripts from the pre-Conquest era, as well as printed books of historic interest. In this part of my work, I had the assistance of Mrs Bridget Johnston, who became a great friend of the family. Canon Armstrong was Vice-Dean and also Treasurer but the day-to-day finances were, in fact, managed by a firm of accountants who sent a clerk to his house every Friday with cheques to be signed. During his last years, Armstrong ran a training course for senior ordinands which was much appreciated. As this scheme was to cease operation with his retirement, he had arranged for Miss Margaret de Bartholome, his secretary and bursar to the scheme, to become Chapter Clerk in place of an elderly and not very competent solicitor whom he had, in turn, persuaded to be secretary of the Friends of the Cathedral. Miss Bartholome was much publicized as the first woman chapter clerk, which appeared rather forward-looking. I could not really object to this manipulation of the cathedral support staff as it occurred before my arrival, but I found Miss Bartholome not altogether easy to work with and I felt rather sorry for the outgoing Chapter Clerk.

Mrs Armstrong, who was, I gathered, a great character, had died the year before and was buried in the garth in the middle of the cloisters. This was an already crowded space but Canon Armstrong had gained permission from the chapter for his wife and himself to be buried there. When I arrived, the chapter was already anxious to prevent any further burials in the space and the following year, I wrote, with some trepidation, to a retired canon (who was also a bishop) to explain that we had decided that there should be no more burials in the garth, offering instead the option of burial in the cloisters. To my relief, he replied that all the time he had been on the chapter he had tried to prevent any more burials in the garth and was delighted that I had succeeded. After his retirement, Armstrong made a nuisance of himself by criticizing all the changes I made, and on one occasion wrote an article for one of the Church papers which was clearly directed at these. My colleagues urged me to protest at what was a clear criticism of what we had been doing and I wrote to him, but all this produced was an angry letter from a lay friend of his complaining that I was persecuting Armstrong in his old age. It was a pity that he should end up so embittered as he had done good work for the Church as a headmaster, first in South Africa and then in England, and in his training of ordinands.

The second canon, who was also Librarian, was Collis Davies, who had been professor of Church History at Trinity College, Dublin. He was a firm evangelical who was very suspicious of my churchmanship though personally very friendly. He was not at all happy when, with the support of Bishop Robin Woods, I persuaded the Crown to appoint

Eric Turnbull to succeed Armstrong as canon. When Davies suffered a heart attack and was out of action for some time, this was attributed to anxiety at my policy in the cathedral. Eric Turnbull brought with him a young priest, Alan Gates, who had been his curate. Alan joined the probation service and, along with my membership of the Education Committee, helped to bring the cathedral further into the life of the city.

The third member of the administrative chapter was the Archdeacon of Worcester, Peter Elliot, a solicitor ordained in middle age who had been appointed, I assumed, at Bishop Mervyn Charles-Edwards' request, as Elliot had been his curate at St Martin-in-the-Fields. He was a very jolly person and more sympathetic to what I wanted to do. His wife, Lady Alethea, was a great support to him, but disliked cathedral services – particularly the music. They made their house very hospitable and were much liked.

The fourth canon was William Purcell, who had been recently appointed, having previously worked for the BBC. He regarded himself as a communicator and was particularly useful when we had to make arrangements for broadcasts. He was anxious to make the cathedral attractive to the general public – in contrast to what it had been. He had himself encountered Dean Milburn's predecessor who, almost unbelievably, had said to him, 'You must understand that this place is the private chapel of the Dean and Chapter.' Purcell had some contact with Geoffrey Fisher and had written a biography of him. On his arrival, he was made Master of the Fabric, meaning he was in charge of all the cathedral works staff and of the maintenance of all the buildings in general, including the houses in the Close. He was liable to be rung up at any time by cathedral tenants complaining about drains, leaks and the like. He was also responsible for the vergers and for cathedral services.

These were the four men with whom I would have to work. To get to know them and to discuss policy and plans before I arrived, I managed to get them to come and stay at Exeter for a couple of days. I had an agenda but so had they. I wanted to talk about worship. It was a time when liturgical revision was beginning to affect the Church at large but so far had made no impression on Worcester Cathedral. The Dean, I discovered, customarily celebrated on Wednesday mornings and I persuaded them to agree that I could use the current revised Holy Communion service, Series 2, as it then was. On their part, they seemed mainly anxious to talk about the problems that they had with the King's School, which was part of the cathedral foundation, supplied the choir and occupied many of the buildings round the Close with its boarding houses and with what was called College Hall, the former monastic refectory. In addition, the headmaster had a fine substantial house and garden adjoining the cloisters.

The chapter told me that Remembrance Sunday was one of the principal days in the cathedral's year; that the commemoration took the place of Matins; that they wanted me to preach at it; and that they had decided to use the new order of service which had just been issued. The Lord Lieutenant, his deputies, the mayor and corporation, and several ex-servicemen's organizations would be present. Not ever having preached at such an occasion before, I was not best pleased. This would be one of my first public occasions and the people attending would form an opinion of the new Dean, so I gave more than the usual amount of thought as to the appropriate thing to say. Taking account of the more positive and forward-looking character of the new service, I spoke about the importance of international law and of the support we should give to the United Nations and the development of peace-keeping initiatives. Nothing was said to me at the time about the sermon, but a few days later the secretary of one of the diocesan committees told me how he had attended a village Remembrance service on the Sunday afternoon. He had found himself standing next to the local MP, who had been in the cathedral that morning, and had overheard his conversation with one of the deputy lieutenants. When the MP asked the deputy lieutenant what he had made of the service he said, 'I don't like these new forms of service and the new Dean preached a very left-wing sermon.' It was not a good start.

Again before I had arrived, the Chapter had decided that there should be no Midnight Mass at Christmas that year – owing to the disturbance caused the year previously by a coach-load of rather riotous people from Birmingham while the Bishop was celebrating. He had thought it necessary to go down to the back of the nave himself to ask them to keep quiet. I felt I had to abide by this decision but in October the BBC wrote to say that they would like to televise Midnight Mass from the cathedral and chapter revised its plans. We had to plan carefully to ensure the service was not disturbed. In this the BBC were very helpful and, in the event, there was no trouble. Thereafter we decided to admit to the service by ticket only and to allow entry through one entrance via the cloisters. One of my colleagues said he would not attend if attendance was to be restricted, another said he would not attend if there was not to be any control.

The first decision I had to make with long-term implications concerned the arrangement and timing of Sunday morning services. At 10.30am during term time, shortened Matins with a sermon took place in the nave. This was attended by the boarders of the King's School, Alice Ottley Girls' School and the Royal Grammar School. Out of term, the service moved up into the choir and became a full cathedral Matins with sermon. This was followed every Sunday by a Sung Eucharist without sermon at 11.30am. The Eucharist had a growing congregation, though we noticed that there was diminution in numbers when the choir was away. The immediate question was how long the schools would continue to insist on compulsory attendance. My own, more personal, problem was that there was no cathedral service suitable for my children and no appropriate church nearby. I met this by starting a simple Series 2 Eucharist with two hymns at 9.30am and was pleased that a number of families in the neighbourhood with small children began to come.

The headmaster of the King's School at this time was David Annett. He and his wife became close friends and I found it easy to discuss problems with him. His wife was excellent with all the boys of the school, as well as with our children. Sadly, she died a few years after he retired. Later, he lived in retirement at Malvern. My wife and I saw him frequently, when he would come to Chichester and go to the theatre with us and we would pay a return visit to Malvern. He died shortly before Easter, 2004. I was ex-officio chairman of the governors of the school and was able to reduce the number of members of the chapter on the governing body and to bring in some useful laymen. The school was a direct grant school, so the governing body also had representatives of the local education authority on it, so it was useful to have lay churchmen as well. Later, when the direct grant system was abolished, we lost the local authority representatives. I was made a member of the Local Education Authority and so witnessed at close quarters the attempt to change policy when, after a local election, Labour members equalled the number of Conservatives on the city council. The balance of power was held by two Independents. The Conservatives agreed that Labour should take responsibility for the education committee so for a year we went through all the consultations preparatory to changing to a comprehensive system, only to have the proposal rejected by the two Independents. I found membership of that committee very instructive and was full of admiration for the amount of time and attention that busy shopkeepers were prepared to give to the government of the city.

My first move with regard to the Sunday services was to get David Annett to agree with me that compulsory attendance should be reduced to three Sundays a term and the boys be given the option of attending my new 9.30am service. He readily fell in with this proposal. In the first year of the new system, one of the compulsory attendance days was Palm Sunday and I arranged that the Passion should be recited dramatically, with the whole school taking the congregational parts. I shall always remember the boys shouting, 'Crucify him, crucify him.'

After this first year, compulsory attendance was reduced to two Sundays a term, and not long after was given up altogether. The Royal Grammar School and then the Alice Ottley School withdrew, so we were left with cathedral Matins and sermon every Sunday at 10.30am and a Sung Eucharist with no sermon but a growing congregation at 11.30am.

The next thing it became necessary to consider was whether we should continue to put on two fully choral services each Sunday, one of which was very poorly attended. We needed to find out the demand for a non-Eucharistic Sunday service in the centre of Worcester. I suggested, as an experiment, that for the following Lent we arrange a special series of Matins sermons by a well-known preacher from Birmingham. In the event, these drew a congregation of not much more that 20 each Sunday so we had to think seriously about what to do. By this time, I had persuaded the chapter that for the first part of our regular meeting we should have with us the organist, Christopher Robinson, the Precentor, Colin Beswick, and another minor canon, who was also chaplain of the King's School. In attendance also was the new Chapter Clerk, Bill Bowen. I was anxious that whatever we decided should be seen by the congregation as the decision of the whole chapter and the cathedral staff. The general consensus of this enlarged meeting seemed to be that we should replace choral Matins with a said service with no sermon and that the principal Sunday service should be a Sung Eucharist with sermon at 11am. This should take place not in the choir but in the nave. After several sessions we all agreed on this except Collis Davis, so I made them continue with the final decision-making meeting with a further hour's discussion until he gave in. We were able to issue a statement signed by all of us. The Series 3 Communion rite had recently been authorized so we agreed that we should begin the new arrangement with the new liturgy. I remember that, at the end of the first Sunday, one of the oldest members of the congregation said to me, 'It is going to take me a little time to get used to this new service but I do like it and if I can try, I don't see why the rest of them can't.'

In addition to the regular choral Evensong on Sunday afternoons during term, there was a second Evensong at 6.30pm with a sermon. This service was sung by the voluntary choir, a most important and useful addition to the cathedral's musical resources. I cannot under-stand why many other cathedrals do not have such a group of enthusiastic volunteers. Our voluntary choir was trained by the assis-tant organist, Harry Bramma, but its mainstay and organizer was a layman called Bollen. The volunteers deputized for the cathedral choir out of term-time and were available, given sufficient notice, for special services. Their annual dinner was always very enjoyable, much more so than that of the bellringers.

The internal ordering of Worcester Cathedral presented its own problems. As a Benedictine foundation, it had originally been arranged according to the traditional monastic pattern with the choir separated from the nave by a substantial stone screen. In Worcester's case, there was a central tower which separated the two major spaces and the choir was on a much higher level. During the Victorian restoration by AE Perkins and GG Scott, the solid medieval screen had been removed and replaced by a metal screen made by Skidmore, but the difference of level remained. Our decision to move the principal service into the nave meant we had to provide a new altar, possibly under the crossing, beneath the central tower. However, it soon became clear to me that the crossing was, in effect, a separate room and that in order to function successfully, the new altar and choirstalls must be in the nave itself. I spent some weeks visiting various churches to get some ideas but a visit to some newly reordered churches in Paris provided me with the most helpful points to ponder. I was able to stay with Roger Greenacre, who was the chaplain at one of the three Anglican churches in Paris, St George's in the rue Auguste Vacquerie. Reporting back on my investigations to the chapter, we decided to provide a substantial platform for a nave sanctuary and a semi-circle of seats for the choir behind it. The Three Choirs Festival and other concerts held in the nave meant that everything had to be movable so that the area could be cleared. We planned the choreography of the service carefully and had it end with the clergy all going to the north door (the main entrance) of the cathedral, so as to be available to speak to people as they left. This all made a great difference to the feel of Sunday morning.

Mervyn Charles-Edwards, the Bishop, was a charming man of whom I was very fond. He had gone down from Keble without a degree but that was no indication of intellectual inadequacy. I heard him preach on at least six very different occasions and it would have been difficult to better what he said on each. He was a member of an agricultural trade union and much involved with farmers and farm workers in the county and diocese. He was not, however, a very good administrator and senior staff meetings, which, as Dean, I attended, dragged on interminably and often ended with the agenda unfinished. There was no suffragan bishop so Mervyn relied on the assistance of various retired bishops from overseas, including Nicholas Allenby, whom I got to know well.

The Bishop lived outside Worcester at Hartlebury Castle and there was much discussion as to whether this was the right place. When the Ecclesiastical Commissioners were set up in 1836, they told the then Bishop, RJ Carr, that he could no longer have two houses and must choose between Hartlebury, about 12 miles away, and the Palace in Worcester. The story is that his aristocratic relatives said to him, 'A gentleman lives in the country', so he chose Hartlebury. When Mervyn was appointed, he and his wife lived for a time in an ordinary country house while the future of Hartlebury was under discussion. It was decided that Hartlebury should be kept, but that the north end should become the county museum, the end including the chapel remaining as the house for the Bishop, and the middle section, the great hall, the Hurd library, and the Prince Regent's bedroom were to be managed as a diocesan resource by the Dean and the archdeacons and used for meetings, receptions and other similar occasions. Mervyn managed reasonably well with this arrangement but his successor, Robin Woods, found the accommodation too small so took over the large bedroom and the Hurd library.

I had been in Worcester for a little over a year when Mervyn told me that he was going to retire and this news came as a great sadness. Inevitably, I became much involved in the arrangements for appointing his successor. It soon became clear that the most influential lay people in the diocese wanted Robin Woods, who was at that time Dean of Windsor. His wife was from one of the principal local families and, as a child, had grown up with the Lord Lieutenant, Lord Cobham, who was Chancellor of the Order of the Garter. Early on, I was telephoned by John Hewitt, the Prime Minister's appointments secretary, to discuss when it would be convenient for him to come down to Worcester to consult various people. Parliament had been dissolved and we were waiting for a general election. It was agreed that Hewitt should go to Hartlebury to stay with Mervyn on the Sunday before the election and come to us from the Monday to Wednesday. He had to be back in Downing Street by the time the election results were out as he had the job of assigning offices to new ministers. He asked me to arrange for him to meet members of the administrative chapter individually, the greater chapter collectively, and various appropriate lay people at my discretion. From the time he arrived on the Monday evening and had had a conversation with me, it was obvious that Robin Woods was the only name in his mind, and I was equally sure that this would be the name he would hear from most of those he met. I was thus not at all surprised when Robin Woods was announced as the choice of Edward Heath, the new Prime Minister. The Queen might have been expected rather to oppose the removal of a dean she liked from Windsor, but it was said she agreed because Heath was newly in office and she rather liked him. I knew Robin from the Anglican–Methodist discussions and we were on friendly terms, so I welcomed the appointment.

The formal procedure for the appointment of a diocesan bishop begins with election by the greater chapter of the cathedral. The chapter receives from the Queen a licence to elect, together with the name of the royal nominee whom they are to elect. I explained this to the chapter and suggested that we treat it as a statement by the diocese that we accepted the Crown's nominee. The election has then to be presented to the archbishop's representative for confirmation. This is usually done for the archbishop by the Dean of the Arches, the presentation being made by the Chapter Clerk, but on this occasion I presented Robin myself as Dean.

The consecration was at St Paul's and, at Robin's request, the choir of St George's Windsor was allowed to sing part of the service. The next stage would be enthronement in the cathedral, so I spent some time looking into the history of this in Worcester. I found that before the Reformation the monks, who formed the cathedral chapter, went in procession to the entrance to the Close and received the new Bishop there. During the eighteenth and most of the nineteenth centuries, no bishop had been enthroned in person so that there was no real post-Reformation precedent. A custom that seemed to have been introduced in recent years was the new Bishop knocking on the cathedral door for admission. I came across a recent article by EC Ratcliff in *Theology* on the enthronement of archbishops in which he criticized this practice as an unjustified importation from the rite of consecration of churches. There seemed to be only two things legally required, one the Bishop promises to observe and respect the cathedral statutes, the other for him to be placed in the throne by the Archdeacon of Canterbury on behalf of the archbishop. We decided to begin with the whole chapter assembled at the entrance to the choir; the Archdeacon of Canterbury then knocked on the door for admittance and presented the Dean with the archbishop's mandate which was read aloud by the Chapter Clerk. We then went to the main door of the cathedral, which was open, and there we received the Bishop as he came across from the palace and welcomed him. He took the oath to observe the statutes and made a promise to be a faithful pastor to the diocese before entering the choir. He was then led to the throne by the Archdeacon of Canterbury and the senior bishop of the province present, who happened to be the Bishop of Gloucester, placed in it by the archdeacon and blessed by the senior bishop. This seemed to me to be a correct way of going about things and later, when I was consulted about my own enthronement at Chichester, I asked if the same procedure could be followed. After the enthronement, the assistant bishop and the archdeacons were commissioned by the new Bishop and other people were presented and given the opportunity to welcome him.

Robin was a very different administrator from his predecessor. Staff meetings were shorter and decisions made. At first the meetings continued to be held at the palace in Worcester, which housed the diocesan office and a sort of diocesan club, but later they generally took place in the Hurd library at Hartlebury. The one difficulty we encountered was that after we had taken a decision that an archdeacon should do a particular task, we frequently found that Robin had already done it himself by the time the archdeacon in question got round to it. Unlike Mervyn, Robin was not satisfied with just an assistant bishop and wanted a suffragan. His idea was to have an area bishop of Dudley, which seemed reasonable and the staff agreed.

Michael Ramsey and the Church Commissioners were more hesitant and Michael asked for my opinion. I told him that, in my view, the area around Dudley was sufficiently distinct for an area system to work, and that the northern part of the diocese had for some time felt somewhat unloved. The creation of a suffragan see might help address this feeling of isolation. In fact, when I first arrived as Dean, I was told that the churches of Dudley felt no-one cared about them so I took the cathedral choir there to sing Evensong and I preached. The suffragan see of Dudley was established and Robin invited Michael Mann, who was a residentiary canon of Norwich, to be the first bishop. There was some difficulty in finding a suitable house so the Manns had to be content with a redundant vicarage outside Dudley. This was a disappointment to Michael, but worse was the way in which Robin continued to work. He did not treat the new bishop as an Area Bishop but insisted on going himself frequently to Dudley and the surrounding parishes. I also felt rather let down in view of the arguments Robin had used to secure the appointment, as I had passed these on to Archbishop Ramsey. Michael Mann was greatly relieved when he was asked to become Dean of Windsor. Robin himself soon became laughingly known as 'Royal Robin' because of the frequency of his references to his time at Windsor. On the whole, he proved to be a good bishop, if somewhat overbearing. I am glad of my time at the staff meetings as I learned a good deal both from him and from Mervyn, in different ways, which proved useful when I had my own staff meetings at Chichester.

My chief joy during my time at Worcester was the cathedral music. Christopher Robinson, who had been assistant organist at Worcester, became organist shortly before my arrival. I remembered him from my Oxford days, when he had been accompanist for the Bach Choir. We worked very closely together and I developed a great respect both for his professional ability and for his instinctive understanding of what was and what was not appropriate in a cathedral. One year, for example, he ruled out Carl Orff's *Carmina Burana* as he regarded the words to be improper. Before going to Worcester, I had not much knowledge of the music of Sir Edward Elgar, but I remember the first time I heard *The Dream of Gerontius* I rather disliked it as it seemed sentimental. It took a very moving performance in Oxford by Kathleen Ferrier as the Angel to convert me, but it was at Worcester that I really discovered Elgar's music. The choir library had unpublished manuscripts of his settings of *O Salutaris Hostia* and *Tantum Ergo Sacramentum* and some other small works which Christopher used regularly. I am also very grateful to him and to Colin Beswick for introducing me to the music of Bruckner. My wife and I both sang in the Worcester Festival Chorus which Christopher conducted very well. We also had, on occasion, Sir Adrian Boult for both choral and orchestral concerts and I recall especially his performance of the Enigma Variations. The Three Choirs Festival was at Worcester twice during my years there and I greatly enjoyed planning it with Christopher. There was a grand opening service on the Sunday afternoon and music had to be provided for the entrance of the city council, the lieutenancy and then the clergy. At one of these festivals, I suggested that we use the overture to *Die Meistersinger*, which we did, and led straight into the opening chorus from the opera as the start of the service.

My first Three Choirs Festival brought with it an unexpected problem. There had not previously been applause at performances in the cathedral but there were some amongst the regular attenders who would have liked it. Shortly before I arrived, the wife of the Bishop of Gloucester had written to the chapter saying that they had recently had applause on an occasion in the cathedral there, how appropriate it had seemed, and could it not be allowed at the forthcoming festival at Worcester? At a meeting, at which I was not present because I had not yet been installed, the chapter had refused. The matter first arose at a concert on the Sunday evening given by the National Youth Orchestra that began with the Brahms Academic Festival Overture. At the end of this piece I sensed some discomfort at the silence. The second item was the Haydn Trumpet Concerto, played brilliantly by a youth of 19. At the end the conductor leaned forward to the soloist and gently clapped his hands, whereupon the whole audience burst into applause. The next morning I was besieged by people saying, 'You must say something to stop this dreadful thing happening again.' I simply replied that we must leave it to the audience and see what happened. During the week there was an interesting discrimination between when the audience thought applause was appropriate and when it did not. Eventually, we came to the Friday afternoon concert conducted by Adrian Boult. Christopher told me that Sir Adrian disliked applause in churches, so I had to make an announcement that in deference to the conductor's wishes there would be no applause. That evening, *The*

Dream of Gerontius was to be given and everyone seemed to agree that I should ask that there be no applause. The following year the festival was at Hereford, and at the opening service Dean Rathbone preached against applause but in spite of his expression of strong views there was applause at the evening concert, led, it was said, by the Worcester contingent. Ever since then applause has been usual, but we had one member of the choir who continued steadfastly to refuse to attend any concert in church at which there was likely to be applause, even when his own son was singing.

When in the process of picking up the reins as Dean, I asked about the financial and material condition of the cathedral and was assured that all was in good order. I soon discovered all was not in such good order as regarded the heating. The cathedral was furnished simply with old, metal Gurney stoves which heated the area immediately surrounding them but left the rest of the building cold. I saw people coming to concerts, and to some services, with travelling rugs and even hot water bottles to keep themselves warm. It was obvious that if we were to make the building more usable we needed to provide better heating. I discussed the problem with Canon Purcell and we both made enquiries about the best thing to do. We concluded that the heating system recently installed at Gloucester would be best for us, but it would cost about £40,000. In 1970 this was a very large sum and it was clear that we should need an appeal. First I got the support of the Lord Lieutenant and the Bishop and then set about finding a suitable appeal agent. We settled on a well-known firm, but almost immediately the senior partner left them and we were assigned a more junior member of staff. What we were not told was that his wife had died recently and that had left him destitute of enthusiasm. In the end, we had to do most of the work ourselves.

When eventually I managed to persuade Miss Bartholome, whom Armstrong had wished on us as Chapter Clerk, to move to another job, Colonel Bill Bowen, the man I had appointed Steward, became also Chapter Clerk. I had revived the ancient office of Steward to help deal with finances and Colonel Bowen proved very competent in this role. As I was also ex-officio Master of St Oswald's Hospital for the elderly, his help in managing that institution was also invaluable. He was the last colonel of the Worcestershire Regiment and had skilfully piloted through the amalgamation of his regiment with the Sherwood Foresters. Their colonel became the first colonel of the combined regiment but the headquarters were in the barracks at Worcester. Bowen and I became friends and he was of the greatest assistance to me. As a soldier, however, he never really understood that I could not command the chapter to do what I wanted.

If we were to have an appeal, wisdom decreed that we needed to find out what other potentially costly work the cathedral was going to require within the next ten years. I felt there ought to be a complete survey of the building. When I broached this with the cathedral architect, he informed me that he intended to retire the following year and so I must find someone else. I consulted the Dean of Gloucester, Seirol Evans, who was most helpful and in the end his architect, Bernard Ashwell, agreed to take the survey on. He became a good friend of Bill Bowen and they worked well together. Ashwell's survey reported that while the building was indeed in good order, the wiring and a few other details needed attention. It was also clear that the organ needed some degree of rebuilding. My conclusion was that we should appeal for £200,000, but the appeal agents argued that we could not hope to raise that amount and beat us down to £150,000. In the end we achieved nearly £175,000. I had to do a lot of the work myself, speaking at meetings all over the diocese and organizing local appeal agents. I have never liked asking for money but it had to be done. Colonel Bowen was invaluable with his many local connections. During my last months, Bernard Ashwell, who by now had become our regular architect, told me of his anxieties about the security of the tower and it became plain that the situation was much more serious than had at first appeared. My successor was perforce involved in what I had hoped we had avoided, an appeal running into millions, and this included the complete rebuilding of the organ, which we thought we had dealt with satisfactorily in 1972-4.

In 1970 I was elected President of the Worcestershire Historical Society and was able to devote some time to the history of the cathedral and its ancillary buildings. Before the Reformation, the tombs of St Oswald and St Wulstan were on either side of the choir with King John, as he had requested, in between them. In the course of my researches I found a seventeenth-century document recording briefly events between 1485 and 1660. Against 1548 it said, 'The tomb of Thomas Becket taken down at Canterbury and his bones burnt there. The tombs of St Oswald and St Wulstan taken down here and their bodies together with that of Bishop John of Constance wrapped in lead and buried at the north end of the high altar.' The chapter agreed that we should investigate this, and when a metal detector indicated the presence of something at the expected place we began to dig. The first discovery was a Victorian gas pipe, but we continued until we unearthed the body of a late sixteenth-century bishop. We regretfully concluded that when that grave was being prepared, the lead bundle containing the medieval saints must have been discovered and removed to the charnel house, where we had little hope of recognizing it. We did not like to disturb the bishop's body to dig further down. The whole of this area of the cathedral must have been subject to a great deal of alteration when the medieval high altar was destroyed, and again later when the present sanctuary was created during the nineteenth-century extensive restoration of the entire building. I encouraged a thorough investigation into the history of all the buildings in the Close and supported the King's School in developing the undercroft of College Hall – which got me into trouble with the Department of the Environment. I also arranged lectures on the history of the cathedral and diocese and was pleased when my old protégé Donald Bullough agreed to come and give a lecture on St Oswald.

The cathedral enjoyed a good relationship with the Lord Lieutenant, Lord Cobham. He was a very distinguished person and had been Governor-General of New Zealand. He had a remarkable knowledge of literature and loved poetry, being able to recite many poems at length from memory. He also had a great sense of humour. It was the custom on certain special occasions, such as Remembrance Sunday and the opening service of the Three Choirs Festival, for the whole lieutenancy to assemble in College Hall and I would then lead them through the cloisters into the cathedral. Lord Cobham would talk to me all the way, usually telling funny stories. On one of these occasions he said, 'Last Wednesday we had a Garter Installation and before dinner on the previous night the Duchess of Beaufort came up to me and said, "Charles, I am sitting next to this man Longford at dinner. I have never heard of him. What do I talk to him about?" So I said, "pornography". After dinner she came up to me again and said, "Charles, I talked to that man about photography all through dinner and couldn't get a word out of him." ' At that point we arrived at the cathedral door and with difficulty I had to compose my face to go in. After the service, we all had to stand outside the cathedral while the Lord Lieutenant, the Mayor and various other people laid wreaths not only at the memorial to the fallen of two world wars but also at the Boer War memorial. There was usually some argument as to how many people should lay wreaths, as representatives of a large number of organizations attended the service. Afterwards, the lieutenancy came to the deanery for sherry and my small son, Edward, had great fun counting the number of spurs being worn. Through the Lord Lieutenant and his deputies, the chapter and I were able to maintain a good relationship with the 'great and the good' of the county and diocese.

I was also on very friendly terms with the MP for Worcester, Peter Walker, and his family. When, in 1970, there was a general election, he was happy to join with me in arranging a meeting in the chapter house at which all the candidates were present to answer questions. I felt it important to demonstrate the Christian community's involvement in the political life of the city in this way.

Another aspect of my responsibilities I soon discovered related to the cathedral bells. I was expected to be President of the cathedral bell-ringers and also of the Diocesan Guild. This involved two annual dinners at which I was expected to speak. After two years I could not think of anything fresh to say about bell-ringing, and the bellringers agreed someone else should propose the toasts.

In 1973, Great Britain entered the European Economic Community (EEC). I suggested to the Bishop that the diocese ought to do something to mark this and we agreed that we should have a special service in the cathedral. We fixed on a Sunday in January that had the added advantage of being in the Week of Prayer for Christian Unity, thus neatly combining two important themes. In consultation with the Precentor and organist, I tried to make the service as instructive and as international as possible. Inside the cover page of the service booklet, I printed a passage from Christopher Dawson's *The Making of Europe* beginning, 'The ultimate foundation of our culture is not the national state, but the European unity.' We chose three lessons to reinforce our theme: the Tower of Babel (Genesis 11), reconciliation and unity in Christ (Galatians 3) and Jesus washing the disciples' feet (John 13). The music we selected was, we hoped, broadly representative of the musical tradition of Europe – from Plainchant to Vaughan Williams. A representative of the Free Churches read the first lesson, Peter Walker, the MP for Worcester and secretary of state for Trade and Industry, read the second, and the third was read by Fr André Lemaire, representing the Bishop of Orléans with whose diocese we had recently

1. Grove House, Waltham, my birthplace.

2. My maternal grandfather,
   Walter Waldram.

3. Me with my mother,
   Florence Kemp, 1917.

4. My paternal grandparents.

5. My mother, Florence Kemp

6. My father, Tom Kemp

7. All Saints', Waltham Parish Church.

8. Bishop Edward King of Lincoln

9. Freddy Hood.

10. Exeter College Chapel.

11. Darwell Stone, Principal
of Pusey House 1909–1934

12. Myself, undergraduate 1933–1936

13. Myself at a St Stephen's House garden party – shades of things to come?

14. Curate at St Luke's, Southampton.

15. Staff at Pusey House 1941–46. R to L Tom Parker, EWK, Freddy Hood.

16. Our wedding, April 7th
1953 at Christ Church. Kenneth Kirk, Pat's father and Bishop of Oxford, married us. Arthur Couratin (far right) was my best man.

7. Sarah, our first child, was baptised by Kenneth Kirk in Exeter College Chapel. Dick Southern (third from right) was godfather.

18. The legal formalities in the Chapter House at Worcester before my installation as Dean.

19. The whole family outside Southwark Cathedral after my consecration, October 1974.

20. The Palace at Chichester from the west. This view is taken from just inside the £700 fence.

21. EWK and Pat in the Cathedral Cloister, 1987.

22. My Golden Jubilee of ordination to the priesthood, in St Michael's, Brighton, 1990.

23. With Pope John Paul II
in Rome, 1978.

24. In the House of Lords.

25. Silver Jubilee of consecration,
October 1999.

26. The Farewell Mass, Worth Abbey
Church, January 2001.

twinned. The sermon was preached by Karl Gunter von Hase, ambassador of the German Federal Republic. It was a great occasion for Worcester and, as far as I was concerned, blessed the inauguration of what I regard as the most important political development of my lifetime. In parenthesis at this point, I would say that I have always been a convinced believer in the development of the European Movement and had often discussed it with my brother-in-law, Peter Kirk, who was the leader of the Conservative group in the European Parliament. At his prompting, I proposed a resolution in Convocation urging the government to make such sacrifices of national sovereignty as might be necessary to progress European union. Ever since George Bell's pioneering work, I have seen the Ecumenical Movement in the European Churches as being an essential support for closer political integration. I have, however, been more hesitant about proposals for the creation of a Federal Europe and the abandonment of national independence.

Prior to this event, I had been thinking about a twinning with somewhere in France and it came to my notice that the Worcester Lions Club had a link with the Lions at Orléans. This existing connection prompted me to contact the Bishop of Orléans, Mgr Riobé, a very positive and liberal-minded person, who responded warmly to my invitation. The priest he sent to represent him, Fr Lemaire, was Professor of Holy Scripture at the Centre d'Etude et de Réflexion Chrétienne in Orléans, which I later discovered was the seminary for the nine dioceses of central France. I also learned later this institution had only nine seminarists – a revelation of the difficulties facing the Church in France and their crisis in vocations. The bishop invited my wife and myself to go to Orléans the following May for the Joan of Arc celebrations. Patricia was not able to leave England but I was free to go and there were also representatives of the Worcester Lions Club attending.

I soon discovered that the annual celebration of St Joan at Orléans is a remarkable occasion, largely, I think, owing to the vision of Bishop Dupanloup in the middle of the nineteenth century. What the city celebrates is its liberation from the English by Joan in 1429, and my first visit was the 544th anniversary of this event. We assembled on the steps in front of the cathedral in the late afternoon of Monday, 7 May, and a group led by the Maire came from the Hôtel de Ville bearing the banner of St Joan which they handed to the Bishop for it to remain in the care of the Church for the duration of the celebrations. The handing over of the banner was accompanied by formal speech-making by Maire and the Bishop before we entered the cathedral for Benediction. Each year, apparently, these speeches contained references to the relations of Church and State during the past year but my French was not good enough to pick up all the nuances. The following morning there was a Mass in the cathedral governed by the strict conventions concerning the relations of Church and State. All the official representatives sat on the north side and did not communicate. Their wives sat on the south side and most of them received Holy Communion. The celebrant was the Abbot of St Benoit sur Loire and the homily was preached by Cardinal Marty, Archbishop of Paris. The Bishop of Orléans was present but the convention was that he did not preside. After the service there was a civic lunch in the Hôtel de Ville. The principal guest was Sven Strayy, Foreign Minister of Norway and President of the European Movement.

In the afternoon the clergy again assembled on the steps of the cathedral and a long procession, led by a girl on horseback representing St Joan, passed in front of us. The procession included the Maire and city council, representatives of the armed forces, judges and lawyers, and members of other such departments of the city's life. It took about half an hour for the procession to pass us and then we joined it at the end. We went all round the centre of the city and across the river to the place where Joan had been wounded. There was then a break for tea, after which we all reassembled and returned to the cathedral at about 5pm. The banner was returned to the Maire, who took it back into his safekeeping in the Hôtel de Ville. In the procession I found myself walking with the representative of Munster, Orléans's twin town in Germany. He and I, a German and an Englishman, together celebrating the delivery of Orléans from the English in 1429 and from the Germans in 1945! The celebration lasted two weeks, with the Monday and Tuesday ceremonies at the heart, and included football matches and similar activities around the city. Bishop Riobé was very welcoming and gave me a book about St Joan which I read with interest, conceiving a great admiration for her. When I became Bishop of Chichester, I ensured her commemoration in the diocesan calendar. Not long after, Bishop Riobé suffered a heart attack while bathing alone in the sea and died.

By the time I went to Worcester, the advent of Pope John XXIII had brought about a major change in Anglican–Roman Catholic relations in England and I soon became very friendly with the parish priest at Pershore, Fr JD Crichton, who was a considerable liturgical scholar. We gathered together a small group of priests from our two Churches which met regularly at the Deanery for ecumenical discussion. I was very moved when I left for Chichester when Fr Crichton presented me with a pectoral cross on behalf of the group.

In the middle of my time at the cathedral, there were some changes of personnel among the Christian ministers of the city and a consequent change of ecumenical atmosphere. The Methodist minister was Derek Greaves whom I had known in Oxford. I deputized for him one Sunday at the Methodist chapel when he had to attend a church leaders' meeting. The new Baptist minister and Roman Catholic priest began to meet with Derek Greaves, Canon Purcell and myself to talk about the state of religious belief and practice in the city. We soon came to the conclusion that a mission would be desirable, but first we would have to persuade the rural dean and the other members of the deanery synod. While our idea was welcome, they were cautious, but we were eventually able to gain their support. It was agreed that the cathedral should play a lead role and we embarked on the planning process. At one point, I thought we were going to fail in getting all the key players to agree as to what was to happen – I recall a most depressing and discouraging meeting one Saturday afternoon. However, at the end of a generally unhelpful discussion, we did agree that everyone should go back to their parish and collect together a small group of neighbours to talk to about, and pray for, the mission. This began to produce results and a change of heart, and I became more convinced of the value of such small groups in local evangelism. We secured the participation of Michael Harper, a charismatic preacher and teacher from the Fountain Trust who was based in Coventry at the time, and also the American group with which he was associated, called the 'Fisher Folk', who had come once before to Worcester during my second year as Dean. The mission actually took place after I had left Worcester, but I was glad to have helped with its inception as it was, I think, a valuable thing for the area. My daughter Alice stayed behind in Worcester to attend school after we left and was able to tell me all about what happened. She became very involved with the Fisher Folk and instead of going to university when she left school, she went to the USA to their headquarters in Colorado, the Community of Celebration, for two years.

In many ways I am glad to have had my five years at Worcester. The work gave me experience which was useful at Chichester, particularly membership of the Bishop's staff meeting. Both Mervyn and Robin were, in their different ways, helpful examples to follow. In other respects, however, it was not such a happy time. My wife and my older children deeply missed their Oxford friends, for nearly six months we were accommodated in a cramped, dark and damp house and when we finally moved into the Deanery, the house turned out to be far less pleasant to live in than I had been led to believe by my predecessor. I missed having any real spiritual and theological unity in the chapter and felt keenly the lack of fellowship after years of college life. I also found that I was still required to occupy myself with central Church affairs and this led to the problem of the allocation of time between London and Worcester. I was enormously busy: one of the 15 deans in the new synod and top of the poll to represent them on the standing committee and the policy sub-committee. There was the Anglican–Methodist Scheme to be dealt with; the Faith and Order Advisory Group; the Intercommunion Commission; the Advisory Council on Religious Communities; the Canon Law Standing Commission; Pusey House; St Stephen's House; school governorships at Worcester Girls' Grammar, Bishop Perowne Secondary, the Abbey School, Malvern; in addition to all the routine administration proper to a dean. Traditionally, those who occupy deaneries are thought to have ample time for scholarly work but I certainly found that the affairs of the cathedral, combined with what I was being asked to do centrally, did not give me much opportunity for that. Of all the above, I regarded the work on the Anglican–Methodist Conversations and the detailed preparations for possible reunion as vital but it was very time consuming. Some account of this work is given in the next chapter. Family life became almost impossible – I found myself working at my desk until 10 or 11pm most evenings during the week. Trying to arrange family holidays or what is today called 'quality time' with Pat was nigh on impossible. I would have liked to have given more attention to the cathedral library and its important historical contents, and in my final year the appeal took up an inordinate amount of time. At the end of four years, when I did not expect to receive any further preferment, I was beginning to think that retirement would be necessary to pursue my calling as a scholar.

10

The Anglican–Methodist Conversations

Following the proposals of the 1920 Lambeth Conference contained in its most important document, *An Appeal to All Christian People*, discussions about closer cooperation and a move towards a measure of unity began between representatives of the Church of England and of the Free Churches. *An Outline of a Reunion Scheme for the Church of England and the Free Churches in England* was produced in 1938 and commended at once by the Convocations for study. Discussion of this outline scheme had not produced any positive results by the time war broke out in 1939, and so after the war Geoffrey Fisher thought it desirable to try to make a fresh start. He used the occasion of a university sermon, delivered at Cambridge on 23 November 1946, to appeal for the Free Churches to reconsider what had been suggested at the Lambeth Conference. In that important sermon, later published as 'A Step Forward in Church Relations', he used a phrase, 'taking episcopacy into their system', which became key to subsequent discussions. The representatives of the Free Churches responded to this initiative and a new committee was set up to consider the implications of what Fisher had suggested. The committee's report seemed to indicate the possibility of further progress but said that such progress must be by bilateral discussions between the Church of England and individual Free Churches. The Convocations expressed their willingness to go ahead on this basis and discussions between representatives of the Church of England and representatives of nine of the Free Churches and of the Free Church Federal Council began in 1947. The report issuing from these discussions on the archbishop's proposal was published in 1950, entitled 'Church Relations in England'. After a period of quiet reflection on this report, only the Methodist Conference decided to proceed further. It is important to understand this background because later in the process, complaint was made that other Churches were not included in the conversations. In the light of his subsequent attitude, it is also important to remember that Geoffrey

Fisher was archbishop at the time the work started, presided over the Convocation at which an interim statement on the conversations thus far was presented in 1958, and again at the Lambeth Conference in the same year, but never gave any indication until after he had retired that he was in any way opposed to what the group he had set up was doing.

The first formal meeting of the conversations was held at Selwyn College, Cambridge, in July 1956. I was asked by Fisher to be a member of the Church of England group but was not able to be present on this first occasion. I learned afterwards that some embarrassment was caused at the entertainment provided by the college because it had not been realized that Methodists were teetotal on principle and only sherry was provided. Thereafter we met twice yearly, alternately in Oxford and Cambridge, in Oxford at my college in Eastertide, and in Cambridge at the Methodist college before Christmas. Cambridge is a very cold place in winter and after one experience of Wesley Hall, I always stayed with my friend Garth Moore at his college, Corpus. Shortly before we started the formal meetings, Norman Sykes, who had participated in the preparatory sessions but was not involved in the conversations, came to see me to talk about what he felt we should do. He was chiefly anxious to say that we could not follow the pattern of the South India scheme because of the very different situation obtaining in England. In South India, the area had been largely divided territorially between the various Churches so that they did not impinge immediately on one another, whereas in England we were all located side by side.

George Bell, the former Bishop of Chichester, was the first Anglican chairman and although I had been under his chairmanship for the South India committee, I had not fully realized the extent of his energy and determination. We all knew that when we retired to bed, he would be sitting up studying his notes of the day's proceedings to come next morning prepared with proposals for the day. I think it was largely due to him that the proposals in the interim statement we produced in 1958 took the shape they did, though I recall a very valuable contribution to the discussion of episcopacy made by HA Hodges, Professor of Philosophy at the University of Reading. With so much experience of the ecumenical movement behind him, George Bell was able to remind us of what had been said on the subject by the 1938 and 1948 Lambeth Conferences and set what we were trying to do in the context of his work in Scandinavia and Germany.

On the last day of our meeting in Oxford in April 1958, we were all assembled for the afternoon session and George did not appear. I went to the room where he was staying to look for him. The door was open and I saw him lying on his back on the floor. I shall not forget those bright blue eyes staring up at the ceiling. He had suffered some sort of stroke. We fetched a doctor and he was taken to hospital. Hetty Bell was in Oxford staying with her brother, Sir Richard Livingstone, and so was able to be with him and, a week later, take him back home to Canterbury. He was able to attend the Lambeth Conference that summer and present our interim report. He felt sufficiently recovered to undertake a round-the-world trip but soon after his return in October he died. George Bell's death was a great loss to us as to many others. His place as Anglican chairman was taken by the Bishop of Oxford, Harry Carpenter. The Methodist chairman was Dr Harold Roberts, in whom I found a good friend. Under their co-chairmanship we resumed our meetings in 1960 and presented a further report in 1963. This followed up the interim report with outline proposals for the coming together of our two Churches in two stages. It was obvious that complete union would involve a mass of legal and administrative problems, not least that of the 'establishment', which would take a long time to sort out. It was equally clear that, meanwhile, it was important to find ways in which the two Churches could share their worship and ministry. We also thought that by worshipping together we would find it easier to come to an agreement on other matters.

My responsibility in this period was to draft a service of reconciliation by which means our two existing ministries could be brought together. In working on this, I had in mind the debates on the South India and North India reunion schemes and the important lessons to be learned from them. In the first of these schemes, all existing ministers, whether episcopally ordained or not, were to function as ministers of the united church but all new ministers were to be ordained by Anglican bishops or by bishops consecrated by them. It was this initial distinction which had caused both the Lambeth Conference and the Convocations to place limits on the degree of intercommunion permitted with the new Church. To avoid this, the North India scheme adopted a different method and a union service was devised which contained the equivalent of Episcopal ordination and was to be used by all who wished to be ministers in the united Church. This approach was approved by the Lambeth Conference but many in the Church of England, particularly the Catholic-minded, were doubtful about it. These doubts needed to be cleared up in any service of reconciliation between Anglicans and Methodists so that there could be no uncertainty about the acceptance of former Methodist ministers by the Church of England. Accordingly, in my draft service I proposed that all Methodist ministers who were to take part in the union should have hands laid on them by Anglican bishops, preceded by an episcopal prayer – the equivalent of conditional ordination. This was to be followed by the Methodist ministers laying hands on the Anglican bishops and priests, preceded by a prayer that all should work together in a united Church. In reaching this solution, I was much helped by two fellow representatives on the conversations, Father Harold Riley, secretary of the Church Union, and Lionel du Toit, Vicar of St Mary's, Windermere and then Dean of Carlisle, who both had experience with the debates over the South and North India schemes. The service of reconciliation was published in the 1963 report on the conversations. However, four Methodists dissented from the report and made clear that what they saw as the implications of the service of reconciliation was the main reason for their dissent.

It was decided to have a two-year break before any further steps were taken, and during that period there were widespread consultations in our dioceses, with the Old Catholic churches, with which we were in Communion, and in the Methodist circuits. There was widespread criticism of the service of reconciliation on the grounds of its apparent 'ambiguity' but the joint committees of the Convocations, in analysing the responses from all consultees, found there to be no ambiguity about its purpose or outcome and commended it as appearing 'to secure completely the very desirable end of the integration of the two ministries from the start'. I attended the Old Catholic International Conference in Vienna in 1966 to explain our proposals and gauge reactions. The Greek Orthodox Metropolitan of Thyatira, whose jurisdiction covered the British Isles, was also present at the conference and expressed strong approval of the service of reconciliation. He saw a parallel between what we had proposed and the Orthodox ordination service in which the newly ordained priest lays hands on the bishop who has just ordained him.

Nevertheless, at the end of the consultation period there was by no means unanimous support for the proposals, so it was decided to set up a new committee to consider the objections raised and make such changes in the scheme as were desirable. The Bishop of London, Robert Stopford, took over as Anglican chairman with Harry Carpenter remaining a member. In 1967 we published a further interim report with a revised service of reconciliation and a proposed ordinal, together with as much explanatory material as we felt was necessary in response to the detailed submissions we had received. This attracted so much criticism that some of us wondered whether it was worth going on. That was not my view and at a rather gloomy meeting in Bristol, I said that I thought we must look again at the service of reconciliation and the ordinal and prepare a statement on the ministry. I offered to do what I could in all this and during the following weeks, I drafted something on the ministry. I had earlier persuaded John Moorman to let me consult a pre-Anglican–Roman Catholic International Commission meeting about the Anglican–Methodist proposals and found some words of the distinguished Roman Catholic liturgist Fr Louis Bouyer very helpful. These I incorporated into my draft, which I then checked with Roman Catholic, Orthodox and Congregationalist theologians. With a few changes suggested during those consultations incorporated, I presented the new draft to what was now called the Unity Commission, which was happy with it.

For the revision of the ordinal we had with us the Old Catholic Bishop of Deventer in the Netherlands, who suggested that we incorporate the redrafted statement on the ministry into the existing preface to the ordinal, which we did, and I think that improved it. While the ordinal gained a great deal of support and approval and, indeed, became the basis for the ordination services in the 1980 *Alternative Service Book*, the Service of Reconciliation remained controversial, even though we had reversed the order in which Anglicans and Methodists laid hands on each other. We had not intended any doctrinal significance by this change. It was simply one of the ways in which we hoped to make the service more acceptable to the Methodists. The Greek Orthodox Metropolitan of Thyatira, who had so approved of the service of reconciliation, said the reversal in the order of laying-on of hands made it no longer possible for him to interpret the service as he had done previously. This illustrates the problem of trying to satisfy a number of different Churches without knowing how they will interpret what one does. I spent most of one Saturday going through the Acts of Reconciliation, as the redraft was called, with Graham Leonard, Bishop of Willesden, and Dr Eric Mascall, as many of the criticisms of it had come from the Anglo-Catholic side for which they spoke. I noted their criticisms and desired revisions and reported them on the following Monday to the commission, which accepted them all. Sadly, later, this gain seemed to Bishop Leonard and his group to be nullified by chapters in the report explaining and defending the process of reconciliation. Harold Riley and Lionel du Toit, who had assisted me with drawing up the original service, no longer felt able to support it. It was not only Anglo-Catholics who had doubts: one of the evangelicals on the commission, James Packer, dissented from the report but for quite the opposite reasons.

In April 1968, the final version of the scheme was published. I suggested, and my colleagues agreed, that it would be wise to test the waters and try and find out what proportion of the clergy of the Church of England was prepared to take part in the proposed service of reconciliation. The survey took place in June 1969 and the result was not as hopeful as we might have wished – only 68.5 per cent were in favour. Nevertheless, it was thought worthwhile to proceed and in July the matter was put to both Churches.

We had always had strong support from Archbishop Ramsey, who was deeply committed to the scheme. He had discussed the proposals with Bishop Christopher Butler, an auxiliary bishop in the Archdiocese of Westminster, and with the Secretariat for Christian Unity in Rome. Both, from the Roman Catholic point of view, thought the scheme was defensible. On our part, we had taken great care to ensure that the ordinal was approved by both Roman Catholic and Orthodox liturgists and there was a good deal of ecumenical support for the service of reconciliation. In the Archbishop's presidential address to Convocation in the January, he warned against the rejection of the scheme and, picking up his enthusiasm, it reduced the required majority for acceptance of the scheme from 80 to 75 per cent. His lengthy speech in the crucial Church Assembly debate was splendidly encouraging. However, when it came to a vote, the Methodist Conference approved the scheme by a majority of 77.4 per cent but the Church of England secured only 69 per cent in favour. This was a great sadness for the Archbishop and for those of us who had been working at the scheme for 16 years and were convinced that if accepted, it would give the unified Church a definite Catholic basis. There was a real sense of disappointment in the parishes where the advantages of working more closely with the local Methodists had been readily seen. On a lighter note, it is worth recalling that the scheme and its related documents were published in very distinctively designed, matching covers, with broad horizontal stripes in black, brown, white and turquoise. Margaret Hewitt, a stylish member of the Church Assembly with distinct Catholic views, often forcefully expressed, was a great wearer of hats. For the debate she wore a hat contrived of exactly the same coloured stripes as the documents. I do not remember if it was at this meeting or another that she told me that whenever she opened a door at Church House I was on the other side!

Throughout the latter part of the process, from his retirement home, Trent Rectory, Geoffrey Fisher consistently agitated against the direction the scheme was taking, both writing for the public press and sending forth a tiresome stream of private correspondence, much of which fell on my doormat. He was convinced that we had all the union that was essential in baptism and was strongly opposed to any sort of organizational union, whether called organic union or anything else. In spite of the fact that the initial principles on which we were working were established whilst he was still in post, when it failed he expressed himself thankful that a scheme along the lines we had proposed had got nowhere and was, to all intents and purposes, dead.

What were the reasons for failure? It is clear to me that many of the Church of England opponents were not willing to accept the key principle of doing what was necessary for the episcopal ordination of Methodist ministers, while leaving it to God to decide whether that was actually required. However, it must be remembered that during the whole Anglican–Methodist discussions there were divisions on both sides. It became clear at an early stage that the union of the Methodist churches in 1931 was not yet fully worked out. The Methodist chairman, Harold Roberts, was a former Wesleyan and represented a position much closer to the Anglicans on the group than his colleague, Norman Snaith, who was a former Primitive Methodist and kept asserting that there was a Quaker element in Methodism. At times it appeared he hardly seemed to believe in sacraments at all, and was full of stories about hostility between Anglicans and Methodists. One such story, which clearly had had a permanent effect on him, related to his childhood. He and his sister were the children of a Primitive Methodist minister in the Yorkshire Dales, where the nearest school was a Church of England school three miles away. One Monday when they got to school, there were a lot of buns left over from a church fête and these were given to the church children, but Norman and his little sister did not get a bun because they were not church children. He said he would never forget walking home that afternoon with his sister in tears because she hadn't had a bun. It was a sad memory, but it is also sad that it should influence his outlook in theological discussion 40 years or more later. On our side, we had a different sort of problem. When I was composing the service of reconciliation, I was anxious to use Methodist material as much as possible and this proved to be mostly hymns. When it came to the offertory in the Eucharist, I found a Methodist hymn by George Osborne Gregory which seemed very suitable. It began, 'Spread the table of the Lord', and so I put it in. When we came to look at it in the full commission, the Methodists said, 'This is a very nice hymn, but it is not one we ever sing.' So we asked them to choose one and after consultation among themselves, they proposed William Bright's 'And now O Father, mindful of the love', and that went in. Later, when Jim Packer had joined the commission, he objected to this hymn as not being acceptable to the Anglican Evangelicals.

When the Synodical Government Measure was implemented and the General Synod brought into being, it was argued that this new body should debate the scheme, which it did in 1972, but the resulting vote produced a yet further reduced majority of 65.8 per cent. Graham Leonard, Eric Mascall, James Packer, Colin Buchanan and Michael Green published a book in 1970, *Growing into Union*, which may have influenced the synodical vote, but little notice was taken of the 1971 report of the Joint Working Group, under the chairmanship of Rupert Davies for the Methodists and myself, which provided further comment on the scheme and acknowledged that conditional ordination was an element in the ministerial section of the service of reconciliation.

In the course of the 1970s, various attempts were made to recover from the defeat and there were meetings with representatives of other Free Churches in a new Church Unity Commission. From these, the so-called Ten Propositions resulted, published in 1976 and debated in diocesan synods the following year, suggesting that these be the basis for a new scheme of a wider ecumenical kind. I was not as directly involved in these later discussion as I had been with the Methodists but friends of mine were. I was in close touch with Graham Leonard and agreed with him that these new proposals were not acceptable.

It must always be remembered that, soundly Catholic in principle as I and others believed it to be, the original scheme was accepted by the Methodist Conference with a substantial majority. The rejection by the Church of England drew attention once again to the difficulties to be faced in any union between episcopal and non-episcopal Churches, and to which I have referred earlier in the context to the North and South India schemes. These had demonstrated that it is usually possible to agree on the ministry in a united Church, the problem is how to get there. From 1958 onwards, we considered four possible models which might have solved this intractable problem.

1. Accept episcopal ordination in the united Church but allow the existing non-episcopally ordained to continue until they die out, all new ministers being episcopally ordained.
2. Get bishops to ordain all the non-episcopally ordained at the outset.
3. Provide something similar to the service of reconciliation as part of the coming together. In this there would be a clear distinction between what is done to the non-episcopally ordained, and can be interpreted as conditional ordination and the prayer of reception and authorization for the rest.
4. Arrange for all who are to minister in the united church to go through a ceremony which some will understand as commissioning and others as ordination. This was the line taken in the North India Scheme.

Model three, the one we tried, failed in the Church of England because some Catholics thought that the service of reconciliation did not do enough while some Evangelicals thought that it did too much. Here in a single issue was encapsulated the problem of Anglican identity.

As I reflect on these things it appears to me that, leaving aside Oxford chaplaincy, the deanery of Worcester and the day-to-day work of a diocesan bishop, that part of my life which has not been bound up with the Convocations and the revision of the canon law has been concerned with the search for Christian unity. This has involved not just 15 years of Anglican–Methodist Conversations but also work in the particular area which has become known as Faith and Order. During my first few years in Convocation there were a number of reunion schemes under discussion in various parts of the Anglican Communion. The Archbishop of Canterbury of the day was frequently asked,

'If such and such a scheme went through, would he be able to remain in Communion with the united Church?' Each time, the archbishop would set up a special commission to consider the matter and I was a member of most of them. Michael Ramsey, tiring of this, decided that instead of setting up special commissions for each case he would appoint a permanent Faith and Order Advisory Group (FOAG). I was the first chairman and remained as such for 20 years. The group had about 15 members for most of this time and was genuinely representative of different shades of churchmanship. When we met for the first time, we decided to discuss the nature of episcopacy and produced a report which pointed to the inconsistency between what the Doctrine Commission of 1938 had said about the subject, emphasizing mono-episcopacy, and the widespread and growing practice of having suffragan bishops in most dioceses. I do not think our report had any effect. Michael Ramsey is supposed to have said, after consecrating a suffragan, 'You are theologically indefensible but we are glad to have you.'

Many proposed schemes contained issues similar to those of North and South India, just as our own Anglican–Methodist Conversations could not avoid the recollection of those processes. We also had the problem of safeguarding episcopal control of doctrine. At one stage I went to France to consult members of the Groupe des Dombes, a group of Roman Catholics and Protestants which had been set up to consider doctrinal questions arising in unity discussions. I eventually wrote a paper on the ministry which FOAG accepted and I think our successors have found it helpful. The last report in which I was involved was on the nature of ministerial priesthood. It was agreed by all the members of FOAG, including George Carey, at that time Bishop of Bath and Wells, but it ran into difficulties in Synod in the House of Laity. Not long after that I resigned and Archbishop Runcie appointed George Carey as my successor. He did not last very long in that post, as on Bob Runcie's retirement he became Archbishop of Canterbury and so appointed John Hind as chairman.

While I was at Chichester two problems arose which I did not feel I could settle myself, and therefore asked if they could be referred to FOAG. Both concerned men asking to be allowed to minister in the Church of England. The first was a minister of the Reformed Church of England, a body which derived from an American suffragan bishop of evangelical outlook who had left his diocese and established an independent Church which had then spread to England. There was no doubt about the episcopal succession but the more we looked at the teaching of the body, questions began to arise about baptism and the ministry, on both of which they seemed to hold very negative views. FOAG eventually recommended ordination *sub conditione*, which I accepted. I was a little worried about the reaction of the congregation to my holding separate ordination services for this man to the diaconate and the priesthood, with an interval between. As I pondered this I remembered a tea-time conversation at one of Claude Jenkins's seminars in his house at Christ Church in which he had spoken of the powers of dispensation available to the Archbishop of Canterbury resulting from the time when he was a papal legate. One of these was the power to authorize the ordination of a person to the diaconate and the priesthood in the same service. I therefore applied for this dispensation and, having assured the Archbishop of the authoritative source of my information, I was granted it. The second case concerned a priest of the Liberal Catholic Church. Here we had much more hesitation than before, as the body was much influenced by theosophy and there were questions about its commitment to belief in the resurrection of Christ. In the end FOAG recommended ordination *ab initio* was required and that is what I did.

The members of FOAG were appointed by the Archbishop of Canterbury and reported directly to him. This was important and helpful to us but later the Board of Mission and Unity of the General Synod became jealous of our independence. I managed to smooth this over but inexorably the hand of the General Synod reached out to take control. The Appointments Committee of the Synod began to influence the appointments to FOAG until it tends now to be treated as yet another committee of Synod. It seems to me this anchoring of FOAG in the Church of England synodical system obscures the position of the Archbishop of Canterbury as the centre of unity of the Anglican Communion. This is yet another of the ways in which the Synod has come to think too highly of its own importance.

11

The Move to Chichester

In September 1973, Robin Woods spoke to me about my future. For some time I had been unsettled, perhaps, in retrospect, for a number of reasons. There was the failure of the Anglican–Methodist Scheme and I could not help but notice that after I had piloted the Synodical Government Measure through the Church Assembly in 1968, I was not invited to take part in any of the arrangements for the inauguration of the Synod or to be involved in framing its standing orders. I rather assumed that, from the point of view of those who controlled those things, I was being put out to grass and being retired from any further participation in central Church affairs. After our conversation, I wrote him a long and frank letter setting out my feelings about Worcester Cathedral and my colleagues. I explained the difficulties I continued to find with the Chapter, which were not simply centred on their lack of spiritual unity but also my problems with getting any one of them to do any real work. The archdeacon, of course, had his job to do but Davis clearly regarded himself as retired and Purcell, though willing, could not be relied upon to remember things. Eric Turnbull was also something of a disappointment as he, like Davis, seemed to regard his canonry as a retirement post. I told Robin of my belief that I should have to retire from the deanery in order to resume my scholarly work and engage with something I felt to be positive.

I think, as events turned out, this conversation must have resulted in a discussion between Woods and Michael Ramsey, who was keen to see me on the bench of bishops. Some time later I had some conversation with Bishop Geoffrey Tiarks, who was Ramsey's senior chaplain at Lambeth. He told me that Michael had for some time wanted to see me a bishop but had not been able to secure an appointment. Owen Chadwick's biography of Ramsey has an interesting account of the Archbishop's dealings with John Hewitt, the Prime Minister's secretary for appointments, who regarded me as a dangerous radical. I can only think that this impression must have been gained at a conference at

Windsor, at which Hewitt was present, when I spoke forcibly in favour of a change from the existing system of Church establishment in England to something on the Scottish lines. Chadwick's biography also reveals that following John Hewitt's retirement, his successor, Colin Peterson, was much more willing to listen to what the Archbishop wanted. Nevertheless, still working on the assumption that being made Dean of Worcester marked the end of my ecclesiastical career, I was considerably surprised when, in May 1974, I received a letter from the Prime Minister asking if he could propose my name to the Queen for the Bishopric of Chichester. I saw Robin Woods later that morning, who obviously knew something about it, and said, 'Oh it's Chichester is it, not Lincoln?' He went on to say that had I been offered Lincoln, he would have advised me to refuse on the grounds that the diocese needed so much pastoral reorganization that all my time would be taken up with it. I do not think that that was quite true or that Robin could really have known very much about either diocese.

Colin Peterson was a very different person from Hewitt, with whom I had dealt over my appointment to Worcester. Gone was all the secrecy and the cloak-and-dagger meetings, so when I went to London to see Peterson, he was quite ready for me to go to Chichester to look at the house and talk to some of the senior staff. He put me in touch with Bishop Lloyd Morrell, the senior suffragan, so I first went to Hove and stayed the night with him. We were joined that evening by Max Godden, Archdeacon of Lewes, and had a good talk about the diocese. I learned that two years or so earlier, John Adair, a leading management consultant, had been commissioned to produce a report with recommendations about the organization of the diocese. He had observed that while other dioceses might be larger in size or in population, in a combination of the two Chichester was the largest in the country. It is certainly one of the most awkwardly shaped, being, like Peterborough, long and narrow, with the cathedral city at one end. The main centres of population are actually in the middle and run north from Brighton. The Bishop's seat is at Chichester, by the cathedral, nine miles from the western end and roughly 90 miles from the eastern end. The diocesan offices were in an elegant square in Hove and had just been enlarged using the proceeds of the sale of a conference house, Elfinsward, in Haywards Heath. For most of the diocese's history there had been two archdeaconries, Chichester and Lewes, which divided the area between them, but there were now three,

Chichester, Lewes and Hastings. There were two suffragan bishops, Lloyd Morrell of Lewes, the senior, with whom I was staying, and Simon Phipps of Horsham, the post Roger Wilson had established. The Adair Report had made a number of proposals, which included the establishment of a third suffragan, but these had not been well received. More recently, the Diocesan Synod had appointed a working party under the chairmanship of Colin Docker, then the Vicar of Eastbourne, to review their application. I was therefore to become bishop in the middle of discussions about the organization of the diocese. They were both keen that I should accept, and Max made it clear he expected me to be there for ten years.

The following morning Mary Morrell, Lloyd's sister, drove me to Chichester, where Roger Wilson, the retiring Bishop, was still in residence and he showed me over the palace. When I arrived, the door was opened by Mary Balmer, the Bishop's secretary, who had been appointed by George Bell in 1951 and went on to stay with me until 1981. I had a thorough tour of the house and so was able to go back to Worcester and give Pat some account of what sort of place we would be living in. All this was very different from the circumstances of my appointment to Worcester, and far more conducive to a sensible and informed decision. I understand arrangements are even better now for those being offered senior appointments. When I got back to Worcester, I gave Pat my first impressions of the Palace and told her of the various things that had been said. We decided that I should accept the appointment but, for good reasons, not move until October – the Wilsons were not planning to leave the house for some little while; we had the Three Choirs Festival to host; and there were things that would need to be done to the palace, particularly dividing a large room on the top floor to make bedrooms for our two oldest children.

During the ensuing months I was able to pay several visits to Chichester, sometimes with Pat. On an early visit with the Commissioners' bishoprics officer and architect, we began to negotiate for the improvements and alterations we needed. We started in the study, which was then at the south-eastern end of the upper floor, and moved along to the rather nice room which the Wilsons used as a drawing room and which I later adopted as my study. For a start we did not like the electrical flexes for the standard lamps trailing along the floor, although they provided all the lighting there was. The architect observed that the proper way to light the room would be with concealed lights above the panelling, but that this would be very expensive and the sensible alternative would be wall lights. The bishoprics officer immediately said, 'The Commissioners do not pay for wall lights', so we continued on. Downstairs, we came to a second sitting room, opening on to the garden. On looking in, Pat said immediately, 'Oh look, wall lights.' We got wall lights upstairs! The only dining room was a big room with an elaborate, sixteenth-century painted ceiling, about 40 yards from the kitchen. With a family like ours, we wanted to make a smaller room next door to the kitchen into a dining room. We asked for a new door through the intervening wall but again there was great resistance for some time on grounds of expense, but eventually they gave way.

There was less trouble about the other two changes that we made a little later. On the inside wall of the passage leading from the front door to the chapel there had been painted a rather amateurish series of incidents from the life of St Richard of Chichester. Several people spoke to me adversely about them and the architect was keen that they be removed. I did not know what sensitivities might be involved so I asked Walter Hussey, the Dean, who said that he had always been keen to see them go. I decided to tell the architect to have them removed but I was disconcerted next morning on going into the Palace to find a lady with paints and brushes touching them up. Plucking up all my courage I said that we thought they were too far decayed and had decided to have them removed. To my great relief she agreed and we had the wall cleared. The other issue was the garden. It had been decided that the greater part should be leased to the District Council as a public park, leaving us with an area just south of the house, which had to be big enough to accommodate a marquee for the Southern Cathedrals' Festival, and another smaller area some distance from the house for use as a kitchen garden. Roger Wilson, we were later told, had said that the actual line of division should be left for his successor to decide, but when we arrived, we found the lawn south of the house cut across by a low open fence. We did nothing about this immediately but one afternoon when my wife was sitting out after lunch she looked up and saw people taking photographs of her from the other side of the fence. We quickly looked at the lease and saw that the District Council was required to erect a close-boarded six-foot-high fence, so we asked for this to be done and the Commissioners' architect arranged for it. I did not know that this would require the agreement of a meeting of the

Council and so I was taken aback a few weeks later to see a newspaper placard which said 'Bishop's fence to cost ratepayers £700'.

On some of these early visits to Chichester I stayed with Walter Hussey, who was most kind and hospitable. This surprised some of the locals as no-one had been known to stay at the Deanery before and few people had been inside. Walter was always on very good terms with me and knew that I appreciated his concern for the Church's patronage of the arts. I was grateful to him for all he had done for the cathedral. On one occasion, however, staying in his house did cause me some difficulty. He had a valuable art collection of his own, related to the great works he had commissioned for the cathedral, which he later left to the city. On the morning of my enthronement I was anxious to go to the early service of Holy Communion, but on coming downstairs I found I could not get out as the door was locked and I had been warned that it was protected, as was the whole house, by a burglar alarm. I had to wait and after a few minutes Walter appeared, having just got out of bed. He let me out but I had the humiliation of appearing late for the service, and in the presence of a number of the canons who were there for the enthronement. On the last occasion I stayed with Walter, I proposed taking him out to lunch, but not knowing Chichester, I asked where we should go. He suggested we went to the Little London restaurant which we did and had a very good lunch, made all the more enjoyable by my first meeting with the proprietor, Philip Stroud, who later became a great friend.

As arrangements for my consecration fell into place, I realized it would be the last at which Michael Ramsey would preside. David Carey, who, as Provincial Registrar, appeared to be in charge of the arrangements, had said that the Archbishop had two dates set aside, October 18 and 23. October 18 was already booked for a new suffragan and they expected a second to be announced soon. As the Archbishop would not consecrate more than two at once, the choice was to be consecrated with the suffragan on 18 October at St Paul's or by myself on 23 October at Westminster Abbey. I chose the latter date, not least because I had heard that Michael Ramsey was not fond of St Paul's, where he felt he was not well treated by the Chapter. David then said that the Abbey Choir did not sing on Wednesdays. This seemed to me to be no problem as I had intended to ask if the Worcester Cathedral Choir could sing part of the service, as the Windsor Choir had done at Robin's consecration in St Paul's. In the absence of the Abbey Choir,

Worcester would be quite capable of doing the whole service. David undertook to speak to the Dean, Edward Carpenter, before I wrote to him. The Dean's reply to my letter began by saying how pleased they were that I was to be consecrated in the Abbey and how much they would put themselves out to make it a memorable occasion. That took three-quarters of the page, and the final paragraph read, 'Our own choir is available on that day and I am sure you will understand that we would much prefer the whole service to be left to them. It would cause difficulty if we began to have outside choirs coming in.' I telephoned David, read the letter to him and said, 'I would rather be consecrated in a London parish church with the Worcester Choir than in Westminster Abbey without it.' David said, 'Leave it to me', and the result was that I was consecrated in Southwark Cathedral with the Worcester Choir singing the whole service. Even this was not without its anxious moment, as the Worcester train was delayed and the choir very nearly did not arrive in time.

Christopher Robinson and I had carefully selected the music for the occasion. The Mass was Lennox Berkeley in Five Parts and the anthems mostly Elgar, but with Wesley's 'Lead me Lord' and a Bruckner anthem to Our Lady. I shall always remember the entrance of Michael Ramsey to the sanctuary as the choir, which was singing Elgar's 'Ecce sacerdos magnus', reached the climax of 'Qui in diebus suis placuit deo'. I was very proud of the Worcester Choir's part in the proceedings. A week or two afterwards Ronald Jasper, who was a canon of Westminster at the time, apologized to me for the difficulties that had been caused about the choir and said it was the Abbey organist, Douglas Guest, who had objected. He had previously been organist at Worcester and Christopher had been his deputy. What none of us realized, but possibly he did, was that in that month's *Gramophone*, a review of the Abbey Choir's recent recording of some Coronation music had said of the Vaughan Williams motet 'O taste and see': 'There is a much better performance of this, with a better soloist, on the Worcester Cathedral Choir's recent record.'

The week of my consecration was extraordinary and one which I shall not forget. We all drove to London from Worcester on Tuesday. Pat and the children left me at St Margaret's, Westminster, and went on to Lambeth Palace where I was to join them later. The Church of St Mary-Le-Bow on Cheapside, where episcopal elections are tradi- tionally confirmed, was under restoration at that time so the confirmation of my election took place at St Margaret's, Westminster. It was performed by the Dean of the Arches, my old friend Sir Harold Kent. I was required to have a barrister with me, presumably to deal with any objections that might be put, and I had asked my former Exeter colleague Richard Buxton, now Sir Richard and a Lord Justice of Appeal, to be with me. When it was over, we all had a drink at the National Liberal Club before I went on to Lambeth. No-one could have been kinder to our five young children than were the childless Ramseys. Edward, who was six at the time, had supper in the kitchen so he could watch television. After dinner, Michael led me off to the study where we sat in silence, as was often the case with him, until he said, 'I don't think I know very much about the diocese of Chichester.' Fortunately, something had already arisen in the diocese about which I wanted his advice and so the conversation flowed. The next morning my youngest daughter had to apologize that she had put her foot through one of the sheets in her bed. Joan Ramsey said, 'Oh don't bother. It's a job lot that we got from Cuddesdon and we are leaving soon.' After breakfast we packed up and drove to Southwark for the consecration.

Because of my connection with the Old Catholic Churches, Michael Ramsey had invited them to be represented at my ordination to the episcopate. Both Archbishop Kok of Utrecht and Bishop Van Kleef of Haarlem were present and laid on hands, saying aloud, 'Accipe Spiritum Sanctum' which is the Old Catholic formula of episcopal ordination. Afterwards they signed the Latin protocol, drawn up for such occasions by Dr NP Williams shortly after communion between the Church of England and the Church of Utrecht had been established [see Appendix 2]. The fact that the two visitors did not quite understand the niceties of English history was evident when, at dinner at Lambeth the night before, they presented me with a picture to commemorate the occasion – it was a drawing of William of Orange! Some years later I showed the protocol to an English Jesuit who wrote to me saying, 'I cannot see how even Cardinal Ratzinger could deny that you are a Catholic bishop.' The Bishop of Chartres, Mgr Michon, also attended, and at the end said to Canon François Legaux, who accompanied him, 'I can have no doubt that that man is now a bishop in the Catholic Church.' Whether that was because of the Old Catholic participation or the general impression made by the ceremony, I have never asked. As it was his last consecration, I had asked Michael himself to preach and I think that that pleased him. I much regret I do not have a copy of his sermon. The details of the service had been largely arranged with his chaplain at a meeting which I had attended shortly before. The service was unusual in that what always seems to me an unseemly scrum when the bishops come up for the laying-on of hands was replaced by their coming up individually and putting their hands on my head saying, 'Receive the Holy Ghost'. The two Old Catholic bishops were at the end.

After the reception and lunch we went to spend the night with our great friends Keith and Mary Hobbs in South Kensington and enjoyed ourselves at the theatre. I said Mass for the first time as a bishop the following morning at TS Eliot's church, St Stephen's, Gloucester Road, where Keith was a part-time curate. Later, Roger Wilson, who was still Clerk of the Closet, came to collect me to go to Buckingham Palace to pay homage to the Queen. I was to be accompanied by the Home Secretary who, at the time, was Roy Jenkins. He showed me the oath that I was to take, which I found a curious mixture of language deriving from the investiture controversy under Henry I and the renunciation of the papacy under Henry VIII. As the last phrase said there was no higher authority in England than the sovereign, I asked Roy Jenkins, with tongue in cheek, what became of the authority of the European Community? He had no sense of humour and just said he did not think it applied.

The homage ceremony consists of kneeling in front of the Queen with hands clasped between hers and reciting the oath. The Clerk of the Closet holds an open Bible on one side and the Home Secretary holds the text of the oath on the other. After this there are a few minutes' conversation. I remember Roger remarked that my wife and I had sung in the Worcester Festival Chorus and the Queen said she hoped we would be able to do something similar at Chichester. I said that my wife would but that I did not expect to have time myself. She then said, 'You must make time. There is too much of bishops not being able to do what they enjoy because they haven't time,' and went on to say that she and her family had greatly enjoyed singing with a local choir at Windsor. That was the only conversation I have ever had with her, other than formal introductions as, unlike most bishops, I have never been invited to preach at Sandringham. A chance comment by the Duke of Edinburgh when the Duke of Norfolk tried to introduce me has made me wonder whether I became confused in the royal mind with an MP for Chichester who made some public comments about the education of Prince Charles which had annoyed the Royal Family.

After lunch we all drove down to Chichester, where the family left me while they went to stay with a friend who was a housemaster at Lancing College. I spent the night at the Deanery and attended the annual dinner of the Greater Chapter where I had to respond to the toast of my health. It was the next morning when I found myself locked in the Deanery and was late for the early service. Work was going on apace at the palace in advance of our moving in, but we were able to use the Tudor Room for lunch where I was glad to meet a number of people who were new to me, including the Bishop of Arundel and Brighton, Michael Bowen, who generously presented me with a pectoral cross. As at Worcester, I had left it to the local civic dignitaries to decide what their visitors should wear and on this occasion the locals had ruled that only the Mayor of Chichester should robe. The Mayor of Brighton took offence and refused to attend but to show there was no personal affront to me intended invited me to a civic lunch at Brighton the following week.

The enthronement service was in the afternoon and was notable for being the first occasion on which the two Lord Lieutenants of the county were together at a service. Although East and West Sussex had been separate authorities for several years, a more recent change had readjusted the boundaries and had created separate Lord Lieutenancies for the two counties. The Duke of Norfolk had been Lord Lieutenant of the whole of Sussex for a very long time and I understood that he was much opposed to the change. He was by this time a sick man, and bravely and kindly struggled out to come to my enthronement. After the service I just had time to greet him briefly before he went home. He died the following January, so one of my first public engagements was to attend his funeral at which I read the Prayer of St Richard. As he was Earl Marshall the funeral was an elaborate occasion, and I recall his horse, with his boots reversed in the stirrups, accompanying the coffin as it was taken from Arundel Cathedral to the eastern part of Arundel Parish Church which is the property of the Dukes and contains their family vault.

On the Saturday morning I went to Brighton to preside at my first meeting of the Diocesan Synod, at which I announced the plans that had been made for the division of the diocese into three episcopal areas following the recommendations made by Colin Docker's Adair Report follow-up group. I cannot now remember what other business was done but I do know it was with a sense of relief after a most exhausting week that I got into the car to drive to Oxford, where I was to stay at St Stephen's House and celebrate and preach on the following morning. I was the first English diocesan bishop willing to admit his connection with the House. There had been one other diocesan, a Bishop of St Edmundsbury and Ipswich who never included his time at the House in his *Crockford* entry. In the evening I preached in Exeter Chapel and dined in hall, and the following morning I drove back to Worcester where, for the first time as a bishop, I celebrated the next morning in the cathedral. I have never had such a series of events within eight days, before or since.

The arrangements for our removal from Worcester were all in hand and I went ahead to Chichester on the Wednesday with my daughter Harriet to prepare for the arrival of our furniture and effects while the final touches to the Palace were being made. Being still unfamiliar with the house, I slipped on an uneven floor and sprained my ankle. When Pat and daughter Alice arrived on Saturday with David Annett, the headmaster of the King's School, who, it being half-term, had come to help us settle in, I met them limping and Harriet and I managed between us to drop the lunch on the floor. So ended an unforgettable fortnight.

12

Chichester – Personalities and Appointments

I was fortunate to have Lloyd Morell, Bishop of Lewes, as senior suffragan when I arrived. He was a long-standing priest of the diocese and had been an archdeacon before becoming bishop. He lived in his own house in Hove and delighted to tell how he had come to know a Roman Catholic bus conductor on the local route who said to him one day, 'I hear you are going to become a bishop so I suppose you will be leaving us now?', to which Lloyd had replied, 'Not if I can help it. They want me to go and live in a great house in Lewes, which would be impossible for my sister to manage so I want to stay here in my own house.' The bus conductor was pleased, 'Quite right, quite right. Bishops should look splendid in church and like everyone else outside.' To my joy, Lloyd stayed until he retired in 1977 and even then he remained in Hove so I was able to visit him frequently and seek his advice. He was a definite Catholic and was delighted at my appointment. With Roger Wilson's agreement, he had begun to celebrate at St Paul's, Brighton, the Holy Week service of the Chrism Mass, at which the holy oils for the year ahead are blessed by the bishop and priestly vows are renewed. He was very happy that the diocesan bishop should take it over from him, which I did in 1975. Later I moved this service to St Peter's, Brighton, and thus opened it to all the clergy. I invited every priest and deacon to come and participate, which many did, with the numbers increasing over the years until the decision of 1992 made it impossible to continue in the same way.

When I was first at St Paul's, Brighton, I noticed that they were to have Evensong and Benediction on Easter Day so I said that I would like to attend and the incumbent, Fr Milburn, invited me to preside and give Benediction. Lloyd and his sister were in the congregation and he said to me afterwards, 'I never thought I should live to see an English diocesan give Benediction.' At St Stephen's House, Arthur taught us the complete Catholic ceremonial on the grounds that it is much easier to leave things out than to remember to put them in. It is also well for a bishop to be well ahead, ceremonially, of any church he goes to because then he can have no difficulty in adapting himself to whatever may go on there. The first time I was to celebrate an evening Mass at St Paul's, I had to go to Brighton for a meeting in the morning so I took all my vestments with me and asked my driver to leave them at the church. When I arrived in the evening, I found a rather abashed parish priest, Fr John Milburn, saying that he had opened the case and found episcopal gloves. He had had to go upstairs to his study to look up what to do with them. I had been left all my father-in-law's pontifical vestments, which had been designed by Arthur Couratin, and I wore them for the first few years in churches such as St Paul's, until everything was simplified. I still have Kenneth Kirk's pastoral staff, given to him by the OUCU when he became Bishop of Oxford, but I placed the vestments on loan at the Castle Howard Museum of Costume. When this collection closed, I gave the vestments to the museum at York Minster.

Lloyd advised me to visit East Sussex as soon as possible after my enthronement. There was a religious community at Baldslow, just outside Hastings, so I arranged to stay with them. The chairman of East Sussex County Council, on learning of this, invited me to have lunch with the council on my way through Lewes, which I did. It was very useful to hear their views about Hastings and its problems before I got there. A few years earlier, there had been plans for a move of the population of part of east London to the town and local arrangements had been made but the plans were dropped. Hastings and St Leonard's-on-Sea, having been an attractive sea-side centre, now faced a number of difficulties. In Hastings, I was shown round by the rural dean, Donald Carter, whom I already knew. He arranged visits not only to the mayor and most of the parishes in the centre and round about, but also to the Mayor of Bexhill. I always found these civic visits interesting and rewarding.

I found that there were two churches in the diocese which the Bishop had not visited for many years, on the grounds, it was said, of their extremes of churchmanship. One, the Annunciation, Brighton, was Anglo-Catholic, the other, Broadwater, was conservative Evangelical. Both the incumbents had been there quite a long time. As soon as I could I went to each, and when it became possible, made both incumbents canons of the cathedral. The Vicar of the Annunciation,

Fr Ronald Bullivant, celebrated his 30th anniversary there and told me that when he was appointed, George Bell had said to him, 'Mr Bullivant, there are some modifications that I want you to make in the services at the Annunciation. There isn't time to discuss them now, but we must make time on some other occasion.' Time passed and every time Bullivant met the Bishop, he said the same thing, until one day when he said, 'Mr Bullivant, we have not been able to discuss the services at the Annunciation yet, and I haven't time now as I am going to Switzerland tomorrow. You had better go and talk to the Archdeacon. He will be able to tell you what I want.' So Bullivant went to the Archdeacon, who at that time was Lloyd Morell, and said that the Bishop had told him to come and ask what he was to do at the Annunciation. Lloyd thought for a moment and then said, 'If I was going there, I think I would try to run it like a little Roman Catholic slum chapel.' Bullivant added, 'That is what I have been trying to do for the last 30 years.' Very successful it had been, too, for most of the time, but, on balance, I think he stayed too long.

Lloyd Morell continued to give me wise help in his retirement but the other person to whom I went for advice, particularly in those first years, was the Bishop of London, Gerald Ellison, whom I had known when he was Cyril Garbett's chaplain at Winchester. He was very wise and tactful. I remember on one occasion when we had been together at a meeting of the Policy Sub-committee of the General Synod Standing Committee, and were waiting for a taxi to take us to the station, he suddenly looked at his watch and said, 'Have any of you heard of the Bishop of Hertford?' We all said, 'No.' He went on, 'His name is Victor Whitsey and it has just been announced that he is to succeed me at Chester.' Victor Whitsey was one of the first bishops to write to me when I was appointed to Chichester. I saw quite a lot of him as we used to meet in the bar of the National Liberal Club after bishops' meetings. Half way through one of the first bishops' meetings I attended Victor stood up at the back of the room and he said with his strong Lancashire accent, 'I've never spoken in one of these meetings before because by the time the Bishop of London, the Bishop of Durham and the Bishop of St Albans have had their say, there isn't any time for the rest of us.' I can't recall what he went on to say, but I do remember the pained look on the chairman's, Archbishop Coggan's, face. Victor always had something useful and trenchant to say.

During a General Synod meeting in the summer of 1974, Michael

Ramsey took me aside and asked if it would make things very difficult for me if Simon Phipps, the Bishop of Horsham I was to inherit, were to be moved to a diocese within a few months. Of course, I was not prepared to stand in his way, and he was appointed soon after to Lincoln. Fortunately for me, he did not move until after Christmas so I was able to have his advice in our discussions about reorganization and especially about moving to a system of designated episcopal areas for the suffragan bishops, of which he was strongly in favour. It might have been more difficult for me if there had not been an obvious successor. Colin Docker, chairman of the group set up to review the Adair Report, was well known and liked in the diocese, and I had seen him many times since I came to Chichester so I had little hesitation in nominating him as Bishop of Horsham. I had forgotten that when a suffragan is translated to a diocese, the Crown appoints his successor. Fortunately, Colin Peterson, the appointments secretary, was much more ready to follow the wishes of a diocesan than his predecessor would have been, so there was no difficulty in appointing Colin Docker. He was consecrated in January at the same time as was John Taylor for Winchester. Colin remained with me until retirement in 1991 and was an excellent colleague. A member of the Crown Appointments Commission told me that he was one of two people being discussed by the commission for Exeter in 1984, but was not appointed because Archbishop Runcie said he did not know him. This bears out the criticism later made by Gareth Bennett in his famous *Crockford* preface of appointments in Runcie's time. Colin was strong in support of the plan for episcopal areas, and to give him freedom of action I kept clear of the Horsham area during my first years, which meant I came to know the Lewes area much better.

The policy I adopted when appointing a suffragan was always to discuss the vacancy first with the other suffragan, then the archdeacons, the Dean, and other senior colleagues representative of the clergy of the diocese. I always had a conversation with the Archbishop of Canterbury and his patronage secretary and with the patronage secretary at Downing Street. This last always insisted that the discussion was purely informal and that he was nothing more than a post box as far as the appointment of suffragans was concerned. Occasionally it seemed to me there were people in the diocese with sufficient knowledge of individuals to be helpful, but not very often. I am sure, in view of their close working relationship, it is important that a diocesan bishop keep the choice of a suffragan firmly in his own hands. When Lloyd retired, I spent some time looking around and collecting names. In the course of my investigations, it came to my attention that Peter Ball, a founding member of the Community of the Glorious Ascension, was well known and liked in East Sussex and was interested in the post. I had got to know Peter slightly in Oxford after inviting him to be resident missioner for a week in college. The more I enquired about him, the more enthusiastic were the comments I received and when I announced the appointment it was very well received. He was anxious to continue his life as a religious and this raised problems about where he should live, as Lloyd had lived in his own house therefore there was no official house for the Bishop of Lewes. Eventually we found a house suitable for community life, but subsequent bishops found it too isolated, so a house in Eastbourne was ultimately found – which I hope will be the Lewes house for some years. Peter's twin brother Michael became Bishop of Jarrow a couple of years after Peter became Bishop of Lewes but in 1990 was translated to Truro as diocesan. Peter became rather restless after this but, nevertheless, when he left in 1992 to become Bishop of Gloucester, it was rather a surprise to me as I had not thought of him in connection with that diocese. He was not well received there and was not happy. Although it was not realized at the time, the circumstances which led to his early resignation were the work of mischief-makers. It was a very sad end to his ministry and his departure was a real loss to the Church which was, no doubt, what those who brought it about intended. Following his departure from Lewes, I thought it would be desirable to have an evangelical as his successor and, as I knew Ian Cundy through FOAG and admired him, it did not take me long to invite him and he fitted into the diocese very well.

When Ian left in 1996 to become Bishop of Peterborough, I looked for another evangelical and the names of several liberal evangelicals were put to me. I had, however, become aware that conservative evangelicals were becoming more influential in the Church and were complaining that there was no bishop of their tradition. As it was unlikely that any other diocese would appoint a suffragan of that outlook if I did not, and the chance of the Crown Appointments Commission putting one forward were negligible, I began to make enquiries of the Archbishop and others. The name which eventually emerged from George Carey, his appointments secretary, the Prime

Minister's patronage secretary and Lady Brentford, chair of our House of Laity, was that of Wallace Benn, who was a parish priest in Chelmsford diocese and member of the Council of Reform, the conservative evangelical political grouping. I got in touch with him and sounded him out, and then arranged for him to have a long meeting with the other suffragan who, though of a completely different tradition of churchmanship, was convinced they could work happily together. Wallace accepted and I have never had any cause to regret the appointment as, despite our differences in churchmanship, he has been very happy in East Sussex and a great pastor there. His wife is a wonderful support and they have become good friends of ours.

Walter Hussey, as I have said, made me very welcome both before and after my formal arrival in Chichester. He was a very distinguished Dean and I am glad to have known him. He had an extraordinarily good eye for contemporary art and was committed to enriching the fabric of the cathedral with the very best work of living artists and to finding affordable ways of commissioning art for churches. John Piper, Graham Sutherland, Hans Feibusch, Marc Chagal, Ceri Richards, Cecil Collins, Geoffrey Clarke and John Skelton were all names in a veritable roll-call of talent employed in the cathedral. The commissions were not limited to the visual arts. Leonard Bernstein's great choral work, *Chichester Psalms*, stands alongside works by William Walton and Lennox Berkeley as an example of the new music Hussey commissioned. George Bell, who as Dean of Canterbury had commissioned *Murder in the Cathedral* from TS Eliot and as Bishop of Chichester had welcomed Feibusch into his diocese as a church muralist, chose Hussey as Dean in succession to Arthur Duncan-Jones. Duncan-Jones had made the Chichester liturgy a landmark for cathedrals to steer by: Hussey made the building an inspiration for others to follow when enriching the worship of God through contemporary art. I was privileged to enter into this inheritance in my cathedral and sorry when Walter retired.

His successor, Robert Holtby, was an old friend of mine who, I am pleased to say, continued Walter's artistic concerns. The Chagal window commissioned by Walter arrived during Robert's first year and was welcomed by him. His own first commission was the magnificent font sculpted by John Skelton from dark green polyphant. It was largely due to Robert that the other great tapestry was provided for the cathedral. It hangs behind the shrine of St Richard and commemorates various aspects of his life. Shortly after becoming Dean, Robert asked me to make a formal visitation of the cathedral, and I did this very thoroughly, issuing a hundred questions as a preliminary. The Charge, when I delivered it, only contained one direction which the chapter were obliged to observe as it concerned the interpretation of the statutes, but there were a great many recommendations, most of which they followed. I could not help comparing the situation at Chichester with that which I had just left at Worcester but I tried not to do so to a boring extent. One very marked difference was in the Sunday morning service. Both Matins and the Sung Eucharist were well attended and there seemed to be no difficulty in maintaining two choral services. The cathedral statutes required the Bishop and the Dean to preach on all great festivals and on the feast of the Translation of St Richard. I arranged that we would alternate between Matins at 10am and the Sung Eucharist at 11am. At Christmas, this left me free to go to a parish for the Midnight Mass. I usually went to one of the villages near Chichester and always enjoyed the experience. It was always good to see an ordinary parish congregation at worship, if somewhat enlarged by Christmas visitors, and to go back to the vicarage or a churchwarden's house afterwards.

I conducted two further visitations of the cathedral during my episcopate. One was at the request of some chorister parents who feared that proposed changes in the accommodation of the headmaster of the Prebendal School would adversely affect the care of the pupils. The other was more general and was about ten years after my first visitation. I think these occasions are valuable. They provide an opportunity both for the congregation and for all members of the cathedral staff to express their views freely and in confidence to the bishop, and for him to take such action about them as seems to him appropriate. Robert, with his great knowledge of church schools, was a great help to me with educational matters in the diocese and was chairman of the Education Committee. He was also active in the celebrations of the centenary of the baptism of George Bell in 1981 which led to the plan to establish a twinning with a city in Germany.

After Robert retired from the Deanery, the Holtbys moved to Huttons Ambo, not far from our cottage in Yorkshire. They were very hospitable and when the General Synod met in York, they always invited the Chichester members to their house. Robert was very keen to keep in touch with what was going on. I was able to help him a little with his book on Eric Milner White, who had been Dean of York from 1941 to 1963, as I had stayed with him twice in 1955 when I was reading the registers, both episcopal and capitular, for my work on the history of Convocation. John Treadgold was appointed to succeed Robert. He had had cathedral experience at Southwell and parochial experience in Nottingham and Darlington, and came to us from a canonry at Windsor, where he had been in charge of the chapel in the Great Park where the royal family regularly worshipped. His wife, Hazel, had been Central President of the Mothers' Union and so brought to Chichester a wealth of experience of engagement with the Anglican Communion and the worldwide Church. They opened their home to the cathedral and diocesan community in a way no previous Dean had done within living memory, and their generous hospitality was much appreciated. John addressed the care and conservation of the cathedral fabric with a seriousness and expertise I acknowledged by inviting him to become chairman of the Diocesan Advisory Committee for the Care of Churches (DAC).

I was very lucky in the archdeacons I found in post. There were three: Guy Mayfield, Archdeacon of Hastings, who had been Diocesan Director of Ordinands; Max Godden, Archdeacon of Lewes, who had had a long ministry in the diocese and was a friend of Lloyd's; and Freddy Kerr-Dineen, Archdeacon of Chichester, who had just been appointed by Roger Wilson. Colin Docker's working party had recommended that the archdeaconries should be coterminous with the new episcopal areas, so one of the first things I had to do was combine the archdeaconry of Lewes with that of Hastings and create a new archdeaconry of Horsham. Guy Mayfield was just about to retire, which considerably facilitated the re-organization, but there were problems with Chichester. The whole diocese had been dominated by Lancelot Mason who, having been George Bell's chaplain, became Archdeacon of Chichester with a residentiary canonry and rather too much influence on the life of the cathedral. To counter this, his successor was given the small parish of Stopham as well as the residentiary canonry, but with only one month's residence obligation each year. Loyally, all fitted in with the various changes I made after my arrival, but Freddy Kerr-Dineen found the three hats rather too many to wear – archdeacon, parish priest and residentiary canon. He had a breakdown and it became clear to me that this combination was too much to sustain. He generously agreed to become the first Archdeacon of

Horsham, retaining the small parish. When he retired I appointed Bill Filby, another leading evangelical in the diocese, who remained in office until after my retirement and was a very good and loyal support. When Freddy took the Horsham archdeaconry, I appointed Richard Eyre, who had again been long in the diocese, to the archdeaconry of Chichester, with the residentiary canonry attached. The diocese bought a house in Canon Lane in the Close which made both canonical residence and full participation in chapter meetings possible for the archdeacon. Fortunately, the cathedral statutes were sufficiently flexible to allow me a good deal of movement.

When Richard left to go to Exeter as Dean in 1981, my first thought was to appoint Keith Hobbs, by then my chaplain, as his successor, but I rejected the idea thinking it would look too much like nepotism. I was still undecided when the Archdeacon of Horsham came to see me and as he was leaving he said, 'We are all wondering why you don't appoint Keith Hobbs as your staff think he is so good.' This, of course, meant his continuing to live in Canon Lane where he and Mary were already well-known and loved. Mary took charge of the cathedral library and later edited a history of the cathedral. When Keith retired, I asked for suggestions from the Bishops of Portsmouth and Winchester and eventually appointed the Vicar of Portsea, Michael Brotherton. He and his wife were very welcome in the cathedral close and she became a most valued figure in the diocese and on General Synod, which I had not anticipated but welcomed warmly.

The Diocesan Secretary is an important person in a diocese, as is the chairman of the Diocesan Board of Finance. At the beginning of 1975, the Diocesan Secretary I had inherited told me that he intended to retire later in the year but in the interim, would like to go away for six weeks to visit his son in Africa. I did not think that we could face a period of that length with aspects of diocesan affairs unable to be touched, so we came to an arrangement whereby his work could be carried on by others and the search for a successor begun. In making this arrangement, I fear I offended the chairman of the Board of Finance, who resigned. This, however, enabled me to appoint David Hopkinson, of M&G Investments, as chairman and it was thanks to his financial ability and skill that, in the 1980s and 1990s, Chichester did not face the financial difficulties some other dioceses did. Indeed, we were able to come to the aid of the diocese of Birmingham and for three years pay for a curate for them. When David retired, I was fortunate in finding Sir John Herbecq and, after him, Hugh Wyatt as successors. It was with David that I set to work to find a new Diocesan Secretary and we were just starting on this when I received a letter from Douglas Smith, the Worcester Diocesan Secretary, whom I had earlier helped to appoint. He had heard of our vacancy and asked if he could be considered. I think he was finding Robin Woods rather difficult to work with. We were delighted to have him and he served the diocese well until his retirement. He was followed by Brigadier John Cooper and he, in turn, by Jonathan Prichard, who masterminded the move of the diocesan offices to new premises and who is still in post.

Chichester was one of those cathedral cities which still had a theological college, but the college's future was very uncertain. From 1960 onwards, there had been much discussion about the decline in the number of ordinands and the consequent empty places in theological colleges. Changes in the balance of churchmanship in the Church at large meant that the Catholic colleges, of which Chichester was one, were suffering particularly. I knew something about what was going on as a Canon Walker had come to see me in Oxford on behalf of the Chichester governing body to discuss a possible merger with St Stephen's House, but that did not proceed. A working party under the chairmanship of Robert Runcie recommended, among other things, the amalgamation of Chichester, Salisbury and Wells colleges. The governing body of Chichester had strongly opposed the proposal and succeeded in keeping Chichester independent, though Salisbury and Wells did combine. Dame Betty Ridley, who was chairman of the Advisory Council for the Church's Ministry at the time, and a friend of mine, lobbied me to persuade Chichester to change its mind. However, as Bishop I had become ex-officio chairman of the governing body and, seeing things from the inside, was not prepared to give way to Betty's wishes. I did, however, resign the chairmanship of the governors of St Stephen's House as I could foresee the possibility of conflict of interest in the House of Bishops.

When I arrived as Bishop, the Principal of the Theological College, Alan Wilkinson, had just resigned so the first thing I had to deal with was the appointment of a successor. After the usual procedures, we appointed John Halliburton, Vice-Principal of St Stephen's House, who made a good start but anxieties about his health made the governing body feel he would not be able to cope with the ongoing threat of closure, which made for a rather tense situation. In 1981, the governors asked me to persuade him to resign, which I did, one of the three occasions when I had to ask friends to resign – the others being Derek Allen from St Stephen's House and Cheslyn Jones from Pusey House. This sort of thing is not easy or pleasant to do, but if you are chairman of an institution you have to be prepared to do things that are not easy or pleasant. We appointed as his successor John Hind, the second of a succession of priests who came from the diocese of Southwark to work in Chichester. Over the next nine years, he did much to renew the life of the college, not least overseeing the sale of most of its old buildings and the complete rebuilding of the college on adjacent land. In 1991, I appointed him Bishop of Horsham but he was not with me in that capacity for long, as he became Bishop of Gibraltar in Europe in 1993. It is a great pleasure to me in my retirement that he has succeeded me at Chichester.

After John Hind, we appointed Peter Atkinson, a young priest who had only just started work in a parish in Bath. Peter made a strong start as Principal but the attack on the theological colleges had been resumed and the anxiety over numbers continued. I had several times to defend the college against misrepresentations of its financial position, as there were always those who wanted to see it closed. Eventually, a new commission was appointed under the Bishop of Lincoln which supported the retention of Chichester but suggested the closure of Oak Hill and Mirfield. This was a mistake as all the powerful forces of evangelicalism rallied in support of Oak Hill, and there were strong arguments for keeping Mirfield as the only college in the north of England. In addition, since the earlier closure of the College of the Sacred Mission at Kelham, Mirfield, run by the Community of the Resurrection, was the only college run by religious, which, of course, made it cheaper than others. Yet another commission was appointed, this time under the Bishop of Hereford. The Chichester governors felt from the start that it was not going to be favourable to us, and, indeed, it recommended the closure of Chichester and Salisbury Wells, and later Lincoln. In spite of the fact that these proposals left no residential college south of London, they were accepted and in 1994 we had to close. This was a great loss to the diocese and to Chichester itself, where the presence of the college had been important in many ways. I was sad for Peter Atkinson, who had made a good start as Principal. I was able to give him an immediate parish appointment in the near neighbourhood, which avoided interrupting his children's schooling, and shortly afterwards I moved him to a residentiary canonry in the cathedral.

I have mentioned a succession of bright priests who came to Chichester from the Southwark diocese. The first of these was Dominic Walker OGS, who came as Vicar of Brighton, at that time probably the most important parish in the diocese. He did valuable work in Brighton for many years before being appointed Suffragan Bishop of Reading, from where he succeeded Rowan Williams as Bishop of Monmouth. John Hind was the second Southwark refugee, followed by a young Australian priest, Lindsay Urwin, who came in 1988 as Diocesan Missioner. He proved so acceptable to parishes of all complexions of churchmanship that when John Hind left to become Bishop of Gibraltar I asked him, in spite of his youth, to become Bishop of Horsham. He is now so widely recognized as a missioner and a pastor that, though the diocese of Chichester would be sorry to lose him, I hope it will not be long before the Church of England recognizes that it has in him a potential diocesan. George Carey borrowed him so many times to lead missions all over the country that I hoped this might have happened before now.

I inherited a part-time chaplain from Roger Wilson, David Grant, who was also Vicar of nearby Oving. I was keen to appoint a full-time domestic chaplain of my own choice as the working relationship between bishop and chaplain is a close one, so when David went to be Rector of Graffham, I appointed Anthony Freeman. I had known him as an undergraduate at Exeter College in my last year there and he had then been ordained curate in Worcester. He agreed to come to me for three years, after which I made him priest in charge of St Wilfrid's, Chichester. Alas, I must at this point say something more about Anthony, as there are misunderstandings and misrepresentations in circulation about what eventually happened. After four years at St Wilfrid's, Chichester, I made him vicar of the rather larger parish of Durrington, where for seven years he did excellent work. I then decided that we needed to create a post which combined being assistant Director of Ordinands with overall responsibility for continuing ministerial education. I consulted the two suffragans and Anthony's name was suggested. We found a smaller base for him than Durrington at Staplefield Common, and he accepted the appointment. All continued well until 1992 when John Hind, in whose episcopal area Staplefield was, reported a conversation he had just had with Anthony about a book that Anthony had recently written called *God in Us* and which he was planning to publish. John had advised him that he ought to talk to me about the substance of the book, so Anthony sent me a manuscript copy which I duly read. What I found in it disturbed me a great deal. Without any of us knowing, he had become involved with a group led by the radical Cambridge theologian, Don Cupitt, calling itself 'The Sea of Faith' after Matthew Arnold's bleak poem, 'On Dover Beach'. The book raised serious questions about the reality and existence of God. Anthony came to see me and I discussed the book with him. I put it to him that if all this went into print, I could no longer allow him to continue with the responsibilities he had for the training of the junior clergy. I gave him a year to reflect on his position and suggested that he talk things over with Professor Charles Moule, who lived in retirement in the diocese, and John Macquarrie, Lady Margaret Professor at Oxford. He agreed to this and spent some time with each of them, after which both wrote to me and said that, holding the views he did, they could not think it right for him to continue in the ministry of the Church of England. Anthony was convinced that he had been delivered from a Christianity which had become oppressive to one which brought him a new sense of freedom and joy so he went ahead regardless of all that had been said and published the book. I consulted the chairman of the Diocesan Synod's House of Laity, some other members of the Bishop's Council, including the archdeacons, before the two suffragans and I had a long meeting with Anthony. Part of our problem lay in his continuing at Staplefield once I had relieved him of his CME responsibilities because it had been chosen for him as a light-duty post. When the three of us saw him at the end of his year of reflection, his views had not changed and what he had written as his own interpretation of the Declaration of Assent to the faith and historic formularies of the Church of England made all three of us feel we could not, in honesty, receive it from him on appointment to another parish. Bishops Lindsay Urwin, Ian Cundy and I were all agreed on this with great regret. Anthony therefore left the diocese. He has not been in touch with me since. I had one or two letters of criticism from some of his friends who, I think, did not realize either the trouble we had taken or the problem presented by the office that he held. I was relieved later to get letters from both archbishops saying that they did not think I could have done anything in the circumstances other than I did.

It was at about the time that Anthony's three years as my chaplain were due to end, that I received a letter from my old friend, Keith Hobbs, saying that he and his wife Mary were about to be made redundant from the training college where they were teaching and asking if I could suggest any jobs. I had no hesitation in offering him the choice of a parish in the diocese or of becoming my chaplain, and he chose the second. He was an excellent domestic chaplain and gained a real insight into the workings of the diocesan administration, which enabled him to be an equally excellent archdeacon when, as I have related above, the time came. When that time did come, I had to look once more for a chaplain, and on one of my visits to St Mary's, Bourne Street, London, the curate there, Freddy Jackson, confided that he felt it was time for a move. I discussed the matter with the parish priest, Fr John Gilling, and with his agreement I offered Freddy the chaplaincy. He was very good, very much liked in the diocese, and we became good friends. He was happy in the job and not at all anxious to move but after five years, I felt that he ought to have a parish and so persuaded the Vicar of Brighton to appoint him to St Michael's, Brighton, where he was much loved and did wonderful pastoral work. Sadly, he was one of those much upset by the decision to ordain women to the priesthood and he left the Church of England to become a Roman Catholic priest. We remain good friends.

Freddy Jackson was succeeded by Grant Holmes, who had been curate in charge of a daughter church in the parish of South Kenton in the diocese of London. Grant was not happy working in the Palace, so when the parish of Mayfield fell vacant I appointed him, and he did good work there as a parish priest for many years. While this was being arranged, Graham Leonard suggested to me a priest in London whom I knew slightly, Jeremy Haselock. Interviewing him, as I recall, in the bar of the House of Lords, I discovered he could not drive. I told him I was happy to appoint him but only if he passed his driving test before taking up the job. He proved to be a very good chaplain both from his knowledge of church history and church buildings, and in his ability to adjust to varied settings of churchmanship. When the time came for him to leave, I was considering how to improve the standard of worship in the parishes and keep the clergy up to date with the new, seasonal, liturgical material that was emerging. At the same time, I had to deal with a vacancy in nearby Boxgrove, a parish with a superb church building, a former Benedictine priory, but which was not big enough to be held as a benefice on its own. Boxgrove had developed a fine musical and distinctive liturgical tradition so I decided to make it the base for a priest who would be a liturgical adviser for parishes and invited Jeremy to take it on, which he did, and made the new office very effective. I made him a canon of the cathedral to underline the importance of the liturgical work he was doing, and when he stood for, and was elected to, the General Synod, he was almost immediately appointed to the Liturgical Commission. He is now Canon Precentor and Vice-Dean at Norwich.

Jeremy was followed by Stephen Masters who, before training for ordination at Mirfield, had been a personal assistant to Derek Pattinson, the secretary general of the General Synod. When Stephen left, I had little hesitation in asking Ian Chandler to take on the job. I had known him as one of the last students at the Theological College and had ordained him as curate of All Saints, Hove. I was uncertain whether he would accept but happily he did, and remained with me until a year before my retirement when I made him Vicar of St Richard's, Haywards Heath, of which deanery my successor has now made him rural dean. For my remaining year, I had the splendid services of Ron Robinson, a priest who had had to leave his parish for medical reasons and was living near Chichester. He also acted as my driver and was a great help. By and large, I have been very fortunate in my chaplains, all of whom have been a great help and some of whom have remained good friends.

13

Out of the Ordinary

The life of a diocesan bishop has a certain predictability and a necessary routine. Early in my first year, I was invited to attend a study week for new bishops at St George's House, Windsor. It provided a few interesting insights into the job but, on the whole, did not seem to me particularly useful. A later occasion of a similar kind was almost a waste of time. Those who organize these things rarely seem to understand the kind of help and advice a new bishop really needs. I am of the view, as should be the case with all the clergy, that undergirding all there must be the firm foundation of daily prayer. My custom was to say Matins in my chapel with my chaplain and usually, once Keith Hobbs had taken over the post, the Archdeacon of Chichester, and then, unless I was to preside at the Eucharist somewhere else that day, to say Mass at 8am. After breakfast I would deal with the post, although the increasing lateness of the hour of its delivery was a frequent source of irritation. After I had dealt with my correspondence, the day would proceed fairly predictably depending on the number and location of meetings, interviews, committees and pastoral visits. Confirmations and the inauguration of new ministries – collations, inductions, licensings and the like – generally took place in the evenings. Visits to London for meetings of General Synod or synodical committees took place fairly frequently and then, when I had taken my seat in the Lords, there was the rota for taking prayers and attendance for any business in which I had an interest, or for which I had been asked to hold the brief.

I was enormously helped in all of this by having the services of a driver. I realized this especially on one early occasion when I had to take an induction at Camber, which is 12 miles beyond Rye in the extreme east of the diocese. Such occasions were almost always the last engagement of a busy day and had I had to drive myself back to Chichester from Camber after 10 at night, I am not sure how safe I would have been. When I was appointed I was told that Charles Monk, chauffeur since 1921, was retiring. Against the Commissioners' advice, I insisted on advertising for a replacement in the *Church Times*. George Reindorp, then Bishop of Salisbury, happened to be preaching at St Margaret's Westminster, arrived early and was reading the *Church Times* in the vestry when he saw my advertisement. He immediately rang to say that his own driver's son-in-law was about to leave the army after ten years' service as a driver and was looking for a job. I interviewed Peter Genever and appointed him. He was with me for 12 years, during which he and his wife became great friends, as they still are. He was lured away from my employment to the Chichester Tennis and Squash Club, who offered a salary considerably more than the Commissioners were prepared to pay. I then found a retiring member of the Royal Marines, Rodney Stannard, known to everyone as Stan, who stayed with me until shortly before I retired, and then left to drive for the Bishop of Exeter.

There was a regular meeting of the senior staff once a month for which my chaplain would act as secretary, writing up the minutes and preparing the agenda. I encouraged my chaplains to participate in these discussions as, once they had become familiar with the diocese and its clergy, they were in a position to offer a useful view on many issues. Having good secretarial assistance in the office at the Palace was also an important matter, particularly as the maintenance of good records and reliable filing there was essential when the diocesan administration was based a good distance away in Hove. When I visited the Palace for the first time in 1974, the door was opened by the bishop's secretary, Miss Mary Balmer. Mary had been appointed by George Bell during the war years. After his retirement, she remained with Roger Wilson, and then with me, until 1981, when she retired and married a year later. It was a joy for me to take her wedding at All Saints, Hove. She was a marvellous secretary and her knowledge of the diocese and of the clergy was invaluable in my early years. She was very discreet and would refrain from comment on my decisions unless she felt I was not being strict enough. She had been able to adapt herself remarkably well to the different ways of working of three bishops. I was very sorry when she retired as it was very difficult to find someone with her degree of specialist knowledge. Mrs Shirley Boak took over and had all the necessary secular secretarial skills but could not be expected to have much insight into the ways of the Church of England. After Mrs Boak, I had a period of some difficulty, until eventually I appointed Mrs Jo Parkinson, who not only understood the Church well but also became, like Mary, a friend. After a while the commissioners funded an assistant secretary and I was lucky to be able to employ Ros, the wife of Bishop Michael Manktelow, when they retired to live in the Close.

Of the things that passed across my desk in the normal run of things there is no need to write, but there were a number of out-of-the-ordinary incidents which are worth recording, if only to show how peculiar are some of the problems with which a bishop has to deal. The first of these began one day in the late 1970s when Richard Eyre, then Archdeacon of Chichester, brought to my attention a complaint from the Vicar of Rottingdean that two men were causing trouble in his parish. They had begun by accusing him of devoting all his pastoral attention to the well-to-do and neglecting the poorer parishioners. Following this, they had started to ring various elderly people during the night, accusing them of behaving badly towards the poor. They walked frequently past the vicarage and made faces through the windows, and now they had started standing at the churchyard gate and shouting at people going to church. My advice was that if personal remonstrance proved ineffective, the vicar should retain a solicitor to take up the matter and the diocese would cover the expense. A week or so later, I received a copy of an open letter from a certain Robin Bryans accusing me of misusing charitable funds to subsidize a malicious prosecution. Thereafter I received several open letters referring to various alleged misbehaviours of the clergy and to things that were supposed to be happening in the neighbourhood of Rottingdean.

Then Bryans must have read my entry in *Who's Who* or some such work of reference because he discovered that I had been a Proctor in Convocation for the clergy of the University of Oxford, but he had confused that with the very different function of being a proctor of the University. He now wrote to me, as he said, in that capacity, complaining about certain of the fellows of All Souls who had allegedly claimed that no-one could be a genius unless they were homosexual. The warden of All Souls at the time, John Sparrow, was also a director of Faber and Faber, which had published books by Bryans, and Bryans subsequently brought legal charges against the firm. The description of these legal actions also included attacks on a judge who, as a barrister, had acted for Faber and Faber. Bryans also circulated a story about a man from Northern Ireland who was alleged to have been disinherited by his father for becoming a Roman Catholic priest, and who had then gone to Milan where he had a relationship with the Archbishop, Cardinal Montini, who, as Pope Paul VI, made him a papal chaplain.

I was able to ignore this farrago until the letters began to be sent to Lambeth Palace to the Archbishop. I then arranged a meeting between the Archbishop's Registrar, my Registrar and someone from Faber and Faber, but there seemed to be nothing that we could do to stop the letters. I even spoke to Lord Hailsham as I learned that earlier, he and Lord Shackleton had both been recipients of letters from Bryans. Lord Hailsham had invoked the Post Office Act and advised me to do the same, but this had no effect. The Brighton police collected a large bundle of open letters but there seemed to be nothing that anyone could do to stop them being written. The most tiresome aspect of all this was that Bryans began to send copies of his letters to priests all over the country, some of whom then wrote to me. There was nothing I could do but explain the situation patiently.

There was, however, a curious end to this story. We had, as a diocese, a relationship with the diocese of Sierra Leone and I was invited to preach in a north London church in connection with a Sierra Leone association. There was the usual sort of tea party afterwards and during it, a man approached me and said, 'I think that the last time we met we were talking about Bishop Bell and his influence on TS Eliot's *Murder in the Cathedral*.' I did not recognize or remember the man and so made some non-committal reply. He went away but came back with a companion a few minutes later saying, 'My name is Robin Bryans and this is my friend George Balcomb. I do want you to understand that there is nothing personal about all this.' They then went off and I heard nothing more for two or three years when there suddenly appeared another open letter about some journalist, but apart from that I have heard nothing since.

Early during my episcopate, I received a good deal of trouble from a group of parishes in the east of the diocese. In the ordinary run of things, these problems would have been dealt with by the Bishop of Lewes but the incumbent insisted on bringing the matter to me. A formal complaint about him was made by 15 parishioners and my registrar advised me that I should see them all individually. Accordingly, I dedicated a whole afternoon to sitting in Church House, Hove, to hear their complaints. The problems were the usual ones which arise when a new incumbent tries to make changes in areas where little change has been seen for ages, and I gave some directions which I felt would be helpful. However, not long after, one of the complainants, an elderly lady, went to visit one of the others who lived on the first floor of a block of flats. At the first step she stumbled and fell onto a large plant pot. The bamboo stake supporting the plant pierced her throat and she collapsed, choking, at the door of the person she was visiting. Deeply sadly, she died as a result of the accident. It was reported that the incumbent had been seen lurking in the darkness near the flats and, wholly unreasonably, he was blamed for her fall. The police were brought in and had to investigate the affair and, as a result, the priest was exonerated from anything to do with it.

Another very strange affair concerning the eastern parishes began a few years later. I was telephoned one evening by Tony Lloyd, who had at one time been chairman of our Diocesan Board of Finance and later became a law lord as Lord Lloyd of Berwick. He was concerned about two friends who had been approached for money by John Baker, the Rector of Newick. He was appealing on behalf of a man who came to live in his parish and was claiming that the man was trapped in a Satanist organization and needed the money to help him get out of it. John Baker was a very reputable priest and a prominent leader of the evangelicals in the diocese. He and Fr Derek Allen had worked together usefully in producing study material for the clergy in a course that I had initiated at the time. I felt sure I had to take anything he said seriously. As I was about to go abroad for a month, I asked Bishop Lloyd Morell and a recently retired civil servant, Sir John Herbecq, to look into the matter for me. By the time I returned they had interviewed the man and John Baker, but found so much in the story implausible they could not make up their minds about it. I saw John Baker myself but the man himself was reluctant to meet me. John was completely convinced of the truth of what he had been told and had raised quite a lot of money from wealthy evangelical friends who seemed only too ready to accept the truth of the man's story. He claimed to have lived at some time with his grandmother at Windsor Castle, and she had made him a member of the Satanist cult in which he had taken vows. He required the money to pay to be released from the vows. I was briefly in Rome about that time on other business and discussed these claims with an expert in the Congregation for the Defence of the Faith. He confirmed the existence of the particular organization but could not tell me anything about its current membership to substantiate the story.

Having received the substantial sum collected for him by John Baker, his parishioner then claimed that another large sum was needed to pay for certain regalia which had to be returned to the Satanist organization. By this time, I was becoming more and more dubious about the whole affair but very influential and important people seemed to accept the truth of it and produced large sums of money for him and, in one case, a Rolls-Royce. I decided I had had enough when he alleged that an Italian cardinal at the head of the European branch of the cult had died and was to be succeeded by a British cabinet minister. The man with whom John Baker was dealing was now in line to become head of the English branch but would need money to do so, presumably to undermine the organization from within. I decided that I must speak to the police, and so got in touch with the Chief Constable, with whom I was on friendly terms. I wrote up an account of the whole affair and gave it to him. John Baker had been very insistent that I should not say anything to the police. However, about this time he telephoned me and read a letter which the Satanist had sent him with the request that he read it to me. It ended with the words, 'You must do as you think best.' I felt I had done exactly that and waited to see what would happen.

It took the police some two months to investigate the matter and identify the man. I was repeatedly visited by the two officers who were dealing with the case. They discovered a whole series of frauds in different parts of the country, and it seemed that he had raised at least £250,000, and probably more, in Sussex. When arrested he had apparently said, 'Well, if someone offers you a packet containing a thousand pounds, you think you are on to a good thing.' The man was tried at Maidstone, convicted of fraud and sent to prison for nine years. I had to give evidence at the trial and was cross-examined by his defence counsel, a man called West, who said to me, 'You will accept will you not that everything you have said is what you were told by others? You never actually met my client.' I said that, in fact, I had met him once when he had driven John Baker over to Chichester but he had refused to come in and talk to me. The barrister then referred to the telephone conversation when John had read the letter ending, 'You must do as you think best.' He said, 'Was not that an invitation to see him?' I replied that I did not understand it as such and, in any case, I had by then brought the police into the matter and did not think I should interfere further. The barrister then said, 'So you washed your hands of one of your flock.' My chauffeur, who was listening, told me that he had difficulty in restraining himself. When all was said and done, what we all found so difficult to believe was the gullibility of the prominent county figures who had contributed such large sums.

In 1980 a member of the cathedral chapter, in London for a session of the General Synod, was arrested and charged with indecent exposure in an Oxford Street department store. He came to see me at the beginning of the following week to tell me what had happened and to inform me that he was to appear in court on the Wednesday. He was willing to resign but I thought it right that I should wait until after the result of the court case. I was due to go abroad the following day, so through the Chancellor of the diocese I arranged for him to have legal representation and I asked the Bishop of Horsham to deal in my absence with anything that needed immediate action after the court hearing. He pleaded guilty and was given a heavy fine. Unfortunately, without consulting the Bishop of Horsham, the Dean issued a statement to the effect that the canon was continuing with his regular duties pending the bishop's return, even though most people, including his chapter colleagues, were expecting him to be suspended. I came back at the end of the week to find that, persuaded by some friends, he had decided not to resign.

There followed a difficult few weeks until Archbishop Runcie persuaded him that the circumstances were such that resignation would be appropriate and so resign he did, on the understanding that another post would be found for him. He took a team vicar's post in another diocese for some years before once again being made a residentiary canon in a cathedral where he did excellent work until his retirement. In the course of the difficulty I discussed the affair with Walter Hussey, who had been Dean when the man joined the chapter. He confided that he had never thought Chichester the right place for the man but Simon Phipps, then Bishop of Horsham, had persuaded Roger Wilson to appoint him to an unexpectedly vacant residentiary canonry. This is the sort of difficult problem that can arise as a result of a decision of one's predecessor.

To succeed him, I was able to appoint Christopher Luxmoore, who proved to be a splendid pastor to the cathedral congregation. His popularity was somewhat resented by Robert Holtby who for a while had alienated a number of the lay supporters over cathedral finance. I was somewhat taken aback when Bob Runcie telephoned me and said he wanted to make Christopher Bishop of Bermuda. The consecration took place at Chichester. We were very sad to lose him. Neither he nor his family were happy in Bermuda, which has often been a difficult diocese to deal with, and I was not altogether surprised when, after a few years, he resigned. I was then able to make him Archdeacon of Lewes and Hastings for the remainder of his active ministry and finally he retired happily to live in Chichester.

Rather different but equally outside the normal run of things was the bomb in the Grand Hotel Brighton in 1983. The bomb exploded the night before we were due to have a Sussex Church Leaders meeting in Lewes. I had not heard the news that morning, so the first I knew of what had happened was when I was telephoned from Lambeth by Archbishop Runcie to ask what I proposed to do about the situation. I rang Bishop Cormac Murphy-O'Connor and we arranged to meet in Brighton and to write joint letters of condolence to the Prime Minister, the Chief Constable and the Chief Fire Officer, which we would deliver ourselves. We took the letter to the Prime Minister to the Brighton Centre where the Conservative Conference was meeting and were rather surprised to be asked to go up to her room to see her. We therefore delivered our condolences personally and she asked us to pray with her. Having delivered the other two letters, we went on to Lewes to meet the other Church leaders and explain what we had done. In the course of our meeting we all decided to go to the site of the martyrs' memorial and pray there. It was distressing to learn later that the Protestant owners of the site had objected to our having prayed with Cormac there. Later in the day, and on the following days, I was able to visit Lord Tebbit and Lord Wakeham in hospital and I was glad to be in the House of Lords the following week when some criticisms were made of the Brighton Police and I was able to speak in their defence.

14

Ecumenical Activities and the Chichester Twinnings

In 1982 I was asked to join a consultation on episcopacy organized by the Lutheran World Fellowship. It took place over five days at the end of November. In addition to myself, I remember it included Paul-Werner Scheele, who was the Roman Catholic Bishop of Würzburg, the Bishop of Oslo and a number of other Lutherans. To my surprise, the Greek Orthodox representative was Emil Timiades whose research degree I had supervised at Oxford in 1949. He had worked on the sacrament of penance in the Orthodox and Anglican traditions. He was now a bishop in Belgium. The Lutherans differed greatly among themselves and came from a variety of different countries and world situations. In one African area, for example, the bishops were appointed for a period of five years and most had little idea of apostolic succession or continuity. Scheele, Timiades and I found very little in common with them and I had to give rather a depressing report to FOAG on my return. The experience was not untypical of other discussions in which I was involved with Protestant bodies. One finds individuals or groups who seem to have a definite Catholic view of the ministry but who share their life with others of a totally different outlook. This makes real difficulty in ecumenical discussion and the acceptance of unity proposals but nevertheless, it is important to persist in discussion and understanding.

With this in mind, I was invited in 1985 to join the group set up by Archbishop Runcie to meet with representatives of the German Protestant Churches and discuss the possibilities of a closer relationship. This process resulted in a common statement in 1988, the Meissen Agreement, which charted the way our Churches could move forward together and established the basis for exchange of ministries. Our first full meeting was in England at London Colney, just outside St Albans. Our second meeting was in what was then the Democratic Republic of Germany in Meissen itself. We had to fly to the Western airport of

Berlin and take the underground through to East Berlin where we were met and driven to our meeting place. The division of Germany into East and West was still very much a reality and we heard much from the East German members of our commission about the difficulties that they were having with their government and the restrictions placed on them. I stayed on in East Germany for a few days after the meeting and preached at the local Lutheran church, which was not well attended. Some members of the local congregation offered to take me by car to Dresden which, as a successor to Bishop Bell, I was interested to see. I was impressed then by the state of restoration that had been reached. Since then much more has been done, with a great deal of help from England, and I have been interested to read glowing reports of the rebuilding of the Frauenkirche and its relations with Coventry. It was on that journey that I experienced the restricted stock available in the shops and found there were only certain garages where my host was allowed to buy petrol.

Through the Meissen connection, my wife and I were invited to Berlin in 1987 to be part of the group of ecumenical guests participating in the Christian celebration of the 750th anniversary of the city's foundation. The city was still divided by the wall and we were accommodated in a comfortable hotel in the West. On the first evening we were entertained by the senior British military officer stationed there. The principal act of worship was in the Kaiser Wilhelm Memorial Church in the heart of Berlin and was genuinely ecumenical, being attended by the Roman Catholic bishop, Joachim Meissner, who was subsequently translated to Cologne and made a cardinal. We spent a day in one of the East German parishes, reaching it through the closely guarded frontier post. The church was encircled with high blocks of flats, giving the appearance of it being shut in. As on the occasion of my previous visit in connection with the Meissen negotiations, we heard much about the secular pressures on the Church and its difficulties. The day concluded with a fine orchestral concert, after which we walked back and had a vivid experience of the division as we passed from the dark and empty streets of the East into the light and liveliness of the West. We ended our time in Berlin by attending another splendid concert given by the Berlin Philharmonic Orchestra. By the time of our next visit the wall had come down and it was moving to be able to walk through freely where before we had been barred.

Links between Germany and the cathedral and diocese had been forged long before through the work of Bishop Bell. The Chapter and I were keen to build on this foundation with personal contacts and some formal twinning. Dean Robert Holtby had come to know a German weaver and designer called Ursula Benker-Shirmer when she was weaving some tapestries for Henry Moore at West Dean College. She came from an East German family but had managed to get into a West German university and had then studied tapestry in France in the Aubusson school. In 1981, the Chapter commissioned her to design a tapestry to hang on the reverse of the screen which carried the Piper tapestry, so as to form a backdrop for the shrine of St Richard. My wife, who had taught German, was called to the Deanery to interpret and we both became involved in the discussion about the new tapestry. It so happened that we were taking our son, Edward, to Germany that summer in connection with a school project. Ursula invited us to call on her at her home in Marktredwitz, where her husband had a large textile factory. We visited the tomb of St Boniface at Fulda and then telephoned the Benkers who invited us to go for the weekend. We enjoyed their hospitality very much and had useful discussions about the projected tapestry.

I had not realized that it was not far from Marktredwitz to Bayreuth, and, to my delight, when the Benkers gathered that I was interested in Wagner they suggested driving over there on Sunday afternoon. There was a performance in the Festspielhaus which we were sure we would not be able to see but as we walked outside, Ursula saw a friend emerging from the stage door. As a result of this chance encounter we were invited to see the first two acts of *Die Meistersinger* from a lighting tower at one side of the stage, and during the interval were given a tour of the orchestra pit and the backstage area, where we met Graham Clark who was singing David. The Benkers invited us to go back again the following year to see the same opera from a regular seat, which Pat and I did.

In addition to helping with Edward's school project, I had also arranged to visit Speyer and meet with the Lutherans there. We were trying to establish a twinning in Germany to balance our twinning with Chartres and as Chartres was twinned with Speyer, it seemed the obvious line to pursue. We had some difficulty in making contact, but it was eventually arranged that we would stay at Mannheim and drive to Speyer on the Monday morning. We arrived at the Church offices at 11am and were received by a secretary who took us to meet Bishop

Kron. We drank coffee and the bishop asked the secretary to tell us their views on the twinning project. He began by saying that during the war, two of their pastors had been prisoners of war in England and had found themselves very much happier with the United Reformed Church, probably at that time the Congregationalists, than with the Church of England, and they would not wish that any connection with us should damage their relationship with that body. Furthermore, they felt their area was really too large for us and it would be better to come to some arrangement with the city itself. The pastor responsible had just retired, his successor would not be known until October and they did not know what his attitude would be. With regret, they felt we must wait until later and they would be in touch with us. All this did not seem very hopeful and, in fact, we heard nothing more from them. The Catholic Bishop of Speyer, whom I knew from Chartres, was away but he had arranged for one of the canons to show us the cathedral. He was a delightful elderly man who made much of Speyer's ecumenical credentials and pointed out things in the cathedral which illustrated his point, including a chapel dedicated to the Pope who had resisted St Cyprian's rigid outlook. He broke off the visit rather suddenly when he looked at his watch and said that his housekeeper would have his lunch ready for him.

Having clearly failed with Speyer, we thought that we had better see what could be done with our new connection with Marktredwitz. It was in the Lutheran Synod of Bayreuth, there was a theological college, and, as we wanted also to explore a Catholic link, it was part of the archdiocese of Bamberg. This seemed promising and after some telephone calls, Robert Holtby and I visited Bamberg and were welcomed and given lunch by Wolfgang Klausschnitzer, who was the ecumenical officer and on the staff of the Catholic seminary. We were able to establish a close relationship between our own theological college, the Protestant seminary at Bayreuth and the Catholic seminary at Bamberg. I am glad that in spite of the closure of our college the relationships continue between the junior clergy. My own personal links with Bamberg have developed over the years, and I have attended the enthronement of three successive archbishops. Wolfgang is now a professor at the university and a residentiary canon of the cathedral. When in revision of our statutes we introduced 'canons of honour' to enable us to have canons of other Churches, I was glad to be able to appoint him as one of the first two. The first archbishop I met was a little hesitant initially but when he found that I was opposed to the ordination of women to the priesthood, he became far more friendly and his successors have been very welcoming. I was greatly taken by the cathedral in Bamberg with its choirs and altars at both ends. It is notable for containing the tomb of Pope Clement II, the only papal tomb north of the Alps. It has also the tombs of the canonized Emperor Henry II and his equally saintly wife, Cunegunda. I put their feast day in the Chichester diocesan calendar. Our relations with Bayreuth were chiefly with the church at Marktredwitz, but there have been contacts with our cathedral and my successor has been there to preach. The tapestry was eventually woven partly at West Dean and partly at Marktredwitz, and the German churches contributed to its cost. It is a symbol of reconciliation of which George Bell would certainly have approved.

Chichester's relationship with Chartres predates my arrival as bishop but the links had developed more on the civic level than the ecclesiastical. After the good experience of the Worcester–Orléans twinning, I was keen for the Chichester–Chartres link to have a solid base in ecclesiastical friendship. I told Roger Greenacre, then Anglican chaplain at St George's, Paris, of the civic twinning when I visited him in the summer of 1974 and he suggested that we get in touch with the Bishop of Chartres, Mgr Michon, and invite him to attend my enthronement. To my delight he asked if he could also come to my consecration, which he did, accompanied by Père François Legaux, as I have already mentioned. During the next few years there were several exchanges of visits and pilgrimages and I came to know the bishop and also some of his principal assistants very well. We soon came to know of the problems the French Church was facing owing to the shortage of clergy. On one memorable visit, again with Roger Greenacre, we telephoned Chartres to see if we could call on the Bishop. Mgr Michon was very happy to see us but deeply regretted the only day he had free was Friday and, as it was Friday in Lent, he would not be able to entertain us in Chartres as he would wish. However, after a moment's reflection he said, 'Let us go and have lunch with my ecumenical officer at Viabon.' This was the same Père Legaux who had been with him to my consecration. So we assembled at the Presbytère in Viabon. What a wise and hospitable bishop! Père Legaux turned out to be the grandson of a famous French chef and had four secret recipes passed down to him, and a cellar of 900 bottles. We sat down to a memorable lunch at

1.45pm and got up at 4pm, but not a morsel of meat had passed our lips and we had observed the Lenten rule.

I was in France again in October 1976, accompanied by Roger Greenacre, whom by then I had invited to become Canon Chancellor of Chichester Cathedral. In Paris we were entertained by Père Berar, the Curé of Notre Dame and his assistant Père Gres-Gayer. We stayed in his apartment high among the roofs of the great cathedral and were able to say Mass the following day. From there we went on to the Abbey of Notre Dame du Bec, at Le Bec-Hellouin in Normandy, where I was to preach on the Sunday morning. Because of its historic links with Canterbury – three archbishops came from there in the eleventh and twelfth centuries – Bec is a great centre for ecumenical relations between French Roman Catholics and the Church of England. When we arrived, we were told that the Bishop of Evreux, in whose diocese the monastery is situated, would be coming to preside. He arrived early so we were able to have some general conversation with him before Mass. I knew he had written two studies of John Henry Newman so I asked him about his research visits to Oxford. 'I worked in the Library at Pusey House,' he replied, 'where I was very kindly received by a Father Kemp.' This was an unexpected compliment and I was able to explain that I was the very same Kemp.

The primary purpose of this journey was to meet with some members of the Groupe des Dombes, a mixed Catholic-Protestant group that had published some important ecumenical studies. I was particularly anxious to hear more of their discussions about the reconciling of ministries as I believed their conclusions would be helpful to some current FOAG work. We went on to visit the Bishop of Autun, Mgr Le Bourgeois, who was, I think, the only French bishop still able to live in the ancient Evêché of his see city. It was moving to be able to stay in a house on the site of the one in which St Augustine had stayed on his journey to England in 597. From Autun we visited Taizé, where we met Brother Roger Schutz, and also Paray le Monial. We returned via Chartres, and we were in time to take part in the celebrations surrounding the restoration of the crypt of the cathedral.

When Mgr Michon died, I was, unfortunately, not able to go to the funeral, but Roger Greenacre represented me and told me of the curious custom at the end of the service – the coffin was taken up to the high altar and bumped three times against it as a sign of farewell. He was followed by Mgr Kuehn, with whom my wife and I both stayed in Chartres. On one occasion Mgr Kuehn took us to Dreux to visit the mausoleum of the Orléans royal family. While we were there a middle-aged lady and her son entered and we were introduced to the Comtesse de Paris and the Dauphin who had presumably come to look at the tombs amongst which they will be buried. It is a curious place, and has, among many others, the tomb of a nineteenth-century prince who had married a German Protestant. She was not allowed to be buried in the church but in a small chapel added to the side. In effigy she lay with her right hand stretched out through an opening in the dividing wall to touch her husband's left hand.

Bishop Kuehn retired to his family home in Lorraine and was succeeded by Mgr Perrier, who was a protégé of Cardinal Lustiger in Paris. He did not stay long but was translated to the diocese of Tarbes and Lourdes. There was then a long interregnum during which our great friend François Legaux, now Rector of the cathedral, was in charge of the diocese. One of our regular exchange pilgrimages occurred during the vacancy and we took our cathedral choir and sang Evensong. I did not know it but François had asked Mgr Perrier before he left to agree to my being made a *chanoine d'honneur*, so it was a real surprise when after the Magnificat he beckoned me forward to join him and read out the protocol declaring me a canon of Chartres and then led me to a stall. It was a great joy as well as an honour. When Chichester revised its cathedral statutes a few years later, it was a pleasure to be able to return the compliment by making François a 'canon of honour'. Such is the state of ecumenical relations, it was possible for François to use *our* cathedral to install Cormac Murphy-O'Connor as a canon of Chartres.

François has a house in Cloyes-sur-le Loir which on one occasion he lent to us for a holiday. Pat and I, with our daughter Harriet, her husband and their daughter Bea all stayed there. On the first evening we were sitting in the cool of the garden after supper when we were nearly drenched by the sudden start of an automatic watering system. François had forgotten to tell us about it. He had moved his legendary cellar there and when we stayed we had to keep a strict record of which bottles we used. He was disappointed that we did not drink more! We were there during August and François was anxious that I should formally attend the Mass in the cathedral on the feast of the Assumption, it being their feast of title. As he was in charge of the diocese, he was able to use the Evêché for a lunch afterwards for the members of the Chapter, to which we were invited. Bea was then quite small and became a great favourite with the canons. I can still see her sitting on the knees of one after another.

François was a great Rector of the cathedral of Chartres and oversaw the commissioning of many great works of art as part of its re-ordering for modern worship. Chichester presented a woven silk chasuble with blue orphreys which is used on feasts of our Lady. I think he also enjoyed his time in charge of the diocese. I hope he is enjoying his retirement at Cloyes. Mgr Perrier was eventually succeeded by the Cistercian Abbot of Lérins, Mgr Bernard Aubertin. I was able to attend his enthronement which was a great occasion with an enormous number of monks gathered together. The representatives of his monastery handed him over to the diocese. The cathedral was crowded, and after his installation he went all round it being warmly greeted. It was clear that this was a popular appointment. He speaks good English and has preached in Chichester both in the Roman Catholic church and in the cathedral. I took him on pilgrimage to Walsingham which he much enjoyed. As I write, he has just been made Archbishop of Tours and Chartres again awaits a bishop. The relationship continues happily.

When Donald Coggan became Archbishop of Canterbury in late 1974, he initiated some discussion about the Archbishop's relations on a personal level with other Churches. He wanted a means by which he could have direct contact independent of the official negotiations of the General Synod's Board for Mission and Unity. The scheme the House of Bishops eventually came up with was for nominated bishops to act on his behalf in relations with specific Churches. Ronald Williams, Bishop of Leicester, was to deal with the Protestant Churches, Bob Runcie of St Albans and Graham Leonard of Truro with the Orthodox and Oriental Churches and I was to relate to the Old Catholics and the Roman Catholics in Europe.

In this capacity, and as the newly appointed President of the Church Union, I became involved in the celebrations of the 50th anniversary of the Malines Conversations. Lord Halifax, the primary Anglican participant in the original Conversations between 1921 and 1925, had also been President of the Church Union so it was appropriate that I represented him. I travelled to Belgium with Bishop John Robinson, who was representing his uncle, Dean Armitage Robinson, another of the original participants. At Malines we were joined by the Archbishop of York, Stuart Blanch, some members of the Halifax family, and

Christopher Hill from Lambeth who was organizing the visit. On arrival, we took tea with Canon Dessain, whose uncle had been Cardinal Mercier's chaplain and a participant in the conversations. There was to be a Mass in the cathedral the following morning and Christopher was rather agitated about whether we were expected to receive Communion. Canon Dessain assured us we were expected to receive but Christopher was anxious not to embarrass Bishop Casey who was representing the English Roman hierarchy. Dessain replied with some asperity, 'Bishop Casey is now in the diocese of Malines.' We agreed to consult the Cardinal who said that left to himself he would be happy for us to receive Holy Communion, but as he would be going to York Minster later in the year and would not be able to receive at the Archbishop's Eucharist it would be embarrassing if Dr Blanch were to have communicated at Malines. As a result, those of us Anglican clergy who robed for the Mass did not communicate but all the Anglican laity did. The Cardinal stood in front of Mercier's tomb with a French bishop on his left and Bishop Casey on his right. The first person to come up was Mrs Blanch who, having received the host from the Cardinal, turned to her left and received the chalice from Bishop Casey.

I have described my relations with the Old Catholic Church in an earlier chapter but I would mention that my trips abroad to visit their bishops often furnished me with the opportunity to talk with members of the Roman hierarchy in the same countries. In 1967, on one such visit to the Netherlands I had tea with the Roman Catholic Bishop of Haarlem, Theodore Zwartkruis, who was very liberal and friendly. He told me he had recently had difficulty with one of his priests who had celebrated a joint Eucharist with a Dutch Reformed minister. The Bishop confided to me, 'Nowadays you can't just say, "You mustn't do that" so I had him to tea and we have sorted it out.' In Amsterdam I went to a weekday evening Mass in the Jesuit chaplaincy. The service was in a lecture room and was conducted by a priest in lay dress. I had some difficulty in following the rite as it bore no relation to what I was expecting, save for the gospel passage appointed for the day. Later I asked the chaplain about this and he boasted that he composed a rite for each celebration. I put it to him that this might be confusing for students, especially when they encountered the normative rite when they got back home. He countered that by the end of their course they would be sufficiently educated in the faith to be able to adapt. Another church with a staff of five priests told me they had dropped the daily

Mass as they felt no need for it. This was typical of the liberal state of things in the Dutch Roman Catholic Church under Cardinal Alfrink, and was soon to be altered by Rome with the appointment of a series of bishops of more conservative outlook.

On the more local level, I was launched into a good relationship with the Roman Catholic community in Sussex through a series of events. The Queen's Silver Jubilee was in 1977 and to celebrate it in Sussex the two Lord Lieutenants wanted to have one service of thanksgiving for the whole county. The problem immediately arose as to where to hold such a service as the cathedral is at the end of West Sussex and not very big. After much discussion it was agreed to use the new abbey church at Worth, which could hold a large number of people, was fairly central and had plenty of parking space. The diocese of Arundel and Brighton was vacant at the time, Michael Bowen having been translated to Southwark as Archbishop, so the Roman Catholic contingent was led by Mgr Iggleden, the Vicar General. I had just begun the work for Donald Coggan with the Roman Catholic Church on the continent and had arranged to go to Rome in December, so I took the opportunity to ask Mgr Iggleden for advice as to where I should stay. He suggested the English College and this was duly settled. Before I set out for Rome, the rector of the English College, Cormac Murphy-O'Connor, was nominated as Bishop of Arundel and Brighton. I arrived in Rome in the middle of his official farewell reception but as he did not leave until two days later, we were able to have a certain amount of time together. Three weeks later I was at his episcopal ordination in Arundel Cathedral. We have been good friends ever since and were able to do much together while we were both bishops in Sussex. He left to become Archbishop of Westminster about the time of my retirement.

On the occasion of that 1977 visit to Rome I also saw Cardinal Eduardo Pironio and Archbishop Jerome Hamer, later a cardinal, whom I came to know well and met on several later visits until his retirement. He was always grateful that we talked in French as he seemed to have few opportunities of speaking his native language. Over the course of the years and while holding a variety of responsibilities in relation to Rome, I met most of those cardinals who headed the main dicasteries. Cardinal Arinze had only just been made a cardinal when I visited him, and as he came to meet me he said, 'I am Archbishop Arinze. Oh no, I keep forgetting, I am now *Cardinal* Arinze.' I had two private meetings with Cardinal Ratzinger, whom I liked very much. In one of our conversations I thought it incumbent on me to try to explain Bob Runcie's views on the ordination of women to the priesthood and I said that, as a priest should be representative of Christ, and Christ was representative of the whole human race, so a priest could be either male or female. I was slightly surprised that this was an argument he had not heard before. He found it very interesting and undertook to ponder it. I found him very open in discussion, and I was grateful when he sent me a book of essays he had written at various times on liturgy and church music. In return, I sent him a recording made by Chichester Cathedral choir of Lennox Berkeley's church music. He thanked me for it and said he had listened to it with pleasure but thought it lacked joy.

I had one long meeting with John Paul II in December 1978, towards the end of his first year. Not long before he had met with Archbishop Runcie in Africa who now asked me to take a message to Rome concerning the future of the Anglican Roman Catholic International Commission (ARCIC), which had just completed the first part of what it had been asked to do. I was to stress the importance of carrying on the discussions and not allowing a gap to develop. From my own experience I was able to reinforce this by quoting the problems that had arisen in the Anglican–Methodist Conversations when there was a two-year gap after the report was published and no provision was made for the two sides to keep in touch during that time.

I was accompanied by a delightful Roman priest, Canon William Purdy, the doyen of ecumenical relations between Anglican and Roman Catholics, and I had about a 40-minute conversation in English, which the Pope spoke well. He seemed to know a good deal about past relations, the history of our dialogues and especially about the Malines Conversations of 1921–5. He seemed to be keen that ARCIC should continue. Canon Purdy noted the Pope said three times, 'My heart is in the Anglican–Roman Catholic Discussions.' He gave me the impression of one who had come out of a Communist country into the West, and did not much like the materialism he found there. I happened to mention the Polish Uniate churches and he said rather sharply that they were martyr churches. He was very friendly and when he gave me his blessing at the end, he presented me with a substantial book on the history of the Vatican. I saw him again when Bishop Murphy-O'Connor invited me to join him in welcoming the Pope to England at Gatwick airport and I attended the magnificent service in

214 SHY BUT NOT RETIRING

Canterbury Cathedral where the Pope and archbishop prayed together for unity between our two Churches. Since then I have seen him two or three times at public receptions, one of them when my wife, her sister and brother-in-law and I were visiting Rome. His last years were a sad story of physical decline and his death was a great loss to the Church but I welcome the election of Cardinal Ratzinger as his successor, Benedict XVI.

The Anglican Communion maintains an Anglican Centre in Rome, set up by Bishop John Moorman with the blessing of Michael Ramsey and Pope Paul VI in 1966 in the heady days of post-Vatican II ecumenical dialogue. The Centre is housed in part of the largest private palazzo in Rome, that of the Doria Pamphilj family, and maintains a good library, study centre and chapel, as well as the offices and home of the Archbishop of Canterbury's official representative at the Vatican. Harry Smythe was director of the Anglican Centre when I first went to the city and he saw to it that my visits to Rome were very enjoyable. He was succeeded by Howard Root who, with his wife, did much to develop the Centre and its influence, particularly in its relations with the Vatican. The Anglican Consultative Council, however, did not seem to understand the importance of the Centre or share its vision, and so it was starved of finance. At the end of Howard's time, the council was beginning to withdraw its financial support and a crisis loomed. Bob Runcie set up a group to consider the problem under the chairmanship of the Primus of Scotland, Ted Luscombe, and of which I was a member. We thought we had found a partial solution in a new and simpler constitution and by appointing as Howard's successor a member of a religious community who would not need so large a stipend. This was all accepted for the next five years. Unfortunately, Douglas Brown SSM, who took charge of the centre, did not keep up the close relations with the Vatican that had been such an important part of the director's work and Brown's successor, Bruce Ruddock, had to build them up again, which he did very well. A group of Friends was formed which has done much in raising financial support from around the Communion. I was chairman of it for a number of years. We set up a new governing body with a more official relationship with the Anglican Communion and under the chairmanship of the Bishop of Wakefield, Stephen Platten, the future now looks more hopeful than for some considerable time.

The continuity of the ARCIC discussions and their results, not least the recent document on the Marian doctrines, show that, with persistence, something can be achieved in dialogue with Rome. Gradually, significant differences can be isolated and sometimes shown to be based on misunderstanding. It remains to be seen, however, whether the papal claim to universal, immediate jurisdiction over the whole Church can in any way be reconciled with the kind of independence claimed by the Orthodox and Anglicans, let alone the Lutherans and other Protestants. But if God wills, he will bring us together.

One of the most ground-breaking things Cormac and I did together came in 1981 when both dioceses were celebrating the 1,300th anniversary of the conversion of Sussex to Christianity by St Wilfrid. We agreed to have a joint pilgrimage to Walsingham. There were some initial difficulties in making the arrangements but it was agreed that we would all assemble at the Roman Catholic shrine the Slipper Chapel for a penitential service, followed by a sandwich lunch and press conference, and then set out on the mile walk to the village doing the Stations of the Cross on the way. On arrival at the village, we were to simultaneously celebrate our Eucharists outdoors on the site of the medieval shrine and, to end the afternoon, to have a joint service at the Anglican shrine before leaving for home. All started well – the initial service, lunch and press conference all happened, and then we set out on the devotional walk. We had only done three of the Stations of the Cross when it began to rain and by the fifth it was pouring so hard that the priest-administrators of the two shrines came along with a car and took Cormac and myself into the village where we all dried and changed. The abbey grounds were now waterlogged so we agreed to use the recently restored Anglican parish church for the Mass. With some difficulty, we all managed to crowd in. We celebrated the first part of the Eucharist together and then Cormac and I separated into the north and south chapels for the Eucharistic Prayer and the administration of Holy Communion before returning together for the post-Communion prayers and blessing. By then the rain had stopped and we were able to have tea and the final service in the grounds of the Anglican shrine as planned. People said that Our Lady had sent the rain to drive us together.

My relationships with the Free Church leaders in Sussex was less close, not least because they changed so frequently and there was less opportunity really to get to know them. We met regularly as the Sussex Church Leaders and did things together. At one such meeting

Cormac suggested that instead of writing letters to the local churches reporting on our Leaders' meetings, we should go to them ourselves, as a 'living letter'. This we did over the next few years, visiting all the main church centres in Sussex. This was especially valuable as it became clear how many people were surprised to see us together and realize that we talked to each other. We began to understand how much there is still to do ecumenically at the local level. My previous involvement in the Anglican–Methodist Conversations was a useful basis for local contact. Numerically speaking, the Free Churches are far less strong in Sussex than Roman Catholics. I remember when I was appointed, I looked at a recently issued report on Church membership and was surprised to see that in Sussex there were more United Reformed Church ministers than Methodists. I have always assumed that this was because the independent chapels which became Congregationalist, and then in our day the United Reformed Church, were so numerous in the sixteenth and seventeenth centuries. The Protestant martyrs commemorated at Lewes were all from such communities, mostly in the Ashdown Forest. Local amalgamation between Methodists and the United Reformed Church continues, and the number of chapels still functioning reduces.

The example of George Bell as an ecumenist is hard to live up to but successive Bishops of Chichester and their Deans and Chapters have endeavoured to maintain old links and develop new ones at home and abroad. Early in my time as Bishop, Robert Holtby had some rooms off the cloister of the cathedral fitted up as a restaurant and reception centre. He had the excellent idea of inviting Pastor Martin Niemoller to declare them open and name them the Bell Rooms. The occasion was a moving one. Niemoller spoke good English and obviously had a great respect for Bell's memory. I hope that memory will continue to inspire Chichester's ecumenical work.

15

Three Tractarian Institutions

St Stephen's House

I had enjoyed my time at St Stephen's House and during my subsequent years at Oxford kept closely in contact with its life. Arthur Couratin eventually arranged for me to join the governing body. This was then a small group of six or seven people with the Principal as chairman and there was little for us to do but endorse what Arthur proposed. However, in 1961 the time came when he told me that he felt he ought to move. My friendship with Maurice Harland, now Bishop of Durham, enabled me to suggest Arthur for a vacant canonry there and he was appointed and installed the following year. It was, for him, a very good move as there were old friends from Oxford already there. John Wild, the Dean, had been Master of University College, and Hugh Turner, formerly Chaplain of Lincoln, was also a canon. They welcomed Arthur and were grateful for his ideas about brightening up the cathedral liturgy. The problem of a successor at the House was a difficult one and we, rather weakly, thought we had solved it by appointing the Vice-Principal, Derek Allen. His first years in the new role were happy and the house flourished. Despite this, the future of theological colleges and ministerial formation generally was coming under discussion, and Derek decided that it would be better if the Principal were not chairman of the governors; someone more independent should deal with the Advisory Council for the Church's Ministry. With his resignation I became chairman.

By the time I moved to Worcester in 1969, there were beginning to be complaints and gossip about the house. Vice-Principal John Halliburton came to see me and as a result, I felt I had to go to Oxford to talk with Derek. The trouble was, as Arthur Couratin had warned us when we appointed him, Derek was not a strong enough leader and had admitted some rather doubtful men into the house whom he could not control. Visitors complained that too much alcohol was being consumed, students were calling each other by girls' names and there was a general atmosphere of high camp and theatricality unsuited to a seminary. Derek promised to speak strongly to the student body about this and make sure that there was a change, but nothing happened and complaints continued to reach me. Then, during a meeting of the General Synod, Michael Ramsey took me aside to express his concern that if Derek Allen remained Principal, there was a real possibility that the bishops might withdraw recognition of the house as a place for the training of ordinands. At that point it was clear I had to go and see Derek and ask him to resign. To my relief, he was quite prepared to do so. Since 1966 he had been Warden of the Community of St Mary the Virgin at Wantage, where his great skills as a spiritual director and confessor were highly valued by the nuns and in the absence of any other job he took up residence there. Later, when I had become Bishop of Chichester, I was able to persuade Keble College as patrons to present him to the living of St Saviour's, Eastbourne, where he did excellent work as a parish priest and was very useful to the diocese in preparing in-service training courses for the clergy. He died in 1991, aged only 66.

Charles Smith, Vicar of St Mary Magdalen's, Oxford, agreed to take charge of St Stephen's House while we looked for a new principal, which was, again, not easy. The name of David Hope, Vicar of St Andrew's, Orford, a parish in Liverpool diocese, was suggested. He had trained at the house in the early 1960s and written a doctoral thesis on a liturgical subject under Leslie Cross but I did not know him. The responses to some enquiries I made and the opinion of one or two members of the governing body persuaded me that he was the right person for the job, and in 1974 he took up the position. Within a year he had disposed of the troublemakers and the house recovered its good name. When the Cowley Fathers (the Society of St John the Evangelist), rapidly reduced in number, decided that they must give up their premises attached to St John's Church and offered the buildings to the house with an endowment, David was keen on accepting and the governors all agreed. In 1980 he masterminded the move from Norham Gardens to Marston Street excellently and a new era in the life of the house began. It was to my regret when, two years later, he accepted Graham Leonard's invitation to go to All Saints, Margaret Street. His subsequent ministry as a bishop, first of Wakefield, then of London, his translation to York as archbishop and his early retirement to become once again a parish priest is well known. St Stephen's House will always be grateful to him.

After David's move to Margaret Street we appointed a former Vice-Principal, David Thomas, who left to take up a parochial appointment in Wales. In 1996 he became one of the corps of 'flying bishops' as provincial episcopal visitor in Wales. David was succeeded by Edwin Barnes – who also became a 'flying bishop', leaving the house to become Bishop of Richborough. Jeremy Sheehy then became Principal and, at the time of writing, still is. He has done a very good job during a rather difficult time, particularly in bringing together the training of men and women for ministerial priesthood. I resigned as chairman of the governors shortly after moving to Chichester, where I found myself ex-officio chairman of the governing body of the theological college there. With so much talk of closures in the air I foresaw possible clashes of interest looming in the House of Bishops. I remained a governor of St Stephen's House until my retirement.

Pusey House

Since 1956, when I became president of the governors of Pusey House, I had been concerned about its future. With Fr Hugh Maycock as Principal things rather stagnated: the House was not much frequented and made little impression on the spiritual life of the university except in the area of individual spiritual direction in which Hugh excelled. When he retired in 1971 Cheslyn Jones, who had resigned as Principal of the theological college in Chichester, was living in Oxford and wrote to me asking if I could try and get him appointed. Some of my fellow governors were initially doubtful but eventually all agreed. At the outset things seemed to improve, but Cheslyn soon made himself very unpopular with the board of the Faculty of Theology by leading the opposition to the changes they were trying to make in the syllabus. I knew that in his day Freddy Hood had privately underwritten much of the activity of the house from his own resources but subsequently the finances had become an increasing worry. The governors began to look round for some other academic institution which could take over part of the buildings and for a while Blackfriars, next door on St Giles, seemed interested but this came to nothing. More and more concerned about the cost of upkeep of the buildings, Cheslyn began discussions with the Master of St Cross College about the possibility of sharing the premises to the mutual advantage of both institutions. The governors as a whole were very keen on this and it was argued that such a link would strengthen the House's standing with the university. We gave Cheslyn the responsibility of working out suitable terms of agreement in consultation with our solicitors. During the negotiations, however, the partner in the firm of solicitors representing the House, and who was initially of great assistance, retired and his successor proved not to be of the same calibre and certainly not equal to dealing with the high-powered solicitor representing the university. None of us realized this at the time, nor did we realize that Cheslyn himself was showing signs of the mental instability which later led to his death. He told the governors that a happy arrangement had been reached which safeguarded the continued use of the chapel, some adjoining rooms and access to the library. At some unspecified time in the future the library building would also pass to St Cross and a new building would be provided by them as a replacement. Substantial funds from America and the Middle East were confidently expected to finance the new buildings. Our solicitor advised us that this was all satisfactory and so we signed the agreement with St Cross without realizing how little of it was legally binding, and how much we were dependent on a so-called 'gentlemen's agreement'.

Cheslyn himself agreed to move out of his rooms into a house in St John Street. No sooner had the agreement been signed than Cheslyn found it was impossible for him to have a telephone link between his new house and the rooms adjoining the chapel, and so refused to move out. This situation lasted for several weeks and resulted in the governors having to pay St Cross rent for the rooms that Cheslyn refused to vacate. Eventually he did move but it rapidly became clear that things were not going to work out as he had said. Good relations between Cheslyn and St Cross no longer existed and he had lost his grip on the situation. It was obvious to me and to the governors that he would have to leave and I, as President, would have to deliver the blow. Thus Cheslyn Jones became the third friend, following on Derek Allen and John Halliburton, for whose resignation I had to ask. The Bishop of Peterborough, Douglas Feaver, was able to offer him a parish and he moved but over the next few years his mental health deteriorated and eventually he died. Thus came to a very sad end the distinguished career of a great eccentric.

We appointed an Australian priest as Cheslyn's successor at Pusey House who would, I think, have been very good, but sadly he fell while changing a light bulb in the chapel shortly after taking up the job and died of the injuries he sustained. We then appointed Fr Philip Ursell, from Emmanuel College, Cambridge, who had to cope with the increasingly difficult situation with St Cross which has only now, under Ursell's successor, Fr Jonathan Baker, begun to be resolved. I ceased some time ago to be a governor. Needless to say, the new funds prophesied for St Cross have not materialized but the relationship between the two bodies now looks promising.

Perhaps Cheslyn's best years were the 14 he spent as principal of Chichester Theological College. He succeeded John Moorman in 1956 and, like John, combined the post with a residentiary canonry in the cathedral. In this capacity he witnessed the installation of many of the contemporary works of art commissioned by Walter Hussey for the cathedral. Famously, he had subtitled Graham Sutherland's version of the encounter between the risen Christ and Mary Magdalen 'Come up and see me some time' and, more notoriously, when the bright John Piper tapestry behind the high altar was publicly unveiled he had slowly and deliberately taken out and put on a pair of sunglasses. Oxford stories also abounded. Never a snappy dresser, he was most frequently seen outdoors wearing a shabby black raincoat and a beret. On one occasion, thus attired and carrying two old plastic shopping bags he encountered Fr Wayne Hankey, one of his colleagues, outside Pusey House. Fr Hankey was wearing a cassock and ankle-length black coat, with a soup-plate hat and carrying a silver-topped cane. 'Aha!' said Cheslyn, 'trying to become an Oxford character, I see.' The two collections he helped edit, *The Study of Liturgy* and *The Study of Spirituality*, have found permanent places on the reading lists of all Anglican ordinands but in his last years in Oxford the effect of any teaching he did was rather negated by his frequent habit of falling fast asleep mid-sentence.

Bishop Otter College

Just as in the 1970s, when theological colleges were under a certain pressure to amalgamate, so it was with Church colleges of education. Chichester had one such teacher-training establishment, Bishop Otter College, which had been founded in memory of William Otter, Bishop of Chichester 1840–2, the same bishop as had founded the theological college. It originally trained only women teachers, but from 1957 admitted male students also. It had had a very distinguished Principal, Dr Betty Murray, who had retired by the time I became Bishop. Shortly after the war, when there was pressure for the provision of new colleges and universities, the West Sussex County Council had established an 'emergency' college of education at nearby Bognor Regis. When this policy was being reversed, as all such policies inevitably are within one's lifetime, it was proposed that Bognor and Chichester be combined. The governing body of Bishop Otter, being unwilling to lose a Church college, had refused to cooperate with this scheme. This was the situation when I arrived and found myself *ex-officio* chairman of the governors, so it was not a surprise when one of my first visitors was the Principal of Bishop Otter, Gordon McGregor, who wanted to fill me in about what had been taking place.

I had been in post for little more than two months when I had to lead a delegation of the governors of Bishop Otter to meet with a similar group from Bognor at the Department of Education and Science. We were received by a senior civil servant who, having listened to us, made it quite clear that unless we agreed to amalgamate he would close both institutions. In the New Year I went to see the chairman of the County Education Committee to discuss the problem, and we decided to set up a working party with Lord Wolfenden as chairman to see what could be done. This took some time and we were not helped either by the Department or by the General Synod Board of Education, both of which refused to agree to the precedents we wanted to use. On the Bishop Otter side, we were greatly assisted by our legal adviser, who succeeded in getting into the proposed scheme clauses which secured the Church character of the body which would result from the amalgamation and so enabled it to be recognized by the General Synod as a Church College of Education. The official name given to the final product was the West Sussex College of Education but as the two separate campuses continued in use the name of Bishop Otter was perpetuated.

We elected as the first Director of the new institution John Wyatt, who had been Principal of Culham College, a church college of education in the diocese of Oxford, and so was personally able to preserve our Church connection. He did a very good job in getting the new college off to a good start and arranged for Southampton University to validate its degrees. When John retired, the governors appointed Philip Robinson, who has so developed the whole institution that it has now achieved university status under the name of Chichester University. The Bishop and the three Archdeacons remain as the Bishop Otter trustees and retain the freehold ownership of the Bishop Otter premises and certain other elements of influence in the University College. There is also substantial church membership on the governing body. As there is now a theology department in place of the former rather indeterminate 'Religious Studies' one, I feel very happy at the way things have developed. The new department has grown out of the Bishop Otter Centre for Theology and Ministry which the Bishop Otter trustees were able to finance. With all the uncertainty about ministerial education still prevailing, my hope is that eventually the new university will be allowed to train candidates for the priesthood as it does now for the diaconate. The proposals drawn up by the General Synod commission, chaired by my successor, for ministerial formation throughout the Church of England may well enable this to happen.

As the future of Bishop Otter College unfolded, we were greatly helped by the then Bishops of Winchester, Portsmouth and Guildford who joined with me regularly in a south-eastern bishops' meeting known to my chaplains by the ugly acronym 'ChiGuPoW'. I remember a splendid occasion when there was a large meeting at Winchester about training for the priesthood and a representative from the General Synod Board of Ministry gave us a typical civil servant speech about why we could not take what we all though should be our next step in training. We listened in silence and when he had finished there was a pause and then Colin James, Bishop of Winchester, broke the silence with words from the current television comedy, *Yes, Minister*: 'Well spoken, Sir Humphrey.' And we all burst into laughter.

16

The House of Lords

Episcopal membership of the House of Lords is restricted to the Archbishops of Canterbury and York, the Bishops of London, Winchester and Durham and 21 diocesan bishops by seniority of nomination to a diocesan see. So, as with most new diocesans, I had to wait for a few years until there was a vacancy to be introduced into the House in 1981. As it happened, shortly afterwards Lord Sudeley drew attention to a recent report on cathedrals and tourism and there was a debate. This seemed a suitable occasion for my maiden speech so, with my experience as a dean, I was able to say something both about the increasing numbers of tourists in our cathedrals and also about their importance as centres of mission. I spoke on a number of other occasions when a contribution from a bishop seemed to be desired, usually on matters to do with schools and education where I felt I had experience. My membership of the House of Lords was particularly useful in connection with the Faculty Jurisdiction Commission as providing useful occasions of contact with ministers and also the ability to speak when the relevant legislation was under discussion.

Peter Kirk, Pat's brother, introduced me to Lord Bessborough early in my time at Chichester. He lived nearby at Stanstead and, with Peter, was closely involved in the Council of Europe. When the referendum on Europe was organized in 1975, the MP for Shoreham asked me to join him on the platform at a public meeting, which I was pleased to do. The other speakers were a Labour peer and Lord Hailsham. During the questions which followed our speeches there was a woman in the audience who was very persistent in her opposition and eventually Lord Hailsham became rather angry. The following January, I was at a New Year's Day party at Stanstead and, as usual, Lord Hailsham was staying. For the sake of conversation I remarked that the last time we had met was on this occasion at Shoreham, at which he immediately said, 'When I lost my temper.' In 1983, we organized a Europe service at Stanstead which was attended by Anthony Nelson, the Chichester MP, and other prominent locals, and I preached. We saw a good deal of the Bessboroughs and I took his funeral, as I had previously done his father's. The house at Stanstead is now open to visitors and there is a substantial garden centre but the little theatre much used by Eric Bessborough in his younger days is rather neglected. He was an enthusiastic supporter of the Chichester Festival Theatre which had been founded by a local optician and councillor, Leslie Evershed-Martin, who we also came to know.

It was through Peter Kirk that Pat and I came to know Philip de Zulueta and his wife who lived not far from Chichester. They became good friends. Philip was private secretary to Harold Macmillan when he was Prime Minister and received a knighthood. Sadly, he died in 1986 at an early age and is much missed. He was a Roman Catholic and I attended his Requiem in the Guards Chapel.

Harold Macmillan became a peer as Lord Stockton. I shall never forget his maiden speech on 13 November 1984. He was very old and his sight wasn't good. As a Privy Counsellor he sat on the front row on the Conservative side of the chamber. When the time came for him to speak he just stood up, leaning on his stick, and spoke without a note for half an hour. It was a most amusing as well as interesting and instructive speech which at this date still repays reading in the proceedings of the House. He started with a reference to his time in the Commons and how he began to feel a lack of sympathy with the policies of his party.

'I was regarded with a certain distaste and even dislike by the leaders of my party. It is an awkward situation. However, I was fortunately able to deal with the matter fairly soon by becoming the leader of the party myself. Noble Lords on the front bench need have no fear as I am too old to repeat that.'

He then said that after his 40 years in the House of Commons, he had had 20 years of complete retirement from politics and began to review what had happened during that period, in an amusing and generally critical way. There was one passage I remember clearly which was not fully reported. He was speaking of the problems that resulted from the oil crisis and the different ways of dealing with them. One, he said, was neo-Keynesian, and then he seemed to hesitate. 'There is this new theory. What is it called? Some think it comes from America and some from Tibet. What is its name? Ah, I have it now, "monetarism".' This was a dig at Margaret Thatcher which the House enjoyed. He continued, 'There are two points of view, and it goes right through. Many of your lordships will remember that it operated in the nursery. How do you treat a cold? One nanny said, "Feed a cold" – she was neo-Keynesian. Another nanny said, "Starve a cold" – she was monetarist.' I think it was about this time that he lamented the fact that miners in the north-east, whom he remembered as a splendid body of men, had been forced into strike action.

I remember some time after Macmillan was elected Chancellor of the University of Oxford, he asked to have a meeting with a number of the college chaplains. He wanted to know what we felt about the state of Christianity in the University and how much support we received from our colleges in doing our jobs. This enquiry was typical of his concerns and shaped my admiration for him, although I am not sure if the query was followed up in any way. I sent him a copy of *Counsel and Consent*, as before a Bampton lecturer can be paid he has a duty to send copies of the published lectures to the heads of houses in the University and to the Chancellor. I did not expect to receive more than a formal acknowledgement, which was what happened with the heads of colleges, so it was a great pleasure to receive a long letter from Macmillan commenting on the book. Michael Ramsey told me that Macmillan had spoken to him several times about it and said how important he thought it was. When I was in Chichester, I met him once in the diocese when I preached at Glynde but we had no conversation. There were a number of other distinguished people there for the occasion, an annual sermon arranged by Max Godden, to which he invited prominent laymen. I used a reflection of the attitudes of JB Mozley and Dean Church to the intellectual problems of their times to consider whether that might help us in contemporary ways of thought. I have often said that today we do not fully realize the difficulties that these two churchmen, along with Bishop King, faced and grappled with.

In 1986, I went to preach at Horsted Keynes where Macmillan lived. He was in church and I was told that I should have to take Communion to him in his pew, so I was surprised when he came up to the altar. I was told after his death that he had said, 'The Bishop is here so I must go up to the altar.' He died only a few months later and I was asked to take his funeral. I was told it was to be a family service but when the time came, there was the whole cabinet and numerous other politicians. The vicar had told me that Macmillan had expressed the wish that some words from Newman's 'Dream of Gerontius' should be incorporated in his funeral so I concluded my sermon with the commendation from that poem: 'Go forth upon thy journey, Christian soul'. Two or three weeks later I was on duty for prayers in the House of Lords and as I got up from my knees beside the woolsack, Lord Hailsham said how pleased he was with what I had said at the funeral and how well it described Macmillan. At the buffet lunch after the funeral I heard some of the current Conservative leaders ask Ted Heath when he was going to come and join them in the House of Lords, to which he replied, 'Someone has to stay and keep the Commons in order.'

I had a real admiration for Edward Heath in government and felt very sorry for him when Margaret Thatcher opposed and defeated him in the election for the leadership of the Conservative Party. As a Liberal, I disliked her and all she stood for. She invited my wife and I to a dinner at Downing Street in honour of the Canadian Prime Minister and we did not find her a very gracious hostess. I was glad when she was turned out of the leadership and I believe it will be some time before the Conservative Party recovers from her leadership. I found I liked John Major much better. Having been a supporter of the Conservatives as a young man, then a member of the Socialist Book Club, I am now a firm Liberal, though I would hesitate to call myself a Liberal Democrat.

In that tradition, I made, I think, my most substantial speech in the Lords in 1999 in a debate started by Archbishop George Carey on religions and international order. In this I was able to draw on what I had written on previous occasions about the contribution of the sixteenth-century philosophers Francisco de Vittoria, Francisco Suarez and Hugo Grotius to international law. I also used Herbert Hart's attempt to restate the concept of natural law and I quoted from Sir Henry Maine that the founders of international law created a law-abiding sentiment not by sanctions: 'They did this, not by threatening punishments but by the alternative and older method, long known in Europe and Asia, of creating a strong approval of a certain body of rules.' Archbishop Carey wrote to thank me most warmly for what I had said. He was a frequent attender at the House and much concerned with its proceedings, and my contribution was welcomed by many peers.

The House of Lords has a proper function to play in the constitution, mainly to correct the mistakes of the House of Commons, but also to provide the opportunity for the discussion of important issues by experienced people who are not all there as politicians. I have heard some very valuable speeches by vice-chancellors, field marshals, a variety of business leaders, and people who could speak with experience and knowledge on agriculture and other important aspects of society. Most of these contributions were from people appointed as non-political peers but some were also by hereditary peers. The contributions of those who sit on the cross benches, such as the law lords and retired law lords, were, I thought, exceptionally valuable and I do not see the advantage of excluding judges on the purely theoretical ground of separating the legislature and judiciary. It can be tiresome when one party has too large a membership in the House but I think that an overwhelming majority in the House of Commons can be just as much, if not more, dangerous to democracy and needs to be balanced by the House of Lords. I did not always vote but if I had any doubts, I followed my instincts and voted with the Liberal Democrats. I must say that of all the changes that retirement brings, I miss the House of Lords most, though I am grateful that retired bishops are invited to use the premises and to hear debates from the steps of the throne.

17

Two Further Preoccupations

Religious Communities

In the 1940s I joined the Advisory Council on Religious Communities, a body set up originally to assist with the relationship between diocesan bishops and the communities in their dioceses. It had developed into an advisory body for the constitutions of the communities themselves and having been already assistant to the Bishop of Oxford in some visitations, I had by now a certain knowledge of the subject. I was therefore put on a small group to draw up the *Directory of the Religious Life* for the use of those concerned with the administration of religious life in the Church of England. It was published in 1943 and the revised edition with which I was also concerned was issued in 1957. Following on the Second Vatican Council's 'Decree on Renewal of the Religious Life' communities became more flexible, simple and with more mutual trust, and all this was reflected in the third edition published in 1976. Other editions followed in later years.

In 1969, the Advisory Council received a request for advice from the Bishop of Lewes as Visitor of a new community which had been established in the diocese of Chichester. Various individuals had tried to start hermit communities but none of them had lasted. Fr Robert Gofton Salmon had a vision of such a community, and was given a wood near Crawley Down with a bungalow into which he settled, thinking others would come and live elsewhere in the wood and there would eventually be a group of hermits. What actually happened was that five others joined him in a community life. When one of them took life vows, Fr Robert saw the chance to resume his solitary life and so resigned, leaving the others with the one in life vows as their Superior. Within a year the new Superior had gone to Rome so that the bishop, as Visitor, was left with four monks in temporary vows. Fr Robert was still living apart and being looked after by a layman, Charles. It was in this tricky situation that the Bishop sought the help of the Advisory Council. The Abbot of Nashdom, Dom Augustine Morris OSB, a Franciscan, the Reverend Donald Allchin and myself were sent to investigate. We recommended that they ask a religious from another community to come and take charge until one or more of the little community could take life vows. We suggested Fr Bryant of the Cowley Fathers (SSJE) and the Visitor saw that this happened.

When I became Bishop of Chichester there were several communities in the diocese, most of them of women. As was the case throughout the country, this picture was one of fairly rapid decline. Professed members were, in the main, elderly and the younger women who came to try their vocation balked at becoming geriatric nurses as well as religious. Two of these women's communities ran girls' schools but economic factors were making these increasingly non-viable. The Society of St Margaret at East Grinstead, which had been founded by John Mason Neale, amalgamated its school with another girls' school as numbers began to drop but this did not stem the decline and eventually both schools had to be closed. The community then decided to sell its fine, Victorian convent building and build a new and more easily run house in the grounds. This they did, and one of my early tasks was to consecrate the new convent. They have now decreased in numbers to such an extent that, as I write, they are proposing to leave East Grinstead and concentrate their energies in the nursing home they run in Chiswick and where their real strength now lies. The other community with a school was at Baldslow on the outskirts of Hastings. After handing the school over to the local authority, they survived for several years as a community but when they numbered just three, they moved to join the sisters at Malling Abbey. The funds from the dissolution of this community have been placed in a trust which considerably assists with Christian education projects in the diocese.

The Community of the Servants of the Cross, a nursing community caring for elderly and infirm women at Lindfield, also found their work unsustainable due to declining numbers and with a community which had itself become elderly and infirm. They moved first to a retirement home in the former premises of the Theological College in Chichester, where they continued a community life, worshipping in the former college chapel. The remaining two sisters finally moved to the community at Wantage. Two other communities which had branch houses in the diocese have closed also. The community at Rottingdean has now ceased to exist.

The Community of the Holy Cross was founded by John Mason Neale's sister to work with Fr Lowder in his parish of St Peter's, London Docks. Feeling called to a more contemplative life, they built a large convent at Haywards Heath and adopted the Benedictine rule. In the late 1980s they decided that it was too big for them and that they must move. My predecessor, Roger Wilson, had become their warden on ceasing to be Visitor and after we had failed to find another house for them in the diocese, he used his connections in the Midlands, where he had been an archdeacon, to arrange for them to take Rempstone Hall, a little north of Loughborough. I remained their Visitor until 2003 when David Hope took over.

All this decline meant that by the time I had been in the diocese 15 years, the only functioning communities were those at East Grinstead and Crawley Down. Lloyd Morell resigned as Visitor of Crawley Down shortly after my appointment, and I was elected in his place. When I went to see them it was ten years after my previous visit on behalf of the advisory council. The situation I found there was not happy. Fr Robert was still living his separate life, looked after by Charles. The other four were now all in life vows, Fr Bryant had gone back to Cowley and they had elected Fr Gregory as Superior. They looked ill and tired and were obviously finding the burden of maintaining the property and running the small farm they had started a great strain. I decided that I must make a formal visitation which I did with the assistance of the secretary of the Advisory Council and the Reverend Mother of the convent at Fairacres in Oxford. We could see no future for them at Crawley Down and so recommended that they should sell it and move to a smaller site. This they refused to do, and as I had no power to compel them, I just had to leave the situation as it was.

Within two years Fr Robert died, and his passing seemed to release much of the tension. Then there was a fire which destroyed much of the community house. This brought them into contact with their neighbours who rallied round and provided them with beds and other necessities. It also made them realize the importance of the society which legally owned the property. I was officially chairman but there were also a number of laymen, including the Secretary General of the General Synod, who were able to deal with the matter of insurance and other such financial problems as they arose. New buildings were put up and the community began to expand. One day when I was there

Fr Gregory said to me, 'I don't know what to do if we grow any bigger as we have only one cell left and it would not be a good thing to become more than ten in number.'

At that time the Archdeacon and I had been much exercised about the future of the pastoral area which lay round the south-western boundary of Brighton and was partly in Hove. The parish church of Christ Church, Brighton, had been burnt down, much to our relief as it was really redundant. This fire happened while I was on holiday at the Three Choirs Festival at Worcester. Someone approached me and said they had just heard on the radio that one of the Brighton churches had been burnt down. When I asked which one and they said Christ Church, they were rather surprised that I was not distressed. There were two other churches in the area, St Andrew's, Waterloo Street, and St Patrick's, Hove. The Pastoral Committee had suggested that St Patrick's be pulled down and St Andrew's made the parish church for the area, but when Keith Hobbs and I went to look at them we both felt that St Patrick's had more potential and should be kept. It then occurred to us that we might find a community to help a new priest to develop it.

We found a good energetic priest in Alan Sharpe but there seemed to be some difficulty in finding a community. The sisters of the East Grinstead community were talking at the time about opening a house in Brighton and I invited the Mother Superior to come and look at the St Patrick's area with me but I am afraid she did not have the imagination to see what could be done. However, while I was in Paris I went into the church of St Gervais and was interested to see that it was run by a community, the Community of Jerusalem, which had been invited by Cardinal Marty to come and make it a monastic centre of urban mission. There was literature about it in English so I took some back and sent it to Fr Gregory, along with a letter saying, 'I wonder if you would be interested in doing something like this in Brighton and Hove?' Rather to my surprise, after discussing it with his community he agreed, and I put him in touch with Fr Sharpe. It was arranged for them to buy a house in the same street as the church and so a partnership began which has done great things, especially in caring for the homeless. Though much must be attributed to the energy and vision of Alan Sharpe, I am convinced that the constant presence and worship in the church was vital to what has been achieved. The church and parish developed to such an extent that the community felt, probably rightly, that they were no longer needed and so returned to Crawley Down where they are now looking for their next call.

Fees and faculties

In Chapter 5, I mentioned my literary conflict with Sir Henry Dashwood over fees paid by a prebendary of St Paul's. I was interested, therefore, to meet him when, in 1953, I was put on a commission on fees and faculties under that chairmanship of Spencer Leeson, the Bishop of Peterborough. Leeson and I had been ordained at the same time, when he was headmaster of Winchester, and I later got to know him as Vicar of St Mary's, Southampton. In the commission there was some discussion about the fees charged to bishops on their appointment, and the chairman suggested that we ask Sir Henry to come and explain them to us. I can still see the table in the conference room at Lambeth with Spencer Leeson at the end and Dashwood at his right. The bishop began by suggesting that Dashwood explain to us the procedure of becoming a bishop and the expenses attached to it. Dashwood began, 'As soon as the name is published in *The Times* I get in touch and arrange a meeting. I usually find that the person in question is totally ignorant of all that is involved. Then when the dates have been fixed, I have to see that he appears for the confirmation of his election. And [turning to Spencer Leeson] you, my Lord, may remember that you forgot the date of your confirmation thereby nearly rendering the journey of thirty bishops for the consecration unnecessary.' Spencer Leeson died shortly afterwards – not of humiliation, I think – and was replaced as chairman by Bob Mortimer, the Bishop of Exeter.

There was strong opposition by the lawyers to our suggestion that payment by fees be replaced by salaries. One of the firmest opponents of the proposal was the Registrar of Exeter diocese, Sir Godwin Michelmore, who said that such a change had recently been made in respect of the clerks to magistrates' courts and had resulted in the appointment of persons of lower standing. The commission was divided, with all the legal members save one voting for the retention of payments by fees and all the clerical members save one voting against. The terms of reference under which we worked included far more than just the revision of fee structures for ecclesiastical lawyers. We were also required to review the system of faculties and the operation of

Diocesan Advisory Committees, which had last been looked at in 1938. We eventually reported in 1959 and our work bore fruit in the Faculty Jurisdiction Measure of 1964.

By the late 1970s the 1964 measure had attracted much criticism from within the Church, local authority planning committees and the increasingly powerful conservation lobby. A private member's motion tabled in General Synod calling for the abolition of the faculty jurisdiction succeeded in gathering 111 votes so many felt that the time was right for a major review. I was asked to be chairman of the resulting Faculty Jurisdiction Commission, which came into being in January 1980. We met 28 times between then and October 1983, sometimes for day meetings and periodically for residential sessions. These were chiefly held in Addington Palace, then the home of the Royal School of Church Music, where we were made very welcome by Lionel Dakers, the director, and his wife Elizabeth.

The complexity of the subject accounts for the length of time our investigation took as well as the size of the final published report, 'The continuing care of cathedrals and churches'. Some might have thought this work a tedious chore but, in fact, we found our inquiries took us into a surprisingly wide range of the Church's life. *Inter alia* we looked at the doctrinal and aesthetic aspects of current ways of worshipping; the relation of the Church to art, artists and craftsmen; the spiritual significance of our built heritage; the functions of archdeacons, registrars, chancellors and the like; and the constitutional relationship of Church and State. New to the agenda was the problem of cathedrals which some wanted brought under the ordinary faculty jurisdiction. It was obvious to most of us that cathedrals had their own special problems as regarded both artistic and liturgical changes, but there was strong pressure for control from English Heritage and such bodies and this involved us in discussion with representatives of the Department of the Environment. I remember visiting the Minister in an office at the top of one of their very tall buildings in Marsham Street, from which there was such a splendid view over London that I have never felt it necessary to go up in the London Eye. The Marsham Street Towers were demolished to make room for the new Home Office building.

I had the advantage of having been a dean and was able to explain the particular problems of cathedrals to the critics as well as carrying some degree of confidence from the cathedral chapters. It was obvious that there would have to be some form of external control, but our task was to ensure that this control should not be too restrictive and prevent aesthetic and artistic additions such as those Walter Hussey had been able to make at Chichester, or make it difficult for new understandings of liturgy to be put into effect. I hope that we produced a reasonable solution, although I have to say that on the part of the national amenity societies there is sometimes a degree of rigidity. I regret that Marcus Binney, the architectural editor of the magazine *Country Life*, who was a useful member of the commission, dissented from much of what we recommended and we included his minority report with ours.

Our report was received by General Synod and inaugurated the process of legislation which resulted in the Care of Cathedrals Measure 1990 and the Churches and Ecclesiastical Jurisdiction Measure 1991 which came into force in March 1993. In the interim I continued to chair the various synodical committees which reviewed the draft legislation, developed the rules and ultimately produced the code of practice to go with the 1991 measure. It was a great deal of work over nearly 13 years but it placed the Church of England in a good position to safeguard the so-called ecclesiastical exemption from secular planning control when the government called it into question. We were able to demonstrate that our house was in good order and little advantage would be gained by making church buildings subject to local authority planning committees.

As I write, the Care of Cathedrals Measure is being revised and amended yet again, and it gives me pleasure that my former chaplain, Jeremy Haselock, who was with me when I was working on the late stages of the 1990 measure, was on the revision committee and is now on the rules committee, as well as being an elected member of the Cathedrals Fabric Commission for England.

18

Chichester – 25 Years

By 1980, having lived in the Palace for six years, Pat and I were finding it increasingly uncomfortable as a home, particularly with all the children gone and there being only the two of us in the house. The house was very difficult to heat and the office accommodation was proving to be not entirely satisfactory. Inevitably, I had to consider the possibility of living elsewhere in the diocese. Brighton was the most geographically obvious place, but any house large enough to have an office and a chapel as well as additional living accommodation for a domestic chaplain would almost certainly be in the most expensive area, where it might not be thought appropriate for a bishop to live. I also had to consider what might happen to the Palace if we did not live in it. Some years earlier, the Prebendal School, where the cathedral choristers are educated, had looked at the possibility of taking it over as they were already using the whole top floor for staff accommodation and the east wing for classrooms. With some regret they had concluded it would prove difficult and expensive to adapt the rest of the building for school purposes. As the only vehicle access to the Palace is along Canon Lane, the main thoroughfare through the Close, the Chapter was not keen on it being put to secular use.

At my request, the Church Commissioners' architects produced various plans for re-arranging the interior spaces but none of these seemed satisfactory so in the end we were told to choose an architect ourselves. As the future of the historic See House was in question, I thought it advisable to bring the Bishop's Council into the discussions. They were emphatic that the Bishop should stay in the Palace and appointed a small group to advise on the appointment of an architect. The firm Carden and Godfrey were approached and a good plan was drawn up which we accepted. We had to move out while the work was being done. Fortunately, The Chantry, one of the houses in Canon Lane, was temporarily vacant so we were able to live there while using one of the Palace stable cottages as offices. When we moved back, Pat and I found the changes a great improvement and I think the staff found it an easier place in which to work.

As I have already mentioned, shortly before I was appointed the diocese had sold Elfinsward, its conference and retreat house at Haywards Heath, and put the proceeds into extending the diocesan offices in Brunswick Square, Hove. The extension had released space for a small flat for the bishop but I found I did not use it very much as it was usually easier and more convenient to go back to Chichester. However, I did hold the monthly senior staff meeting there in comfortable surroundings. The cost of upkeep of the Brunswick Square property was high and eventually the Diocesan Board of Finance advised its sale. With the proceeds a purpose-built diocesan office was put up on the site of a former vicarage at the western end of Hove. This had open-plan office space, ample parking space for staff and visitors and, from my point of view, was far more convenient to get to from Chichester.

When I arrived in the diocese, I discovered that the Diocesan Synod was held in a different place each time it came together. This did not seem to me to be a good idea. The staff had to transport all that was needed for the meeting to a place that was strange to them and where the logistical problems were different each time. It always took some time for the synod members to settle down to new surroundings and a variety of arrangements. Furthermore, I wanted to begin each meeting with a celebration of the Eucharist, at which I would give my presidential address in the form of a homily. This would prove difficult, I felt, in some of the suggested venues. In the summer of 1975, we met at the end of the pier in Hastings and I used the experience of that to persuade people we should always meet at the same place. For some time we used a large lecture hall at the University of Sussex, and then later a Roman Catholic school in Hove which was very conveniently near the new diocesan offices.

In addition to the normal complement of regular Church and local authority day schools, I found that the diocese had a substantial number of public schools with boarders and a tradition of hosting their own confirmation services. The Bishop of Chichester has a special responsibility for the schools of the Woodard Foundation. Nicholas Woodard was a priest of the diocese and the first of his schools was at Shoreham, later moved to Lancing on the hill above. The magnificent chapel of Lancing College, gloriously completed during my tenure of office, serves as the 'cathedral' of the whole foundation. The Bishop is

Visitor both of the southern division of the Woodard Schools and of the whole corporation. This did not cause me any great difficulty but I was concerned, as were a number of the Fellows, that the governing body of the corporation, as well as those of the individual schools, should keep in mind and observe the religious and distinctively Anglican intentions of the founder, particularly in the matter of appointments. Some felt there was real risk of the schools becoming just like any other boarding school. There was not much I could do about this, but when I was appealed to about some incident I used my charge to refer to the distinctive ethos of the Woodard Schools and the need to preserve it. I had copies circulated to all members of the corporation in the hope that it would have some influence on the appointment of heads and senior staff.

I was in close touch with the other public schools in the diocese and visited them for confirmations fairly frequently. I found that my predecessors had cultivated a special relationship with Christ's Hospital. The custom had developed whereby the bishop administered confirmation on Saturday, had dinner with some of the Grecians (sixth-formers), stayed overnight and then presided at the Eucharist on the Sunday morning when those who had been confirmed would receive their first Communion. The headmaster in 1975 was David Newsome and the chaplain John Robson, and I was filled with admiration for both of them for their knowledge of individual boys, in particular. David had been a fellow of Emmanuel, Cambridge, and was a distinguished ecclesiastical historian. When he left Christ's Hospital he took on the mastership of Wellington College, from which he retired in 1989. The circumstances of his departure from Christ's Hospital distressed me but I was very pleased when my godson, Peter Southern, became head.

In the course of the 1960s and 1970s, various links were established between English dioceses and other parts of the Anglican Communion, chiefly in Africa, India and Papua New Guinea. Chichester had formed an East African link and, I think, Roger Wilson had been out on a visit but nothing permanent had been forged. In 1976, David Brown, the Bishop of Guildford, wrote to me and to the Bishop of Portsmouth about a visit he had just made to the dioceses of the province of West Africa. The diocese of Guildford was supposed to be twinned with that province, but David suggested that our three dioceses should share the twinning as it was a very big area. I put this to our Bishop's Council and was glad when they agreed. Two years later this led to an invitation to visit Sierra Leone to attend the centenary celebrations of the cathedral at Freetown. The archbishop of the province, Moses Scott, was an interesting and physically very substantial figure. He was having a new episcopal residence built so I was not able to stay with him but was lodged instead with the Ghanaian dean. I have to say, to my disappointment, the celebrations were not very exciting. I presided at the Eucharist, which was more or less the English Series Two rite, but the chief celebration at Freetown Cathedral was Book of Common Prayer Evensong with music by Charles Villiers Stanford. There were Victorian hymns, sidesmen in frock coats and the Mothers' Union paraded in white frocks and straw hats, looking for all the world as if they were at the annual garden fête in a large English parish. The church at which I preached the following Sunday was of the same colonial mould. During the following week I visited some of the rural areas, which were more interesting and vibrant.

Freetown itself, it seemed to me, was waiting for revolution. There was one main street through the centre and on either side small shacks, partly homes and partly shops, all inhabited by the poorer element of the native population. On the hills above them were grander houses which had been built by the British when Sierra Leone was a colony. They were inhabited by the Creoles and the grander part of the population. From Freetown I went to Accra in Ghana for a week. While the liturgy there was more up to date, again I was disappointed to find how little the worship generally had been influenced by African ways. The bishop, I am afraid to say, seemed chiefly interested in getting money and materials from us to build himself a new house. After a few days I went to Ashanti in the north of Ghana, to the diocese of Kumasi, where I found things much more lively and interesting. I understand from those who have served in that diocese that it has always been more forward-looking in that respect. Since that visit there have been great changes, the revolution in Sierra Leone has happened and there are now more Anglican dioceses. The liturgy of the Church has taken much more note of native culture and worship is, I understand, more indigenous in feel. At the time of my visit I found it all rather depressing.

I did not come back from West Africa filled with any great enthusiasm for the work of the Anglican Communion overseas, and this feeling was not greatly changed later that year by my first experience of a Lambeth Conference. It was much overshadowed by the issue of the ordination of women to the priesthood – on which the Americans had already taken their own line. I spoke in the main debate on the subject and afterwards Archbishop Coggan said that my speech had been very good but on the wrong side. Unfortunately, a few years earlier Michael Ramsey had told the Anglican Consultative Council that he was prepared to accept such ordinations in other provinces, and this was very much on the record so, in spite of opposition from a considerable minority, the conference could do little else than give its approval. This decision marked the beginning of a series of events which, I think, will in the end lead to the dissolution of the Communion.

The 1978 conference was of a manageable size, I felt, and consisted only of diocesan bishops and a small number of individually chosen others. I was glad to renew my friendship with James Schuster, Bishop of St John's in the province of South Africa. The 1988 conference was much bigger as all the suffragans were invited. It was remarkable in that, for the first time, all the provinces had authorized it to commit the whole Communion to something, viz. the Statements of Agreement issued by ARCIC on the Eucharist and the Ministry. I am not aware of any pronouncement since then that has such authority. It was useful to me in the case concerning the Henry Moore altar at St Stephen's Walbrook. The third conference in 1998 was still larger and many of us had to live in houses on the University campus. For the first time there were women bishops present, bringing us a step nearer the dissolution of the Communion, which I now see as even more certainly impending following on the independent action of the North American and Canadian churches in matters to do with homosexuality. As I write, the nature and future of the Communion raises enormous problems and I feel very sorry for Rowan Williams as he struggles to cope with them. I cannot say that I enjoyed any of the Lambeth conferences nor do I think they did much good, but it was an opportunity to meet a certain number of friends and particularly to make contact with orthodox Catholic Anglicans from America and elsewhere and give them some support.

It has always struck me as strange that anything to do with the diocese of Chichester always seemed to meet with opposition and often misrepresentation from the central offices of the Church of England and consequently from elsewhere. There is a common misapprehension that Sussex is, in general, a rich county and, in consequence, that we are a rich diocese. The first of these is untrue. When a survey was undertaken for the Church Urban Fund many people were surprised at the large areas of poverty shown to exist in Hastings, Brighton, Worthing, and elsewhere in Sussex. As regards the second, we are not a rich diocese but, as I have said earlier, we have been fortunate in that our finances have been managed by a succession of prudent and competent chairmen so we have always been able to do what was needed and to help some others.

Shortly after I became a bishop, Mervyn Stockwood, the Bishop of Southwark, invited me to join a discussion group of bishops and academics called 'Caps and Mitres'. This was a lively and interesting group in which the most positive person was Hugh Montefiore, then Bishop of Kingston but later, in 1978, translated to Birmingham. Although we met for several years I do not think we accomplished anything significant. However, after Hugh moved to Birmingham he wrote to me about the allocation of deacons to dioceses which the House of Bishops was trying to regulate. Hugh had been allocated 11 but his diocese could not possibly afford so many. I discussed this with David Hopkinson, the chairman of the Diocesan Board of Finance, and between us we persuaded the diocesan synod to give Birmingham the stipend of a curate for three years. I believe this to have been a far better way of helping other dioceses than making grants to central funds, a method of which I have always been suspicious.

In this respect, it is worth recording what the archbishop's officer for Urban Priority Areas wrote to me in 1988.

> I just wanted to say how appreciative we have been of the Chichester response to 'Faith in the City', not least for the careful consideration given by your Bishop's Council to the nature of the diocese's approach both to the issues raised in the report and to the financial challenge of the Church Urban Fund. I have been heartened to hear from your stewardship officer of the concern to view the diocesan response as an opportunity for spiritual renewal of parishes and people in Sussex and not just as a means of giving much needed financial support to those struggling in the Urban Priority Areas. I sincerely hope that others may follow the 'Chichester way' in their response as faithful disciples to the challenge presented by the Archbishop of Canterbury's Group on Urban Priority Areas.

Pastoral reorganization is something for which bishops are frequently criticized, particularly in the use of the pastoral measure to suspend presentation to livings and introduce an element of rationalization into the deployment of the clergy. One of the parishes with which I had to deal at an early stage was Boxgrove and Tangmere. The incumbent, Richard Ratcliff, came to see me to inform me of his wish to retire. The patron of the living was the Duke of Richmond but matters were being dealt with by his son, the Earl of March, whom I knew well from the Church Assembly. Charles March came to see me and we consulted about the problems and complications of the two very different villages and I gathered that the two congregations were rather at odds with one another. Boxgrove was 'high church' and had then, as now, a very fine choir and a tradition of polyphonic church music, neither of which was to the taste of the Tangmere people. The curate, Michael Rose, a retired naval officer, was popular at Boxgrove, where there was a group in favour of the idea of him taking over as parish priest, but not so well liked in Tangmere. As he was leaving my study, Charles March turned around and said, 'My father and I would not be displeased if you decided to suspend presentation and take the matter into your own hands.' I did exactly that and spent a whole day seeing various individuals and ending with the first ever joint meeting of the two parochial church councils. I think the arrangements I made were satisfactory for the time being and Fr Rose became priest-in-charge until his untimely death. Later, I was able to separate the two villages, join Tangmere with a more suitable neighbour and make Boxgrove the base for a priest who was to be the liturgical adviser for the diocese. As I have already mentioned, the first person whom I appointed to that post was my then chaplain, Jeremy Haselock.

The other parish which caused me much anxiety at an early stage was Moulescombe, a working-class development on the eastern side of Brighton. At that time, it had a very bad reputation for vandalism and disorder and I was told that all other denominations had withdrawn from it. I was able to set up a team ministry there and send deacons there for training. The area improved and the parish is now doing well. From the start of my episcopate I urged such parishes to form small groups for discussion and prayer and as a basis for local evangelism. I had learned the value of this during the preparation for the Worcester Mission and hoped that something similar would work on a diocesan basis. I am not sure how many parishes took up my suggestion, the diocese is so large and diffuse, but I hope that there are parishes where this is still being done.

During my episcopate I dedicated two long periods to visits to every deanery. This was an invaluable means of getting to know what was going on at a parish level and of delivering some encouragement and advice. I delivered an address in each deanery and at the end of each cycle of visits, I published the address I had given, one of which I called 'Milk without Guile' (1 Peter 2.2). This was one way in which I tried to keep in touch with the whole diocese but, as I have said elsewhere, I visited individual parishes both for confirmation, anniversaries, institutions and licensings, and also just for occasional visits, so that nowhere should feel they never saw the diocesan bishop. I did, however, find that there were places where no bishop had visited within living memory. That is not a comment on any of my predecessors, but rather on the size of the diocese and the difficulty of visiting every parish. The Episcopal Area Scheme has done much to meet these difficulties.

By 1980, I had begun to think that we should devise some occasion to which all the parishes could be invited. I put this to the Bishop's Council and we decided to have what we called the Festival of Sussex Saints on the Saturday nearest to St Richard's Day. We held this in Chichester in the cathedral and Palace grounds. About 5,000 people attended and it was felt to be a great success. We repeated it two years later, and on that occasion I persuaded Lord Tonypandy, who as George Thomas had been speaker of the House of Commons, to come and preach which, as a Methodist lay preacher, he did very well. Later we rather outgrew the cathedral and decided to hold these gatherings at the county showground at Ardingly. This formula worked well and it was repeated several times before I retired. These days were tiring but always very enjoyable as they brought the diocese together, not only in worship but also in many other activities, both edifying and entertaining.

In 1977, I was invited to preach at the national pilgrimage to the Shrine of Our Lady of Walsingham. I had not been there since many years before when, as a member of the Advisory Council on Religious Communities, I was appointed to go with Fr O'Brian SSJE to report on the embryonic community there. Fr Alfred Hope Patten, the reviver of the shrine, was trying to have some men exempted from military service on the grounds that they were novices in a community of St Augustine which he had founded. I remember being greatly impressed by what Hope Patten had already done in re-establishing the shrine and his imaginative plans for the future, but we were not able to recommend recognition of his community and, indeed, it came to nothing. By the time I was invited there to preach, Fr Patten was long dead and the administrator of the shrine was a friend of mine, Fr Alan Careful. I enjoyed the visit enormously and was surprised and pleased to be elected as an honorary guardian. Since then I have been able to get to Walsingham most years, sometimes three times in a year, and have become devoted to it. It is a great centre for Marian devotion but, as Bishop Maurice Wood of Norwich once said, it is a great witness to God. The congregation of several thousand that gathers for the National Pilgrimage is as wide a representation of laypeople as you will ever find at Anglican services. Two archbishops of Canterbury have led pilgrimages there, a good number of diocesan bishops have been, and there are regular diocesan pilgrimages from a number of dioceses, including Chichester. I believe it is one of the great centres for the promotion of the Christian religion in England today, with its theological work, its work with children and young people, with the sick and with the good people of a large number of affiliated parishes. It is a force for good throughout the Anglican world with centres of devotion to Our Lady of Walsingham in America and elsewhere. In recent years, two young and visionary administrators, Fr Martin Warner and Fr Philip North, following one another in office, have not only supervised the enlargement and improvement of the buildings surrounding Fr Patten's original shrine complex but also extended its outreach work. While both have sought to integrate the shrine more firmly into the life of the Church of England, the distinctive, slightly exotic atmosphere and ethos which contributes so much to the fascination of this holy place remains.

A couple of years after my first National Pilgrimage to Walsingham, I was invited by one of the guardians, Fr David Diamond, to preach at the Deptford Festival. He was a great and charismatic parish priest, and I was greatly impressed by what I saw and the extent to which the whole festival was a community occasion. A year or two later, David brought his parish brass band to Walsingham for the pilgrimage and, after it played for the Mass, stationed it opposite the Protestant protestors in the common place to play rousing hymns. It was a most effective way of dealing with them and I have wondered why nothing similar has been done since.

By the end of 1984 I had been a bishop for ten years, and there was a desire that my portrait should be painted to hang along with those of my predecessors in the palace. Fortunately, I was given a voice in the choice of artist and, in preference to other names suggested, I chose Andrew Festing, who had recently painted the master of Emmanuel College, Cambridge, and I thought captured a good likeness. It was a good choice and I enjoyed the sittings which began with photographs one Sunday in March 1985. I decided to be painted in my Oxford Doctor of Divinity robe rather than the conventional bishop's rochet and chimere, which I think was a good idea. Later in the year, the finished portrait was presented to me by Colin Docker, Bishop of Horsham, on behalf of the diocese. David Hopkinson, who had supervised the arrangements, said that far more money than was needed had been contributed, so Andrew was asked to paint a smaller version for the family. Later Andrew was asked to paint a third version for the National Liberal Club.

I decided to commemorate my anniversary and, as the diocesan crozier was wobbly and unsatisfactory, I decided to commission a new one. After making some enquiries, I asked John Poole of Pershore to make it. He took some time to decide how to approach the commission, and eventually came to the decision to copy the head of one of the medieval croziers in the cathedral treasury. The result was very successful. I used it for most of the rest of my time and left it to my successor. Along with his episcopal vestments, I had inherited a crozier presented to Kenneth Kirk in 1938, to which I had myself subscribed, and I use this from time to time still. I also took the opportunity of the anniversary to have a new tabernacle for the Blessed Sacrament installed on the window sill at the east end of the private chapel in the Palace. This became very useful when I arranged with the Theological College to have Benediction in the chapel once a month on Monday evenings.

In 1985 I was 70 years old and, ordinarily, would have retired but having been appointed in 1974, the year before the legislation requiring all clergy to retire at 70 was brought in, I was exempt from that requirement and could choose for myself when to retire. I had suffered a bout of prostate trouble in 1981 which had been successfully treated surgically. Apart from that, nothing serious had occurred and I felt well and in good heart. I was still enjoying the work, but I would have been happy to go had it not been for the lurking question of the ordination of women to the priesthood. At that stage, the proposed legislation allowed those in office who were opposed to women priests to remain until their retirement so when, at a meeting of the diocesan synod, the clergy had voted in a majority against the proposed legislation and the laity had supported it by only a small majority, it was obvious to me that from the diocesan point of view I must stay and see what happened. Consulting with others, I found there were also many people outside the diocese who wished me to remain. So I stayed on.

In 1990 I celebrated my 75th birthday, the 75th anniversary of my baptism and the 50th anniversary of my ordination to the priesthood. My former chaplain, Freddie Jackson, and my then current chaplain, Jeremy Haselock, organized a special mass in Freddie's church, St Michael's, Brighton, which is perhaps my favourite of the great Brighton churches. I presided, assisted by the deacons I had ordained that year, and the church was full of clergy, religious and layfolk. I wore the chasuble my parents had given me as an ordination present and Anthony Caesar preached, recalling the days I spent as his father's curate in Southampton all those years before. It was for me a moving occasion. Curiously, it was thought worthy of an article in the *Independent*, which was written by Toby Forward, a priest of the diocese, as a parting shot before he moved to York. I believe he is now a residentiary canon and Precentor at Liverpool Cathedral.

I have been a frequent visitor to Europe but had never been to the USA and had no particular desire to go, though Pat was quite keen on going. In 1991, however, I was told of a priest called James Hiles who organized a conference or gathering every year around the feast of St Patrick on 17 March to encourage Catholic and Protestant reconciliation in Northern Ireland. In the following year he was expecting the two Archbishops of Armagh, Anglican and Roman Catholic, to participate and wanted an Anglican bishop to give a lecture which would help forward the purpose of the gathering. Bishop Michael Marshall, who was then based in St Louis, suggested my name and so Pat and I agreed to go in March 1992. When that date came, it emerged there was no question of the two archbishops attending but as plans for our visit had been made we went.

We stayed one night in St Louis and then flew to Sarasota in Florida on Friday and stayed with the Reverend Jack Iker, since elected Bishop of Fort Worth, and I preached twice on Sunday and spoke to an adult education class. The next day I had a discussion with a group of the clergy, mainly about the problems caused by the ordination of women to the priesthood, and we then flew back to St Louis. We then went to Boston where at All Saint's, Ashmont, we attended Evensong and I gave my lecture. On Saturday we had an interesting tour of Boston and I preached twice on the Sunday in the Church of the Advent. I was told later the Bishop of Massachusetts was unhappy about my visit because I was opposed to the ordination of women to the priesthood and that the Archbishop of Canterbury had intervened to vouch for my respectability.

At Boston, Pat and I diverged. She went to stay with friends in Texas and I flew back to St Louis and then on to Milwaukee to stay at Nashotah House. There I preached on the Feast of the Annunciation and later repeated my lecture. I had some interesting conversations with members of the staff and was given a very depressing picture of the state of the American Church. Everywhere I went, I found people seriously worried about the state of the American Church and the serious divisions caused by the ordination of women to the priesthood, a warning of what was going to happen in England.

On Saturday, 28 March I flew to New York to stay with John Andrew, Rector of St Thomas, Fifth Avenue, and preached there on the Sunday. John had been chaplain to Michael Ramsey, first at York and then for many years at Lambeth, so we enjoyed many hours of happy reminiscences of the great man. I saw quite a lot of Michael Ramsey in his retirement as he came frequently to stay at the theological college and lecture. He preached on the text 'A man greatly beloved' at one of the various commemorations of George Bell. On one visit he was asked to celebrate on the Sunday and had not brought a mitre with him. I have photographs of him sitting in our garden trying on several of my mitres for the occasion. The House of Bishops held a dinner for him on his 80th birthday and it happened to be a day when the House had passed some motion in support of the ordination of women to the priesthood. He took me aside to say how much he sympathized with what I was feeling.

Pat rejoined me in New York having had an enjoyable visit to her friends and we had two interesting days sightseeing in the city. On 1 April we flew via Philadelphia to London. Altogether, it was an exhausting but thoroughly enjoyable visit.

On 11 November 1992 General Synod decided to proceed to the drawing up of legislation to enable women to be ordained as priests in the Church of England. I have written of the effect of this decision in the next chapter when giving some account of my involvement with the Church Union. I had opposed this deeply wrong course of action at every stage and finally, as the last piece of opposition I was able to exercise, I spoke against the legislation in the House of Lords. I did not think it right, however, to exclude women from the diocese, although I was not able to ordain them myself. Chichester, contrary to what some have claimed, did not become a 'no-go area for women priests'. When the Act of Synod made it possible, I allowed them to be ordained and licensed by the Archbishop, and later made an arrangement with the Bishop of Guildford so that he or his suffragan could ordain women priests for Chichester. There is much illogicality about all this but logic does not have a proper place in all matters of Christian communion.

On Saturday, 23 October 1999, I celebrated the silver jubilee of my episcopal ordination with a Sung Eucharist in the cathedral. I presided and Colin Docker came up from Devon to preach. In the afternoon there was a teaching pilgrimage around the cathedral called 'In the Steps of the Apostles', a break for tea and then Evensong. We set up an altar in the forecourt of the Palace and after Evensong we gathered there and I gave Benediction. It was an altogether splendid and moving day.

By 2000 things seemed to me to have settled down. As far as Chichester was concerned, the arrangements outlined in the Act of Synod were working and there were women priests in the diocese in those parishes which chose to accept their ministry. The diocesan Vacancy in See Committee made it clear that they wanted a successor of my views and the Archbishop shared that opinion about the appointment, along with some other bishops, so I decided that I could go without causing any great upset. I therefore decided to retire at the end of January 2001.

My farewell started in the Worth Abbey church where Lindsay Urwin had made all the necessary arrangements with the courteous and hospitable assistance of the abbot and community. I celebrated the Eucharist in the morning, assisted by two women deacons, my suffragans, the Dean and the Archdeacons, and I preached. My family gathered from all over to be present, as did a large number of episcopal friends, the clergy and thousands of laypeople from the diocese and beyond. After the Mass there were speeches and presentations, and I was glad that Pat was included in the thanks and good wishes. A lunch had been arranged at which not only other retired friends such as Max Godden were present, but also one of my godsons, David Wickstead, and his wife. On the following Sunday I presided and preached for the last time in the cathedral.

I was delighted when John Hind was appointed as my successor. It was a great pleasure to be present at his enthronement and to be able to hand over the pastoral staff to him. I have also been very glad to give him the pectoral cross and ring which had belonged to Humphrey Beevor when he was Bishop of Lebombo. His widow had given them to Freddy Hood as Humphrey's closest friend with the proviso that they should always be given to a bishop. Freddy gave them to me and I handed them on to John Hind.

19

The Church Union

Ever since I went back to Pusey House in 1941 and began to know first hand what Gregory Dix, Kenneth Kirk, Robert Mortimer, Freddy Hood and others were involved in, it was clear to me that to maintain the Catholic revival in the Church of England some sort of political organization was needed. In the nineteenth century, the English Church Union had been founded to protect Catholic priests and parishes which were under attack from the militantly protestant Church Association. Other associations, such as the Society of the Holy Cross (SSC) for priests and later for particular devotional purposes soon came into being. Then the Society of Ss Peter and Paul, to which I referred previously, was started by Ronald Knox, NP Williams, Maurice Child and others and published a number of pamphlets and tracts. In 1920, the first Anglo-Catholic Congress was held and became a formal organization. In 1933, the centenary of the start of the Oxford Movement, Lord Halifax persuaded the English Church Union and the Anglo-Catholic Congress to unite and the Church Union was started. I joined soon after the amalgamation. The function of the Church Union was not purely political, though for many years it had to act for priests and parishes against persecution, but it had also a valuable positive role in teaching through the publication of books and tracts and the organization of congresses and other teaching occasions.

There are always people whose hearts are in the Catholic revival but who hold aloof from any kind of positive action which they regard as political. This along with personality differences has been a great weakness in the Catholic Movement and has led to some opposition to the Church Union. The recovery of confidence among evangelicals in the 1960s, and their growing influence in the Church of England, made the Church Union think very seriously about its future. Not long after I became a bishop I was approached by an old friend, Fr Charles Smith, who was chairman of the Church Union, to invite me to become president, in the hope that I might be able to inspire some renewal. I hesitated somewhat and had a talk with Archbishop Coggan who, although an evangelical himself, said that the Catholic Movement had an important place in the Church of England and encouraged me to accept, which I did.

I gave my first presidential address in December 1976 stressing the importance of wholeness, tolerance and understanding. I also quoted the words of Maurice Reckitt: 'Men may celebrate no second centenary of our movement if we do not determine now to stand in social or in doctrinal issues plainly upon our own ground, with a message and a philosophy for the whole range of human life, and a true order of ends and values, which men may reflect indeed, but the distinctive character of which they can no longer mistake.'

I emphasized that we must be concerned with Christian unity in all its aspects and I concluded by saying:

My first word to you, therefore, as your president is that we should all try to understand more fully what it means to be a Catholic Christian, to see the wholeness of the faith, its focus in the Eucharist, the form of its communication, its bearing upon the problems of society, the riches of its spirituality, its call to unity, and all this inspired by the love of which we speak so readily but in the exercise of which we are so often found wanting. If we can come to understand this true Catholicity, I believe that we shall recover the joy, the enthusiasm, and the spiritual power which we see in the story of our fathers in the faith; we shall become apostles and evangelists proclaiming the good news of the reconciliation and healing offered to all men through the love of our Lord.

Over the next few years as time allowed, I tried to get together men and women of Catholic outlook to consider what we should do and I travelled the country speaking at a number of meetings. People were kind and receptive because I was a bishop but I did not feel that there was a great body of enthusiasm for Catholic renewal just waiting to be released. Nevertheless we persevered, and on Ascension Day 1977 issued a statement of faith which was well received, though some said that there was nothing distinctively Catholic about it. One of our number was in touch with Michael Ramsey and told us that he had suggested we write to *The Times* asking all who agreed with us to make contact. As a result it was decided to hold a Catholic Renewal conference in March 1978 and the place chosen was the University of Loughborough. This was in the diocese of Leicester and the then Bishop, Ronald

Williams, though not of our outlook, was happy to come and encourage us. The chief speakers were Richard Holloway, later Bishop of Edinburgh, and Michael Marshall, the Bishop of Woolwich, both of whom gave us exactly what was needed, and the conference was accounted such a success that it was proposed, I think by George Timms, that we hold another in 1983 to commemorate the 150th anniversary of the Oxford Movement.

This second Loughborough conference, 4–8 April 1983, was by no means as united as the first. From the beginning there were complaints that we had not provided a place for discussion of the issue of the ordination of women to the priesthood. We had some good addresses but the new Bishop of Leicester, Richard Rutt, who was one of us, caused some upset by criticisms that he made of Catholics. It was urged on me by Graham Leonard and others that in my speech at the end I must do something to balance this. I spent a long time in the preparation of that speech, which was eventually published under the title of 'The Catholic Future'. Graham said that he thought it the best speech he had ever heard me make. I have printed it in the Appendix as it represents my outlook on the Catholic revival.

A number of us had been working together at a revision of the constitution of the Church Union in order to enable it to carry out more effectively the ideas that had developed in the preparation for the second Loughborough conference. We had some valuable new people on board, including an ex-headmaster, John Lello. We wanted to place more emphasis on mission and evangelism. To this end, there were to be sub-committees into which we could bring some new people who had important things to say. We approached several people who expressed their willingness to help. Peter Geldard, as General Secretary of the Union, was to write formally to ask them and others to serve on the sub-committees. We hoped to get the whole Union organized by 1985 and to have a really new start.

I went back to work in the diocese pleased with what we had done and looking forward to a more encouraging future. I was disturbed when, some months later, I found that none of those we had selected had been approached. I spoke to Maurice Chandler, the chairman of the executive, and he said that he had asked Peter several times what was happening and always received the reply that Peter was going to write but had not yet had time to do so. This dragged on until most of those who had promised to help assumed that the plans had been shelved, and became involved in others things. So what seemed a great opportunity was lost.

Meanwhile, the movement for the ordination of women to the priesthood was gathering strength and as the Church Union did not appear to be doing anything, other organizations were formed that eventually united as Forward in Faith, which the Union supported but had lost the opportunity to take the lead itself. There is a wide belief among influential people in the Church that the Church Union has an important place as a teaching and evangelistic body maintaining and spreading the Catholic faith, but that it should leave what needs to be done politically to Forward in Faith, which it would support but from which it could be distinct.

The decision in General Synod on 11 November 1992 to ordain women came as a shock to many of us but was, of course, a great joy to others. The rejoicing among members of the Movement for the Ordination of Women was understandable but not always charitable. A friend told me that as he came out of Church House after the debate, he heard two women saying to one another, 'I hope this means that they [meaning those of us opposed to women priests] will get out now.'

The House of Bishops met in Manchester in the New Year and I remember it as a very dismal meeting. Those of us who were opposed could not make out how much freedom the majority was prepared to let us have. The only source of relief was that John Habgood, the Archbishop of York, seemed to be sympathetic to our plight and secured a decision to have further detailed discussion before the final legislation was drawn up. This was the only crumb of comfort for the group waiting at the Church Union headquarters to hear the result of the bishops' deliberations. Noel Jones, the Bishop of Sodor and Man, who went to tell the Union did not get a very enthusiastic reception. I remember a series of meetings of Catholic societies wondering what, in the circumstances, we were to do. I went to the meeting of the Wal-singham Guardians to help them consider what to do as the shrine had always kept clear of political action.

John Habgood produced the document called 'The Bonds of Peace', and a group of bishops including David Hope, then Bishop of London, and chaired by John, met together to consider the way forward. In June 1993 they presented what became known as the Act of Synod which was passed unanimously in the House of Bishops with few dissentients in the other houses in the Synod session of November that year. The intervening period seemed very long and drawn out, and one was very conscious of losing friends from the Church of England to Rome and Orthodoxy.

The Act of Synod concerned itself with arrangements for pastoral care, following the ordination of women, for those who in conscience could not accept their ministry or the ministry of those bishops who had ordained women. As I continued to function in office as a diocesan bishop under its provisions, it is worth briefly outlining its ecclesiological basis. Whereas the Church of England had determined to ordain women to the priestly ministry of the Church, it admitted that there needed to be a period of reception by the Church which might or, however remote the possibility, might not, indicate that the right thing had been done. 'Discernment of the matter,' said the preamble to the Act, 'is now to be seen within a much broader and longer process of discernment within the whole Church under the Spirit's guidance.' In presenting the report to the Synod, John Habgood spoke of both 'discernment' and 'reception': 'We are trying to think of this within the context of the Church universal and "reception" implied to some that we had to move inevitably in one direction. We believe we are moving in that direction, but we have also to be sufficiently open to go on listening to what our fellow Christians in other traditions are saying. That is why the word "discernment" is in.' In theory, therefore, the Act of Synod provided space for this 'reception' or 'discernment' to take place. For this to be genuine discernment of the will of God, there had to be an admission that it was possible that in this matter the Synod had made a mistake and might even find itself, at some time in the future, undoing what it had purported to do.

To make room within the one Church for those who supported the ordination of women to the priesthood, and those convinced it was wrong, the Act of Synod attempts a *modus vivendi*. It outlines how the dioceses and the local churches can continue to live together within a situation of radical difference on a fundamental matter. It allows that a diocesan bishop might remain opposed to women as priests, but permit another bishop to ordain and license women within his diocese. A diocesan bishop in favour might invite a bishop who does not accept women's ordination to minister to priests and congregations in his diocese who themselves do not accept it. This would express the collegiality of a House of Bishops which 'accepts the legitimacy of both positions'. What is more, each diocesan bishop is to ensure that pro-vision continues to be made for the care and oversight of everyone in his diocese, including those opposed to the ordination of women to the priesthood.

Those of us who remained and were opposed to the core legislation were somewhat divided as to the right course, even in the light of the Act of Synod. Some regarded themselves as totally out of communion with all who received Communion from women priests or received Holy Communion alongside them. Some felt that those bishops who ordained women to the priesthood were somehow tainted, so one could not receive Communion from them. I have never felt able to take that line and believe that we should all remain in communion with one another as far as possible while not being able to recognize women as priests and consequently not able to receive the Sacrament they have celebrated. In every other way, it is important to retain communion and to keep friendship and courtesy. It is, however, disturbing that there are those who are actively campaigning for the withdrawal of the provisions of the Act of Synod, and therefore in principle wish to see those of us who cannot accept women's priesthood leave the Church. This situation will become grave when, as now seems likely, there are women bishops.

There is no doubt in my mind that the decision that women can be ordained priest in the Church of England was the most devastating thing that has happened to the Church in my lifetime. Not only did it mean that we lost some valuable bishops and priests, but it clearly put an end indefinitely to any hopes of unity with the two largest churches, Rome and the Orthodox, which together make up the majority of the Christian world, and this at a time when the movement towards closer unity seemed to be making progress.

It is important to emphasize that most of us who oppose the ordination of women to the priesthood do not do so on anti-feminist grounds. We have supported the ordination of women to the diaconate and I have myself ordained a number of women deacons. Our oppo-sition is based on the grounds that the tradition of the Church has from earliest times not ordained women to the priesthood and as Cardinal Ratzinger, now Pope Benedict XVI, said to me on one occasion: 'The question is: "Does this rest on the decision of the Lord or is it purely sociological?" If it is the first we can do nothing about it. If it is the second it is intolerable.' Only the whole Church can decide and make such a major change. The Anglican Communion, let alone the Church of England, ought not to do this by itself, even provisionally as the Act of Synod allows, and there is no sign of the two major churches moving on this matter. Since the recent decision to proceed to the consecration of women to the episcopate, the question is now even more sharply put: whether the Act of Synod will be allowed to continue as an act of toleration in the Church of England or whether a majority will decide that opponents must be driven out.

In 2000, a great millennium celebration, sponsored by Forward in Faith, the Church Union and the other Catholic societies, was held in the huge arena in Docklands under the title 'Christ our Future'. I presided at the Mass which was attended by thousands of people including bishops, priests and deacons. Five years later the principal society for priests in the Anglican Communion, the Society of the Holy Cross (SSC), celebrated the 150th anniversary of its foundation by the Exeter College man, Fr Charles Lowder, with a mass in the Royal Albert Hall. It was packed out. Geoffrey Rowell, the Bishop of Gibraltar, presided, and the Bishop of London, Richard Chartres, was present and made an encouraging and supportive speech at the end, giving unqualified support to the Society and to the Catholic Movement. There were a good number of other bishops there but I did not feel strong enough to concelebrate so, wearing choir habit, I sat in the Royal Box with the other Walsingham Guardians. What I was not prepared for was that, towards the end of the afternoon, the Master of the SSC, Prebendary David Houlding, drew attention to my presence. He told the assembly I was only days away from my 90th birthday and the whole 5,000 or more who were present clapped and cheered. I was greatly moved. I had resigned as president of the Church Union in September of the previous year after 27 years and so, perhaps, this was why the assembly was kind enough to give me so great an ovation.

I am led to believe by all this that the Catholic Movement in the Church of England is not in terminal decline, and those who were hoping after the ordination of women to the priesthood that it would slowly disappear must be disappointed. It remains to be seen how the decision to ordain women bishops will affect the situation but I, for one, am not prepared to be driven out of the Church of my baptism. Something more clearly defined and with a permanency not apparent in the Act of Synod needs to be provided for the strong minority who choose to stay and bear witness to the Catholic faith of the Church of England.

I am often asked where I should go if it really became necessary to leave. I have always been clear that I could not become a Roman Catholic because I cannot assent to the canon which defines the universal, immediate jurisdiction of the Bishop of Rome. I respect the papal primacy but do not believe there is any authority for the Pope to appoint and depose bishops throughout the whole Church, nor do I accept the doctrine of papal infallibility. So, if I had to leave the Church of England it would be to the Orthodox churches I would look.

Epilogue

Toby Forward, in his article on my golden jubilee of priestly ordination in the *Independent*, wrote of diocesan gossip that Pat and my daughters were all supporters of the ordination of women and remarked that conversations in the Palace must therefore be interesting. I do not recall that the subject was common currency around the Aga, but my wife and family have always been a vital link with the world beyond what might seem to some the limited vista of an academic, a dean and a bishop. Family life in Oxford was easy in the house we liked so much in Davenant Road. Schools were no problem as there was good primary school nearby and when Sarah and Katharine were old enough for secondary school, Milham Ford seemed appropriate. In Worcester things were more difficult. We did not enjoy living in the Deanery very much and pressure of work meant I saw little of the children and Pat, and I found it difficult to find time to spend on our own. We found a good primary school, however, and the girls went to the Girls' High School.

After leaving school, Sarah went to Newcastle University to read Spanish and Katharine to Manchester to read History of Art. Alice spent some time in America with the Fisherfolk, as I have said in my account of the Worcester mission, and then went to the University of Kent at Canterbury to read Social Psychology. Harriet went to her mother's old college, Lady Margaret Hall, in Oxford and read Greats. When we moved to Chichester, we left Edward behind as he had just been admitted to the cathedral choir and was therefore a pupil in the junior school of the King's School, Worcester. Later he was elected a King's Scholar and went on to New College, Oxford. During the summer before entering the sixth form at school, he suddenly switched from science to arts, largely because of his developing interest in the theatre, so at Oxford he read English. His subsequent career in the theatre, as what is best described by the embracing term 'dramaturge', has been a great delight to me.

This wide variety of family interests has been a great antidote to stuffiness. Towards the end of my time in Worcester, Roger Wilson, as Clerk to the Closet, nominated me to be one of the Chaplains to the Queen and as a consequence we were invited to a Royal Garden Party. When I became a bishop this became a regular annual event and the invitation always included any unmarried daughters. This usually meant Katharine, and I remember one year she was working in a student hostel near Wormwood Scrubs. She arrived at Buckingham Palace on her bicycle, which the officials there were quite happy, though I think surprised, to take charge of. She also collected quite a lot of food to take back to the hostel.

Family holidays were important times. When Bob Mortimer went to Exeter diocese I did a *locum tenens* in the parish of Pinhoe. This was our first experience of living for any length of time in someone else's house. The children were very young and we carefully put out of reach the huge number of nick-nacks with which the downstairs rooms were littered, and then had to remember when we left to replace them in the correct position. Later, through some personal contacts, I was able to arrange a regular locum holiday at Long Houghton in Northumberland. The north-east sea is lovely and there was a quiet beach at Long Houghton. We went there for several years, and then for two years to Nawton and Beadlam, and to Gilling in north Yorkshire.

We liked the whole area so much we began to think of getting a holiday house there and investing in it some of the money we had from the sale of our Oxford house. Pat's brother, Roger, was also looking for somewhere to live outside York so we began looking together. We found what we wanted in the little hamlet of Oulston – a row of empty cottages belonging to the Newburgh Priory estate. There were, in fact, two cottages made out of what had been three or four little fifteenth-century houses, each with two stories at the front and one at the back, with some outbuildings and quite large gardens behind. The whole was being offered for £1,500. The smaller one suited Roger best and the larger one at the east seemed ideal for us and our five children. We put in a bid and waited for something to happen. After some weeks with no news, we made some enquiries and learned that the trustees were trying to find out if we were respectable. By chance, Pat and I were having tea with her godmother and we told her about this. When she heard where the property was she said she would write to another godchild of hers who lived at Crayke

Castle, a couple of miles from Oulston. This she did and within a month our bid was accepted.

We both made extensive renovations. As Roger was proposing to make his cottage a permanent home it was more completely modernized than ours initially, though later we both had extensions made. We moved in for our first holiday in 1970. The Worcester Cathedral Choir, who were travelling on tour, came to visit us and we took them to sing a Sunday Mass at St Martin's, Scarborough, where I preached. A curious incident occurred on the way there – I was driving our Volkswagen van and I was so intent on finding the way that I did not notice I was exceeding the speed limit. On the outskirts of Scarborough, I was stopped by a policeman on a motorcycle who pointed out I was doing 40 miles an hour in a 30 miles an hour, built-up area. I apologized and said that I was trying to find the way to St Martin's church, whereupon he said, 'Oh I was confirmed there. Follow me,' and led us to the church. The Vicar at that time was Morris Maddocks, who later became Bishop of Selby and then moved south to be the representative of the archbishops for healing ministries. Holding that office, I made him a canon and prebendary of Chichester, and when he retired he moved into Canon Lane. He had been a student at the Theological College and had there married his wife who was assistant organist of the cathedral. This is one of many strange coincidences in my life.

We had very many happy holidays at Oulston for the next 20 years. We found that in Helmsley there was a riding school and there the children learned to ride. They very much enjoyed the cottage as a place to get away to, as I did, either on my own or with Pat. I would generally stay there whenever General Synod met in York. There were several of Pat's school friends living nearby, so we had people to visit when we were up there. In addition, the Holtbys were at Huttons Ambo, not far from us, after Robert retired from the Chichester deanery. Roger married in Oulston in August 1975 and did great work as headmaster of the nearby Easingwold School. In his retirement he was useful to the universities of both Durham and York and also developed a clergy assessment scheme for the York diocese. Sadly, he developed cancer and died in February 2003. York was about to give him an honorary doctorate but he died before the ceremony. The university, however, included his name in the degree ceremony and asked his wife, Christine, to attend formally. The Chancellor, Janet Baker, spoke movingly of him.

When I finally decided to retire we had to come to some decision about Oulston as our original idea was to live there in retirement. With this in mind, we had extended the cottage somewhat over the years and I had added a library and transferred a good number of my books there. We now began to realize how impractical it would be to live there in our old age. Oulston has no church, shop or pub, all of which are two or three miles away in Coxwold, and it would be necessary to use the car to do anything. Regretfully, we decided that we must sell the cottage and purchase a house elsewhere. We were having tea one day with Max Godden and his wife, who had retired to Chichester, and we were talking about the problems of retirement when Max suddenly said, 'Why shouldn't you retire to Chichester?' Somehow this had never occurred to us, but nagging away was the thought that this was not quite the proper thing to do. Friends assured us that it was perfectly proper, so we began to look around. We soon found our present house which we were able to adapt and add to using the proceeds of the sale of the cottage. We moved in during April 2001 and have been very happy here. I am still able to see the cathedral but I have joined the congregation of St George's, Whyke, which is a flourishing parish church not too far away. The parish priest, Fr Paul Seaman, is very kind and allows me to say Mass every Friday. Apart from that, I have done very little except when there was a long vacancy in the parish of St Wilfrid's, Chichester, and I took several services there. I see my successor occasionally at meetings, and of course know him well, but I think I have avoided being a problem to him.

We no longer have to think about holiday homes for the children as they all have their own houses and families, and we have enough space to put up two of them at a time with children. Sarah is the furthest away in Northumberland. She and her partner run a small theatre company called Theatre sans Frontières, performing plays, mainly French but some Spanish, in schools, colleges and small theatres. Sometimes they come south and we are able to see them and their small daughter Eleanor. Katharine lives in Bath with her two sons and is involved with local schools. Alice is not far away from her in Box with her husband, a consultant at Bristol General Hospital. They have two children. We are able to visit these two families fairly easily. Harriet has been living in Switzerland with her two children and her husband and working for a chemical firm in Berne, but has now returned to England to work for ICI and is living at West Byfleet.

Edward, at present, lives in north London with his partner and two children, but as he is much involved in the theatre as a dramaturge, he has for the last few years been spending a lot of time in Chichester. He has written an adaptation of Lessing's *Nathan the Wise*, a new stage version of *The Master and Margarita* by Bulgakov, a musical version of the life of war photographer Lee Miller, and a play commemorating the Gunpowder Plot of 1605 under the title *5/11*. Pat still works at the theatre, which she enjoys – in many ways we are rather a theatrical family.

My 90th birthday was a very special occasion. Just before it was the great Royal Albert Hall rally I mentioned earlier. My actual birthday was on 27 April and we had a number of friends to a buffet lunch. In the afternoon, Sarah and Harriet unexpectedly appeared and took us out to dinner. On a Saturday in June, the whole family – children and grandchildren – all assembled at Box and we all went on a cruise on the Kennet and Avon canal. Later that month, the general committee of the National Liberal Club gave a dinner for me, and towards the end of the month some of my former chaplains and members of SSC entertained Pat and me at lunch in the Athenaeum. The year 2005 was full of significant birthdays: Katharine was 50 and Edward 40 so we had joint celebrations. John Hind, my successor, was 60, and Lindsay Urwin 49, so we had a joint luncheon party at the Palace. At St George's, Whyke, we had cake and a glass of wine after Mass on the Sunday before my birthday. Altogether, it was a splendid celebration of 90 years which I had never expected to reach.

I have been a member of the Church of England all my life and hope to remain so until I die. The Church of England can be very trying to its members at times but it offers faith with great freedom. I am glad to have been prepared for confirmation by Mr Horn at Waltham, whose teaching I still remember and think about. I am grateful for the teaching and example of Freddy Hood in so many ways but particularly in enabling me to remain steady through the trials of 65 years of ministry and with confidence in the divine providence. Throughout my life I have been inspired and guided by the memory of Bishop Edward King and his sermons and writings, to which I still constantly refer. When I was an undergraduate I bought a volume of the *Pastoral Lectures* of Edward King. I took it to Pusey House chapel when I went for my afternoon meditation and, feeling the need for growth in humility, I thought of the humble bishop and opened the book at random. 'Castles in the air:' I read, 'smash them up, for your own arms are sure to be emblazoned over the castle door.' Finally, I am deeply grateful to my wife and to the children for keeping me sane and, I hope, sensible. God has been good to me throughout my life and for all that I am profoundly thankful.

Appendix I

PROTOCOLLUM consecrationis episcopalis Rm̃i Dñi Erici Waldramni Kemp episcopi Cicestrensis, in ecclesia Cathedrali S.
Salvatori Apud Southwarkiensi, die a Rm̃o Dño Marinus Archiepiscopo Ultra-
jectensis una cum Rm̃o Dño (archi) episcopo peractae.

IN NOMINE SANCTISSIMAE TRINITATIS, AMEN. Harem prae-
sentium litterarum tenore Nos, Marinus Archiepiscopus Ultrajectensi
in Ecclesia Vetero-Catholica Bataviae, cunctos Christifideles ad quos
haec pervenerint certiores facimus, quod die XXIII et mensis Octobri
qui fuit Festum, anno salutis Nostrae MCMLXXIV in ecclesia Cathedrali S. Salvatori Nos, Episcopus praedictus, consecrationi episcopali
Reverendi Domini Erici Waldramni Kemp electi episcopi Cicestrensis a
Reverendissimo Patre ac Domino Domino Michaeli (archi) epsicopo
Cantuariensi celebratae in propria Nostra persona interfuimus atque
adstitimus, necnon et impositionis manuum super caput praedicti
Domini Erici Walramni Kemp participes fuimus, quippe qui in illum
ipsum finem (approbantibus Reverendissimis in Christo Patribus ac
Dominis) venissemus, ut antistitibus Ecclesiarum Anglicanae atque
Vetero-Catholicae coniumctim atque aequeprincipaliter novum epis-
copum consecrantibus caritatis fraternae exemplar omnium hominum
oculis praeberetur.

Porro ne futuris temporibus quaestiones vel controversiae circa
modum externum consociationis Nostrae cum praedicto Domino
(archi) episcopo Cantuariensi et cum Reverendissimis confratribus
eius Episcopis Anglicanis in dicto consecrationis episcopalis actu
oriantur, testamur Nos ambas manus, utpote consecratorem aequeprincipalem, in caput praedicti Reverendi Domini Erici Waldramni
Kemp simul cum Domino (Archi) episcopo Cantuariensi et assis-
tentibus eius episcopis imposuisse, atque verba consecrationis episcopalis quae in Pontificali Ecclesiae Vetero-Catholicae Batavuae

praescripta sunt, scilicet Accipe Spiritum Sanctum, non arbitrio Nostro privato sed legibus Ecclesiae Vetero-Catholicae obtemperantes, calra voce, ita ut a circumstantibus audiri possent, et Latina lingua protulisse, uno atque eodem tempore quo praedictus Dominus (Archi) episcopus verba consecrationis in Ordinali Anglicano praescripta, scilicet 'Receive the Holy Ghost for the Office and Work of a Bishop in the Church of God' et caetera quae ibidem sequuntur, pronuntiaret.

Ad abolendam denque atque radicitus tollendam omnem quae oriri posset circa intentionem Nostram dubitationem, Nos, Episcopus praedictus, declaramus atque profitemur Nos in supradicta manuum impositione atque in simultanea verborum Accipe Spiritum Sanctum proclatione praecise et formaliter intendisse

1 esse, Secumdum Ecclesiae Vetero-Catholicae leges quae supra commemoratae sunt, comministrum consecrationis episcopalis dicti Reverend Domini Erici Waldramni Kemp cum Domino (Archi) episcopi Cantuariensi aequeprincipalem, et non tantum merum assistentem vel consecrationis testem;

2 eidem Reverendo Domino Erici Waldramni Kemp conferre ordinem episcopatus iuxta mentem Sacrosanctae Matris Ecclesiae Catholicae et Apostolicae necnon et Ecclesiarum Vetero-Catholicarum Unionis *Ultraiectensis*, atque eundem characterem episcopalem quo Ipsi et confratres Nostri Ecclesiarum Vetero-Catholicarum praesules gaudemus, id est, *plenitudinem sacerdotii cum omnibus et singulis functionibus, potestatibus et facultatibus in eadem inhaerentibus,* in eo praeciso sensu quo plenitude sacerdotii in Ecclesia Catholica *ubique, semper, et ab omnibus* intellecta est;

3 in eiusdem Reverendi Domini persona tanquam duos rivulos eius successionis quae est ab Apostolis coniungere, illum scilicet qui per antistites Ecclesiarum Vetero-Catholicarum derivatur et illum qui per hierarchiam Anglicanam usque ad praesens tempus deducitur.

IN QUORUM FIDEM hanc chartam chirographo Nostro necnon et sigillo Nostro episcopali munivimus. Datum Apud Londinium, die XXIII mensis Octobri anno salutis nostrae MCMLXXIV

+ ....

De mandato RmI mei Dñi/Archiepiscopi

Et ego, ... testor me consecrationi supradictae adfuisse tanquam presbyterum Reverendissim Domino Archiepiscopo Ultrajectenso .... assistentem, impositionemque manuum eiusdem Episcopi Vidisse prolationemque verborum Accepe Spiritum Sanctum audivisse, sicut suprascriptum est.

IN NOMINE DEI, AMEN.

Ego, Marinus, Archiepiscopus ecclesiae Ultrajectensi, per has praesentes cunctos Christifideles ad quos haec sive nunc sive in futurum pervenerint certiores facio, quod anno salutis MCMLXXIV atque die XXIII Octobri ego, Episcopus praedectus, consecrtioni episcopali Rm̄i Dn̄l Erici Waldramni Kemp, episcopi ecclesiae Anglicanae a Rm̄o in Christo Patre ac Domino Michaeli archiepiscopo Cantuariensi (totius Angliae Primate atque Metropolitano) in ecclesia cathedrali S. Salvatori apud Southwarkiensum peractae adstiti atque manuum impositionis supra caput dicti R. Dn̄i Erici Waldramni Kemp particeps fui, cum ea intentione quae verbis sequentibus exponitur: scilicet, cum charactere episcopali non tantum per eam successionem quae ab Apostolis derivate in ecclesiis Anglicanis constanter et ligitime traditur sed etiam per eam quae in ecclesiis Vetero-Catholicis hucusque asservata est ipse ego potitus sum, quippe qui A.S. MCMLXXIV die 23 Octobris in ordinem episcopatus iuxta mentem S. Matris Ecclesiae Catholicae et Apostolicae simul a Michaeli archiepiscopo Cantuariensi atque Gerhardo episcopo ecclesiae Vetero-Catholicaie Harlemensi apud Batavos [per successionem ecclesiae Vetero-Catholicae consecrato] tanquam consecratoribus aequeprincipalibus ipse consecratus sum, volui atque intendi dicto R. Dn̄o Erici Waldramni Kemp hunc ipsum characterem episcopalem atque sacerdotii plenitudinem conferre quem ipse non tantum ab episcopis Anglicanis sed etiam a praesulibus Vetero-Catholicis accepi, ita ut dictus R. Dn̄us successionis episcopalis non Anglicanae solum sed etiam Vetero-Catholicae particeps fieret: ad quem finem ambas manus in caput dicti R. Dn̄i Erici Waldramni Kemp simul sum Rm̄o Dn̄o Michaeli archiepiscopo Cantuariensi imposui, atque verba consecrationis episcopalism a Pontificali ecclesiarum Vetero-Catholicum desumpta, videlicet ACCIPE SPIRITUM SANCTUM, clara voce protuli: dictumque R. Dn̄um Ericum Waldramnum Kemp sic in episcopatum in Ecclesia Catholica ubique semper et ab omnibus intellectus est.

In quorum fidem chirographum meum subscripse, die 23 Octobris A.S.
MCMLXXIV

+ Marius Kok
Archbishop of Utrecht

Testis chirographi praedecti Dñi Episcopi,

+ Gerhardus van Kleef
Episcopus Harlemensi

_____

Appendix II
The Catholic Future

I have been reflecting on some of the contrasts between the two Loughborough conferences and I would like to begin this afternoon with that.

At Loughborough I we were all, I think, a bit edgy. It was the first big Catholic gathering for many years and some thought that it should not have happened at all. The issue of the ordination of women, due to be debated in General Synod later in the year, overshadowed our sessions. The programme was overcrowded and we wasted a lot of time trying to find the various rooms in which the discussion groups were to meet. And yet, at the end, in spite of all the mistakes and weaknesses, there was, I believe, a new confidence in what we were doing as Catholics.

At Loughborough II many of us have come as to a familiar place. There has been no overshadowing controversy. We have not been afraid to face the disagreements that exist among us, to bring them out into the open and to find that yet there is unity. At the first Loughborough conference, in my opening address at the first session, I set out five points which I thought necessary to Catholic renewal which I shall refer to in the course of this address at various stages. The fourth of them was that we must recognize that Catholicism is not a monolithic structure and this is quite as clear to us to be the case in the Roman Catholic Church as it is in our own. I think I quoted on that occasion Fr Faber's hymn:

> But we make his love too narrow by false limits of our own,
> And we magnify his strictness with a zeal he would not own.

Let us not allow ourselves to be divided into hostile camps because we disagree on some points of practice or theology. Above all, let us not be divided on grounds of personalities.

Now the title given to me is 'The Catholic Future' and I am glad that it is put in that form. The Tractarians did not set out to make the

Church of England Catholic. Rather they set out to persuade it that it *is* Catholic and should act accordingly. But what is it to be Catholic? I am going to start with what I have always regarded as, in a sense, the title deeds of the Catholic renewal movement, that is the statement called 'A Basis for Renewal' issued on Ascension Day in 1977. This statement is in the form of a creed, a Trinitarian form, but nearly all creeds betray a particular concern at the time with certain aspects of the faith and I draw your attention to certain phrases. 'God entered into a new relationship with the material world by becoming man in Jesus the Christ.' 'The flesh and matter which God created are the very stuff in which we already begin to share his life of Glory.' 'The Catholic religion is not an abstract body of principles but is embodied in a living and historical Church, Christ's Body, with its Bible, its apostolic order, its sacraments, its priesthood and its life of worship and prayer.' 'God's kingdom of *justice* and peace.' 'New heavens and a new earth in which justice dwells.'

Here is the materialism which alone makes possible the incarnation, the Church, the sacraments, and is the basis for concern about the right ordering of society. Whether we all draw the same political conclusions is another matter, but we are agreed in social concern, not just as ambulance work, but going to the roots of society. And we stand here in the line of the Christian Social Union, Scott Holland, Charles Gore, Maurice Reckitt, Dr Demant, who sadly died the other day, and if you read his commentary on the Minor Prophets, you will see that we stand in the line of Dr Pusey also.

That was one main emphasis. The other is on wholeness, and the last paragraph of the statement is this: 'The renewal of Catholicism, in the Church of England, as in the rest of the Christian world, is the recovery of wholeness. Catholic means whole, integral, complete: its opposite is partial, unbalanced, sectarian. Today, as we see the decay of narrow and inadequate forms of Christianity, and the revival of pietistic and harmful byways of belief, the renewal of Catholic truth and life will not occur without a struggle. But it is essential if the true God is to be preached.'

Case for tracts

What do we need for this struggle? One of the greatest needs for the future of Catholicism is to find a means of producing and distributing widely Catholic literature. The demise of *Christian World* was a tragedy from which lessons are to be learned and no-one should underrate the difficulties of publishing at the present time. We know that there are new means of communication being rapidly developed and it is important that Catholics avail themselves of the opportunities of being trained for these and try to make the most of them. Nevertheless, I think it will be a long time before there is any complete substitute for the tract, the pamphlet, the booklet and the journal as means of popularizing the knowledge of the faith. We need also to find effective channels of distribution. You will remember that the Tractarians rode on horseback up and down the length of England distributing their tracts and we need to find ways in which to become the new Tractarians.

We need an instructed and committed laity. The Catholic Movement is seen from outside, and we must acknowledge with some truth, as very much a clerical movement. The Tractarians had to start by emphasizing the spiritual authority of the priesthood derived through apostolic succession and this emphasis has been continually necessary, but it can easily give the impression that we regard the Church as being principally the clergy. Along with our emphasis on ministerial priesthood, we need to speak and teach about the royal priesthood of all the baptized. We need to emphasize, as the Good Friday collect says, that every member of the Church has his vocation and ministry. For the ordinary lay person his primary calling is to live and do his job as a Christian and it ought never to be suggested that some particular form of 'church work', whether as server, choirman, churchwarden or whatever, is necessary to being a good Christian. The holy people of God in the Catholic Movement, that is repenting, confessing and worshipping in the Eucharist, living their lives and doing their jobs in the inspiration of the Catholic faith, filled also with a desire to communicate that faith.

We need laity of all ages, but we need specially to give attention to our children and young people. We, but not only we, the whole country, has been through a terribly enervating period in respect of religious education and youth work. The vogues of experiential learning and emergent leadership, to mention just two of the slogans in recent educational jargon, have gone a long way to destroy any idea of communicating knowledge and the result is that an increasing number of young people have little more than a vague, sentimental conception of what the Christian religion is about, of the discipline involved in it, what the sacraments are for and so on; and if children are not taught the right things they will learn the wrong things. But how often have I heard priests and teachers lament the lack of suitable material. This is not just a grouse. The kind of thing which was represented by the Childermote manuals of the Faith Press and Haggerston Catechism does not seem to exist any more. There are popular books of Bible stories, but the Bible is the Church's book and needs to be accompanied by Church teaching. We need more lay people who are prepared to learn how to teach and to give time to teach, more people prepared to be trained as youth leaders, more people prepared to give time to Catholic Scouts and Guides, more people who having found for themselves the fun and the how of the Catholic religion are keen to share it with others.

More Priests ...

From the laity we need more priests. There is a great deal of talk today about new patterns of ministry and new patterns of training. There are those who say that the time is coming when we shall have to make do with a very small number of full-time professional priests, each responsible for a wide area served under his guidance by a large number of part-time stipendiary priests. Some think this would be a good thing and see it as a way of breaking down what they regard as a mischievous and frustrating clerical domination of the Church. Others think it is a development for which we should prepare, made inevitable by the rise in cost of training and clerical stipends. When changes as revolutionary as this are urged upon us for financial reasons we need to stop and think hard about the reasons for these financial constraints. We need to ask why it is that certain areas of the life of the Church do not feel them, why, for example, the charismatic and other movements show no sign of shortage of money where it is needed, and we need to ask questions about faith, about stewardship, about discipline and about self-denial. The evidence suggests that if we are a converted believing people, the money will come.

In any case, we must not let these gloomy forecasts silence now our call for more men to consider whether they have a vocation to the priesthood. The bishops have accepted a target of 430 stipendiary deacons a year as what is necessary to keep the ministry at its present strength. We must use all our efforts to see that the Catholic

Movement contributes a high proportion of that total. Nor must we allow these gloomy forecasts, or financial constraints which the CBF tries to impose from time to time, to dilute the quality of training for the priesthood.

The establishment of theological colleges was among the first fruits of the Oxford Movement. The training of priests in circumstances which will give them the most thorough theological and spiritual formation continues to be a priority. Our theological colleges still have their enemies and need support. And I can tell you from personal knowledge over the last eight years or so that two of our leading colleges have been saved by the support of the Anglo-Catholic Ordination Candidates' Fund when they might easily have been axed along with others.

The development of dedication and discipline is vital, for there must be a clear understanding that personal and priestly life cannot be separated. We need priests who will go where they are needed and tackle difficult tasks. I have great sympathy with what the Bishop of Leicester said about the problem of finding priests who do the kind of steady unexciting teaching jobs without much in the way of externals.

The Church of England has accepted the legitimacy of a married priesthood such as was known in the early centuries in the West and throughout the centuries in the East, but is has also kept before the eyes of young men the possible vocation to a celibate priesthood, with the sacrifice and discipline involved in that. Much of the great work done in Catholic parishes in the last century and the first quarter of this was only possible because such a vocation was accepted. The work of the Company of Mission Priests has been a continuation of this and there have been priests who were prepared to remain unmarried for a period to devote themselves to this kind of work while not feeling a vocation to celibacy. That kind of renunciation, self-sacrifice and discipline is still needed. It is important that we do not lose sight of it.

Committed Scholars

Then we need scholars, men and women trained in the various academic disciplines, for whom, as the motto of Pusey House says, 'The Lord is a God of knowledge'; men and women who will put their academic skills at the service of God's people like good scribes bringing out of their treasures things new and old for the confirmation, exposition and enlargement of the faith; men and women who will make time to help us with their knowledge and their writing in the controversies which threaten the foundations of belief and the controversies which threaten the Catholic structure of the Church. Most of us dislike controversy and engage in it only when it is thrust on us. We have the right to appeal to Catholic scholars not to shrink from helping us. We are grateful to those who are here, grateful to Brian Horne, Rowan Williams and others who have helped us and are helping us in this way. But I am aware of many others who are not here and who stand aloof from these things.

Being realistic about the Catholic future we know that there will be controversies, and we must face these squarely. We have had the most recent one over the rejection of the proposed services for the blessing of the oils and for penance. I am not myself too deeply grieved about all that and I do not think it will have been altogether a bad thing if it discourages the Liturgical Commission from producing any more new services which take up synodical time and money and discourage that liturgical freedom for which the Bishop of Leicester was pleading.

But over penance, remember that the issue as it was presented in the General Synod was the issue of priesthood and that lies at the root of many other differences. There is a need, an urgent need, for dialogue within the Church of England on ministry. We are all going to be asked to spend a lot of time over the next few years studying the Lima and ARCIC Reports, and Catholics must play their part in that. I would like to see Catholics also taking the initiative in the dialogue with the Free Churches.

At Loughborough I we had Michael Green commenting on our proceedings as an Evangelical and there is far closer friendship than there used to be. But there is still much need for greater understanding and I hope we shall not lose sight of the vision of a Catholic–Evangelical conference for renewal which we talked about at Loughborough I. Perhaps we might think about that as something to happen in five years' time on the occasion of the next Lambeth Conference in 1988 and as a preparation for it.

My fifth point at Loughborough I was that if we are really looking for renewal we must expect to be shown something new. The former Bishop of Leicester, welcoming us here five years ago, spoke of his appreciation of what he called the two wings of the Church, Catholic and Evangelical. But he spoke also of the interaction of the two to produce, not a dull central churchmanship, but what he liked to call 'classical Anglicanism', and he listed Hooker, Ken, Gore, Temple and some others as examples. I suspect that it is in learning from one another, which will only come in dialogue, that we shall find the things that are really new – new perhaps to us but in fact new understanding of the truth that is old.

As I said earlier, the first Loughborough Conference was over-shadowed by the controversy over the ordination of women to the priesthood which a few months later brought the Church of England nearer to a split than anything that has happened in my lifetime. Shortly after that was avoided we had the further division caused by the covenant proposals. We must be prepared for both these issues to be raised again in the coming years. We must recognize as I said at the beginning, that Catholics do not all take the same view of them but let me make a few comments on them without entering into the detailed theological arguments.

Unilateralism

Both these issues raise the question of what it is proper for the Church of England, or indeed any of the various parts of the Anglican Com-munion to do by itself. Both involve theological issues concerning the nature of Christian priesthood, both involve substantial changes in what has hitherto been regarded as requisite for ordination into the historic ministry. The question is by what authority can such changes be made in what is a part of the structure of the whole Church not just the possession of any part or parts of it. It is the claim that the Church of England has the right to take such decisions by itself that, more than anything else, arouses Catholic opposition. This is a different matter from just saying that this or that course of action will make union with Rome or the Orthodox more difficult. It is a question of one's understanding of what the Church of England is. The Tractarian assertion was that the Church of England is but one small part of the whole Catholic Church and that in defence of our separation from the two great historic churches, Eastern and Western, we appeal to the teaching and practice of the undivided Church of the first thousand years. There in scripture and that early tradition we find our standards for the structure and sacramental practice of the Church. In any decisions that we take we must be faithful to those principles.

It is of course possible that in the course of time and under the guidance of the Holy Spirit the whole Catholic Church may come to a new understanding and new interpretation of those principles. It is possible that particular local churches may lead the way in argument and in persuasion. But that is very different from local or national churches taking decisions by their own authority to alter what is the common possession of the whole Church. I have expressed a view which, as it seems to me, the writer of the recent Crockford Preface wholly fails to appreciate. There is a triumphalism about some Anglican utterances, even by some of our leading scholars, which is deeply offensive to those who try to see the Catholic Church as a whole and care passionately about her unity.

There is still about a great deal of Dr Arnold's reductionist view of the Church which prompted much of what the Tractarians did. Let me tell you what that view was as summarized by Dean Church:

> He divided the world into Christians and non-Christians: Christians were all those who professed to believe in Christ as a Divine Person and to worship Him, and the brotherhood, the 'societas' of Christians, was all that was meant by 'the Church' in the New Testament. It mattered, of course, to the conscience of each Christian what he had made up his mind to believe, but to no one else. Church organization was, according to circumstances, partly inevitable or expedient, partly mischievous, but in no case of divine authority. Teaching, ministering the word, was a thing of divine appoint-ment, but not so the mode of exercising it, either as to persons, forms or methods. Sacraments there were, signs and pledges of divine love and help, in every action of life, in every sight of nature, and eminently two most touching ones, recommended to Christians by the Redeemer Himself; but except as a matter of mere order, one man might deal with these as lawfully as another.

Well, I would have thought that there is a lot of that about today, and there is need, great need, for a real renewal of our understanding of the doctrine of the Church, of ecclesiology. Contrast what I have just read with the last paragraph, or indeed the whole of the Ascension Day Statement about the Church.

English Traditions

Now, having said that let me remind you that the Catholic Movement is a movement within the Church of England and the Anglican

Communion, and that there have been and there are distinctive Anglican contributions to theology, notable works resulting from the Catholic revival, many of which tend quite wrongly to be overlooked. I have mentioned some writers who have been important in developing the Church's social teaching. I hope that the celebrations of this year will bring back to our attention some who contributed in other spheres. JB Mozley, for example, was among those who had to re-examine their positions as disciples of Newman. His writings on predestination and baptism deal with fundamental questions in ways that are still instructive and fruitful. Dean Church, himself, to whom I have referred already. His *Life and Letters*, edited by his daughter, is a goldmine of balanced and penetrating thought on fundamentals. He deserves to be remembered with thanksgiving in this anniversary year as the young don who, in 1845, persuaded his fellow proctor at Oxford to join him in vetoing the proposal to condemn Tract 90. Then RH Moberley's works on the Atonement and on Ministerial Priesthood remain classics. Kenneth Kirk's *The Vision of God* is a masterly guide to Christian spirituality. These are just a few out of many whose writings can give us instruction and inspiration more than the passage of time might suggest.

There is nothing wrong in buying an alb in Paris, a mitre in Rome, or candlesticks in Vienna, and I have done all three, but remember that there is also good native craftsmanship here. We must not suppose that it is only Roman Catholics who write good theology or Orthodox who write good spirituality. In considering our needs and our duty for the future it is right that we remember our past with thanks and faithfulness.

The need for spiritual renewal was my first point at Loughborough I. In seeking it we need to remember that there is a great tradition of English spirituality. We all know about the revival of interest in Julian of Norwich, but there are others of that period equally worthy of our attention, others of the seventeenth century, and others nearer our own day.

Let me remind you again of the last paragraph of the Ascension Day Statement with its emphasis on wholeness and the need to recover wholeness. But how can any of this be done without an organization or organizations to promote it? This is a proper form of the application of the sacramental principle. God uses human agencies for his purposes as he uses material things as channels of his grace. It is also in line with the history of the Church of England. All the great things in our history have been achieved by groups and societies formed for particular purposes.

Contributions of Societies

Now I should be the last person to knock synods, for I piloted the Synodical Government Measure through the Church Assembly, but synods have their limitations. They have accomplished and accomplish little that is of constructive value. They are there to keep the machine oiled and provide for the letting off of hot air and to do a certain amount of tidying up. All the things that matter most have been done and are done by the SPCK, the SPG, the CMS, the National Society, the Mothers' Union, the CPAS, the ACS, and a host of others of what are essentially private societies.

Look at the recent life of Fr Lowder, that great hero among the parish priests of the Oxford Movement, and read there of the foundation of the Society of the Holy Cross, an English adaptation of S Vincent de Paul's Company of Mission Priests to provide disciplined clergy in the establishment of home missions to preach the gospel to, as they put it 'the masses of our working population, and to publish tracts and pamphlets to defend and extend Catholic faith and practice'. Read of the foundation of the Confraternity of the Blessed Sacrament to promote and defend the truth in doctrine and devotion about the Eucharist following on the adverse judgment in the Denison case. Read also about the foundation of the English Church Union 'to defend and maintain the doctrine and discipline of the Church of England and to afford counsel and protection to all those suffering under unjust aggression'. Read about the foundation of the Christian Social Union, which I mentioned earlier, and a host of other such societies.

Times have changed certainly, and the situation of the Church of England is in many ways different from what it was then, though when I return from Bishops' Meetings and I read the words of Fr Mackonochie during the East End riots, when he wrote: 'So we dragged on, the bishop enlivening the monotony by coming down unexpectedly whenever the rector was away, with some monition of an illegal kind, removing at one time the choir, at another the hangings, at another the cross', I think – shades of scarlet cassocks and some other things – and I wonder.

My point is that the real work of the Church of England has always been done in the parishes and with the support of a variety of what are essentially private societies – people who have banded themselves together to promote a particular good. That is part of the genius of the Church of England and I cannot see why it should ever cease to be so. The Catholic societies are part of this picture. It is easy to knock them but it is far better to get in and try to improve them. In the last 20 years I have more than once thought seriously of resigning from the Church Union, but on reflection I did not think that that would do any good; division always causes weakness. So I stayed, and then out of the blue they made me president.

Renewed Church Union

The new Aims and Objects of the Church Union represent the biggest and most radical reconstruction of that body since 1933 when the amalgamation of the English Church Union and the Anglo-Catholic Congress took place.

There is to be set up a structure of groups to carry them out. There will be a renewal and mission group, a theological group, a Church Literature Association to deal with publications, a children and young people's group, a group for social concern with special responsibility for that end, and those groups are to be constituted with people who are best qualified to serve them, best able to serve them, and we hope that those who are interested in serving on them will let the General Secretary know so that their names may be kept in mind. The Church Union will be looking for people who are concerned for those things so that it may be in the fullest possible way Catholic. Let me emphasize also that the Church Union as reconstituted is a fully democratic body. It rests upon local elections, and every level rests upon elections, so if you do not like it, it is the same as with trade unions – get in, get in and change it.

Let me say also that this revision provides for people who are not members of the Church Union and have difficulties about it but are nevertheless keen on the aims and objects to share in the work. It provides for those areas where Catholic renewal is strong and the Church Union scarcely exists, nevertheless to be associated with the work.

Now this is one bit, just one bit, but it is one bit, of what Catholic renewal has achieved, but it depends on the participation and support of each one of us to ensure its realization, that it becomes more than just a piece of paper.

Personal Testimony

And now let me conclude with what I think is unusual in Catholic circles, a personal testimony. At about the age of 16 I went through what many people do and have done, a period of scepticism. In that period I was suddenly set to write an essay on the Oxford Movement by my history master. I found it an interesting story, interesting enough to pursue it by searching out churches that had been influenced by the movement. In those days such churches had tract cases and the cases were full of tracts – the John Bull tracts, the Congress tracts and some more substantial things, all produced by the CLA. I bought some of these and read them and my religion came back, came alive, and I learned to make my first confession.

Shortly afterwards I went to Oxford and I was in touch with Pusey House, another Catholic organization. Freddy Hood taught me more about the Catholic faith, emphasizing its social teaching and its concern for Christian unity. I became aware of the Church Union, then recently founded by the amalgamation of the ECU and the Anglo-Catholic Congress, supporting and promoting all this.

It was the aim of the first Anglo-Catholic Congress in 1920 'to bring all men to a true realization of the Lord Jesus Christ as their personal Saviour and King'. That is what the Catholic Movement and Catholic organizations did for me, and I want there to be societies, unions, agencies, organizations, call them what you will, to make all this in its renewed, and continually being renewed, form available to other young people, and old people, as it was to me. And for that I am prepared to spend my time and money.

Bibliography

1937 'The Augustinian Tradition in the Religious Life', *Church Quarterly Review*, 125

1943 A Group of the Clergy, 'The Discipline of the Church: Canon Law and the Ecclesiastical Courts', *Thy Household the Church: Proposals for Government and Order in the Church of England* (London)

1943 'Reconstruction in the Church of England', *Agenda*, reprinted as part of the Church and Realm series, The Church Literature Association

1945 'Pope Alexander III and the Canonization of the Saints', *Transactions of the Royal Historical Society*, 4th series, 27

1946 'Zeger Bernhard Van Espen', *Theology*, 49

1947 'Legal Reform in the Church of England', *Illuminatio*, 1

1948 *Canonization and Authority in the Western Church* (Oxford)
EG Wood, *The Regal Power of the Church: or, the Fundamentals of the Canon Law*, with a Preface and Supplementary Bibliography by EW Kemp (London)
Canon Law in the Church of England, Church Literature Association of the Church Union (London)

1950 'Das Buch of Common Prayer', *Internationale Kirchliche Zeitschrift*, 40

1952 'The Origins of the Canterbury Convocation', *The Journal of Ecclesiastical History*, 3

1953 'Laity in Church Government', *Parson and Parish*, 17
'Round Table Conference', *Parson and Parish*, 20
'The Roman Catholic Doctrine of Marriage', *Theology*, 56

1954 *Papal Decretals Relating to the Diocese of Lincoln in the Twelfth Century*, W Holtzmann and EW Kemp (eds), The Lincoln Record Society, 47 (Hereford)
'The Canterbury Convocation', *Parson and Parish*, 22
NP Williams (London)

1955 'The Attempted Canonization of Robert Grosseteste', in DA Callus (ed.), *Robert Grosseteste* (Oxford)

KE Kirk, *Beauty and Bands, and Other Papers,* prepared by EW Kemp (London)

'Bishops and Presbyters at Alexandria', *The Journal of Ecclesiastical History,* 6

1957 *An Introduction to Canon Law in the Church of England,* Lichfield Cathedral Divinity Lectures for 1956 (London)

'Apostolic Succession', *Faith and Unity,* 4

1959 *The Life and Letters of Kenneth Escott Kirk, Bishop of Oxford 1937–1954* (London)

1961 *Counsel and Consent: Aspects of the Government of the Church as Exemplified in the History of the English Provincial Synods,* The Bampton Lectures for 1960 (London)

1964 *The Anglican–Methodist Conversations: A Comment from Within* (London)

1965 'The Canterbury Provincial Chapter and the Collegiality of Bishops in the Middle Ages', in *Etudes d'histoire du droit canonique dédiées à Gabriel Le Bras* (Paris)

1966 'The Anglican–Methodist Conversations', *Internationale Kirchliche Zeitschrift,* 56

1967 'The Church of England and the Old Catholic Churches', in EGW Bill (ed), *Anglican Initiatives in Christian Unity* (London)

1968 'Anglican Orders', *One in Christ,* 4

1969 'Die Anglikanisch–Methodistische Unionsplan', *Internationale Kirchliche Zeitschrift,* 59

'Augustinianism', in EW Kemp (ed.), *Man: Fallen and Free, Oxford Essays on the Condition of Man* (London)

The Anglican–Methodist Unity Scheme, published with F Colquhoun, *Evangelicals and Methodist Unity* (Windsor)

1970 'Das Primatsverstandnis in der Anglikanischen Theologie', *Internationale Kirchliche Zeitschrift,* 60

1974 'The Organization of the English Episcopate from the Reformation to the Twentieth Century', *Aspects de l'Anglicanisme,* Colloque de Strasbourg, 14–16 June 1972 (Paris)

1976 *Inaugural Address to the General Council of the Church Union as President,* Church Union (London)

1977 'Jubilee – Jollification and Holiness', *The Server,* 10

'The Art of Worship', *The Occasional Journal of the Alcuin Club*

1980   *Square Words in a Round World* (Glasgow)
        'The Structure of Theology', Birmingham Additional Curates
        Society, *Kairos*, 2
1981   *Milk Without Guile: Address to the Deanery Synods of the Diocese
        of Chichester* (Chichester)
        'History and Action in the Sermons of a Medieval Archbishop',
        in RHC Davis and JM Wallace-Hadrill (eds), *The Writing of
        History in the Middle Ages: Essays Presented to Richard William
        Southern* (Oxford)
        'Bonn Agreement Golden Jubilee Celebrations', *Internationale
        Kirchliche Zeitschrift*, 71
1982   'Mary and Right Belief in Christ', in A Stacpoole (ed.), *Mary's
        Place in Christian Dialogue* (Slough)
        'Personal Memories', in C Van Kasteel, PJ Maan and MFG
        Parmentier (eds), *Kracht in Zwakheid van een Kleine Wer-
        eldkerk. De Oud-Katholieke Unie van Utrecht. Studie Aangeboden
        aan Marinus Kok, Aartsbisschop van Utrecht* (1970–1981)
        (Hilversum)
1984   *Joy in Believing: Sermons Preached by the Lord Bishop of Chi-
        chester on the Occasion of the Tenth Anniversary of his Con-
        secration* (Chichester)
1986   'The Creation of the Synod', in P Moore (ed.), *The Synod of
        Westminster: Do We Need It?* (London)
1987   'The Spirit of the Canon Law and its Application in England',
        Ecclesiastical Law Journal, 1 (1–2)
1988   'The Problems of Church Relationships Facing the Anglican
        Communion in the Coming Lambeth Conference', *Inter-
        nationale Kirchliche Zeitschrift*, 78
1989   'Legal Implications of Lambeth', *Ecclesiastical Law Journal*, 1 (5)
1992   T Briden and B Hanson (eds), *Moore's Introduction to English
        Canon Law*, 3rd edn, with a Foreword by Bishop E Kemp
        (London)
        'Fede, ordine e strutture ecclesiastiche nell' Anglicanesimo
        contemporaneo', in C Alzati (ed.), *L'Anglicanesimo: Dalla
        Chiesa d'Inghilterra alla Comunione Anglicana* (Genoa)
1995   *The Bishops Address to the Deanery Synods 1994–95* (Chichester)
1998   'Unity – Lessons to be Learned; Issues to be Faced: Anglican–
        Methodist Conversations 1956–72', *Ecclesiastical Law Journal*, 5

Lightning Source UK Ltd.
Milton Keynes UK
09 December 2010
164085UK00002B/6/A